D1250117

LIBRARY USE ONLY

FLORIDA STATE
UNIVERSITY LIBRARIES

MAR 25 1997

TALLAHASSEE, FLORIDA

INTERNATIONAL ORGANIZATIONS SERIES
Edited by Jon Woronoff

Historical Dictionary of the World Bank

Anne C. M. Salda

International Organizations Series, No. 11

The Scarecrow Press, Inc.
Lanham, Md., & London
1997

SCARECROW PRESS, INC.

Published in the United States of America
by Scarecrow Press, Inc.
4720 Boston Way
Lanham, Maryland 20706

4 Pleydell Gardens, Folkestone
Kent CT20 2DN, England

Copyright © 1997 by Anne C. M. Salda

All rights reserved. No part of this publication may be reproduced,
stored in a retrieval system, or transmitted in any form or by any
means, electronic, mechanical, photocopying, recording, or otherwise,
without the prior permission of the publisher.

British Cataloguing-in-Publication Information Available

Library of Congress Cataloging-in-Publication Data

Salda, Anne C. M.
    Historical dictionary of the World Bank / Anne Salda.
            p. cm.—(International organizations series; no. 11)
    Includes bibliographical references.
    ISBN 0-8108-3215-1 (alk. paper)
    1. World Bank—History—Dictionaries.   I. Title.   II. Series: International
organizations series (Metuchen, N.J.); no. 11
HG3881.5.W57S25   1997
332.1′532′09—dc20   96-9151
                                                                          CIP

ISBN 0-8108-3215-1 (cloth: alk paper)

♾™ The paper used in this publication meets the minimum requirements of
American National Standard for Information Sciences—Permanence of
Paper for Printed Library Materials, ANSI Z39.48-1984.
Manufactured in the United States of America.

*To my husband, my parents, and my grandparents
with thanks for their help over the years*

Contents

Editor's Foreword

Foresighted as they were, the founders of the World Bank nevertheless could not have imagined how it would grow and flourish. Founded after the Second World War, mainly to provide some stability and assistance to shattered economies, the Bank has become a major source of aid to most of the developing countries. Not only does it lend money, the Bank also approves or rejects projects and keeps an eye on their implementation. On occasion it has influenced the broader economic and financial policies of borrowers. And it helps shape the world economy in many ways. Not surprisingly, this has won friends for the Bank, while creating enemies as well.

Alas, many of those who like the World Bank, and many of those who dislike it, as well as the vast majority of the uncommitted, know much less about the Bank than they might. This book helps them all. Whether or not it changes their views, it certainly provides a wealth of information, which is its main purpose. It shows how the International Bank for Reconstruction and Development (IBRD), better known as the World Bank, has evolved from the early postwar years to the present. It describes many of the Bank's activities, most of its institutional components, and all of its presidents. It also presents its various affiliates: International Development Association, International Centre for Settlement of Investment Disputes, International Finance Corporation, and Multilateral Investment Guarantee Agency. The evolution is summed up in a chronology, and a list of acronyms assists the reader through the documentation. The bibliography, which is particularly useful, introduces those who want to know more to the Bank's own copious literature as well as to general works by outsiders: friendly, unfriendly, and neutral.

This book was written by an insider, a very special insider. Anne C. M. Salda was for many years a librarian for the Joint Bank-Fund library in Washington, D.C. She has no policies to defend and no axes to grind. Instead, she tries to provide information on the World Bank, what it has done, what it is doing, and what has been written about it. Since her retirement she has produced two major bibliographies covering the International Monetary Fund and the World Bank. In this Historical Dictionary of the World Bank she has acquitted herself extremely well.

Jon Woronoff
Series Editor

Acknowledgments

It would have been impossible for me to complete this book without the help of many kind friends and colleagues. First, I would like to express my gratitude to the Librarian and staffs of the Joint and Sectoral Libraries. I have been fortunate to enjoy access to these unique collections on the Bank and its affiliated institutions, and I appreciate all the help I have received in locating books and other material. Special thanks also to all the librarians and their staffs in the Bank/Fund Library Network, including Yvonne Liem, Linda Thompson, and Amokrane Touami, and to the staff of the World Bank Bookshop, especially Jesse Parker. Susan Turner and her staff and Gabriel Arturo Martinez have given me useful assistance in connection with the mysteries of the computer. I owe many thanks to Goddard W. Winterbottom, formerly editor in the World Bank's Publications Department, who encouraged me to undertake this book, and very kindly gave me access to his excellent collection of material on the Bank and its affiliates. Finally, I am grateful to all those kind people who have helped me in the tasks of proofreading and correcting errors, especially Chrisona Schmidt, who did much useful work on the draft of this book. The editor of this series, Jon Woronoff, has had a difficult task, and I thank him for his patience and help.

While collecting material for this dictionary, I have made extensive use of books, periodical articles, and papers on the World Bank Group, and have tried to cover as many aspects as possible of its many and varied activities. The Bank is a very active publisher of books, papers, periodicals, reports, and studies dealing with its work and many other important development issues, and I am very grateful to the Bank and its authors for all the useful information they provide. For their scholarly study of the Bank's first twenty-five years, *The World Bank Since Bretton Woods: The Origins, Policies, Operations, and Impact of the International Bank for Reconstruction and Development and the Other Members of the World Bank Group,* I am indebted to Edward S. Mason and Robert E. Asher. A 1994 publication by the Bretton Woods Commission, entitled *Bretton Woods: Looking to the Future,* was also helpful, as were the papers and proceedings of numerous conferences on the Bank's operations.

Although the material in this book has been drawn as far as possible from "official" sources, I should add that errors or omissions are my responsibility only.

Abbreviations and Acronyms

AfDB	African Development Bank
AIDS	Acquired Immunodeficiency Syndrome
ASAL	Agricultural Sector Adjustment Loan
AsDB	Asian Development Bank
BIS	Bank for International Settlements
CDB	Caribbean Development Bank
CGIAR	Consultative Group on International Agricultural Research
DC	Development Committee (Joint Ministerial Committee of the Boards of Governors of the World Bank and the International Monetary Fund on the Transfer of Real Resources to the Developing Countries)
EBRD	European Bank for Reconstruction and Development
ECA	United Nations. Economic Commission for Africa
EDI	Economic Development Institute (Washington, D.C.)
FAO	Food and Agriculture Organization of the United Nations
FIAS	Foreign Investment Advisory Service (IBRD/IFC)
FSAL	Financial Sector Adjustment Loan
G-3	Group of Three (Germany, Japan, U.S.)
G-5	Group of Five (France, Germany, Japan, U.K., U.S.)
G-7	Group of Seven (Canada, France, Germany, Italy, Japan, U.K., U.S.)
G-10	Group of Ten (Belgium, Canada, France, Germany, Italy, Japan, Netherlands, Sweden, U.K., U.S.)
G-24	Intergovernmental Group of Twenty-Four on International Monetary Affairs (Group of Twenty-Four)
G-77	Group of Seventy-Seven
GATT	General Agreement on Tariffs and Trade

GDP	Gross Domestic Product
GEF	Global Environment Facility
GNP	Gross National Product
HRO	Human Resources and Operations Policy Vice Presidency (IBRD)
IBRD	International Bank for Reconstruction and Development
ICSID	International Centre for Settlement of Investment Disputes
IDA	International Development Association
IFC	International Finance Corporation
IMF	International Monetary Fund
ISAL	Industrial Sector Adjustment Loan
LDC	Less Developed Country
LSMS	Living Standards Measurement Study
MIGA	Multilateral Investment Guarantee Agency
NGO	Non-Governmental Organization
OECD	Organisation for Economic Co-operation and Development
PA	Poverty Assessment
PTI	Program of Targeted Interventions
SAL	Structural Adjustment Loan
SECAL	Sectoral Adjustment Loan
SDA	Social Dimensions of Adjustment
SPA	Special Program of Assistance (for sub-Saharan Africa)
UNDP	United Nations Development Programme
UNEP	United Nations Environment Programme
WB	World Bank (IBRD, IDA)
WBG	World Bank Group (IBRD, ICSID, IDA, IFC, MIGA)
WHO	World Health Organization

Chronology, July 1944–December 1995

1944

July 1–22   The United Nations Monetary and Financial Conference,
            attended by delegations from forty-four nations, was held at
            Bretton Woods, New Hampshire. The Articles of
            Agreement of the International Bank for Reconstruction
            and Development (IBRD) and the International Monetary
            Fund were drawn up during the conference.

1945

December 27   The Bank's Articles of Agreement entered into force, after
              signature by twenty-nine governments.

1946

March 8–18   The inaugural meeting of the boards of governors of the
             Bank and the Fund was held in Savannah, Georgia. The
             Bank's bylaws were adopted, the first executive directors
             were elected, and it was agreed that the headquarters of
             the two institutions would be in Washington, D.C.

June 18   Eugene Meyer took office as the first president of the Bank.

June 25   The Bank opened for business.

September 27–   The first annual meeting of the Bank's Board of Governors
October 5   was held in Washington, D.C. At that time, the Bank
                had thirty-eight members and a staff of seventy-two.

October 14   Applications for loans were received from Chile,
             Czechoslovakia, Denmark, France, Luxembourg, and
             Poland.

December 4   Eugene Meyer resigned as president of the Bank.

1947

March 17   John J. McCloy took office as the Bank's second president.

May 9   The Bank's first loan, $250 million, to Crédit National of
           France, was approved by the executive directors. In real
           terms, it remains the Bank's largest loan.

| June 10 | A small fact-finding mission to Poland was announced (the Bank's first mission). |
| July 15 | The Bank offered $250 million in bonds on the U.S. market (the Bank's first bond offer). The issue was oversubscribed. |

1948

| March 25 | The Bank's first loan to a developing country (Chile) was approved by the executive directors. |

1949

January 6	The Bank lent $34.1 million to two Mexican government agencies for electric power development (the Bank's first sector loan).
May 18	John J. McCloy resigned as president of the Bank.
June 30	A mission to Colombia was announced (the Bank's first comprehensive economic survey mission).
July 1	Eugene R. Black, who had been the U.S. executive director since March 1947, became the Bank's third president.
August 15	The Bank made a loan of $34 million to India (the Bank's first Asian loan).

1950

January 25	Bank bonds in the amount of $100 million were sold to a syndicate headed by Chicago banks.
March 6	The Bank announced that its Swiss franc bond issue had been sold to a group of Swiss banks.
June 15	A loan of $12.8 million was made to Iraq for the construction of a flood control system on the Tigris (the Bank's first loan to the Middle East).
August 22	The Bank lent Australia $100 million (the Bank's first program loan).
September 13	The Bank made two loans to Ethiopia, one for road construction and one for the establishment of a development bank (the Bank's first loan to Africa, and the first development bank loan).
October 6	The Bank and the Food and Agriculture Organization of the United Nations (FAO) sponsored an agricultural survey mission to Uruguay (the first sector survey).

1951

| May 23 | The IBRD's first public offering outside the U.S., a £5 million issue of 20-year Bank bonds, was offered on the London market by Baring Bros. |

1952

August 13–14	Japan and Germany became members of the Bank and Fund.
September	The first reorganization of the Bank took place, and three area departments (Asia and Middle East; Europe, Africa, and Australasia; Western Hemisphere) and a department of technical operations were established.

1953

September 8	Eugene R. Black was appointed president of the Bank for a second five-year term.
October 15	The first three loans to Japan, totaling $40.2 million, were approved.

1954

December 10	Representatives from India and Pakistan took part in discussions on the Indus River system.

1955

March 11	The Bank announced the establishment of its Economic Development Institute (EDI), with support from the Rockefeller and Ford Foundations.
June 21	An interim agreement on irrigation use of the Indus River was signed by India, Pakistan, and the Bank.
November 3	Indus Waters Agreement extended to March 31, 1956.

1956

January 9	The Economic Development Institute began operations.
June 30	Bank staff grew in number to 511.
July 11	The International Finance Corporation (IFC) was established.

1957

June 20	IFC made its first investment ($2 million) which was in Siemens do Brasil.
November 6	Eugene Black visited Egypt in connection with the High Dam project.

1958

March 28	Discussions were held concerning compensation for shareholders in the Suez Canal Company.
July 14	Suez Canal compensation agreement signed in Geneva.
August 25–27	Following a deterioration in India's balance of payments, the first meeting of the India Aid Consortium was held in Washington, D.C.

1959

July 1	For the second successive fiscal year, Bank lending exceeded $700 million.
September 16	The Bank's authorized capital was increased from $10 billion to $25.3 billion.

1960

September 19	The Indus Waters Treaty was signed in Karachi by India, Pakistan, and the Bank.
September 24	The International Development Association (IDA) was established.

1961

May 12	IDA's first development credit, for $9 million, was extended to Honduras.
September 5	IFC's Articles of Agreement were amended to permit the Corporation to make equity investments.

1962

September 17	An IDA credit of $5 million was approved for school construction in Tunisia (first World Bank financing of education).

1963

January 1	George D. Woods became the Bank's fourth president.

1964

June 29	IDA's first replenishment came into effect, amounting to $753 million.

1965

June 30	For the first time, World Bank commitments exceeded $1 billion.
December 17	The Bank's Articles of Agreement were amended to allow the Bank to make loans to IFC of up to four times IFC's unimpaired subscribed capital and surplus.

1966

March 16	The Bank and representatives from nine countries met to establish the Nam Ngum Development Fund for financing a hydroelectric power project on the Mekong River, the Bank to be administrator.
May 4	The agreement establishing the Nam Ngum Development Fund was signed.

August 10	The Bank's capital was increased to $28.9 million.
October 14	The International Centre for Settlement of Investment Disputes (ICSID) was established.
December 8	IFC made its first investment in tourism.

1967

October 27	In an address to the Swedish Bankers Association in Stockholm, George D. Woods proposed the establishment of an international commission to examine world development.

1968

April 1	Robert S. McNamara became the Bank's fifth president.
May 2	The Tarbela Development Fund Agreement was signed, providing nearly $500 million in external financing for the Tarbela Dam Project in West Pakistan, the Bank to be administrator.
August 19	Lester B. Pearson accepted chairmanship of the proposed commission on development issues.

1969

July 1	The Bank and IDA announced total loans and credits of $1,784 million in fiscal 1969, compared with $953.5 million in the previous fiscal year. IFC lent $93 million, compared with $51 million in fiscal 1968.
July 23	IDA's second replenishment was agreed, amounting to $1.4 billion.

1970

February 12	Japan's first loan to the Bank (equivalent to $100 million) was announced.
June 16	The Bank made a loan of $2 million to Jamaica to support the government's family planning program (the Bank's first loan for family planning).
June 30	The Bank Group's commitments for the fiscal year 1970 exceeded $2 billion for the first time.
July 22	Agreement was reached on IDA's third replenishment (approximately $813 million for three years).
September	An operations evaluation unit, with responsibility for evaluating Bank Group operations, was established by President McNamara.

1971

May 18	A loan agreement ($15 million) was signed for river pollution control in Brazil (the Bank's first loan for pollution control).
May 19	The newly established Consultative Group on International Agricultural Research (CGIAR) met in Washington, D.C.

1972

June 30	World Bank lending exceeded $3 billion for the first time in fiscal year 1972.
October	The second major reorganization of the Bank took place. Five new regional offices were created, incorporating seven former area departments and eight projects departments.

1973

April	Robert S. McNamara was appointed as president of the Bank for a second five-year term.
September	Agreement was reached on IDA's fourth replenishment, for $4,500 million.

1974

October	The Joint Ministerial Committee of the Boards of Governors of the World Bank and the International Monetary Fund on the Transfer of Real Resources to Developing Countries (Development Committee) was established.

1975

December 16	The Project Preparation Facility was established. Through this, the Bank provides funding to borrowers for project preparation and institution building.
December 23	An intermediate financing facility, ("Third Window") came into effect, enabling the Bank to provide financing on terms between those of the IBRD and IDA.

1977

May	The Bank's authorized capital was increased to $34 billion.
November	The fifth replenishment of IDA came into effect, providing $7,500 million. IFC's capital was increased to $650 million.

1979

June 30	World Bank lending exceeded $10 billion for the first time in the fiscal year ending June 30.

1980

January 4	The authorized capital stock of the IBRD was increased by $44 billion to $85 billion.
March 25	The first structural adjustment loan, to Turkey for $200 million, was approved.
July 1	A new system of currency pooling, intended to equalize exchange rate risks for Bank borrowers, was introduced.

1981

July	A.W. Clausen became the Bank's sixth president.
August	IDA's sixth replenishment, for $12,000 million, came into effect.
October	The Bank's authorized capital stock was increased to $86.4 billion.

1982

September 8	IDA donors, with the exception of the United States, agreed to make special contributions, equivalent to one third of their total contribution to IDA's sixth replenishment. These were needed because of legislative delays in the United States and a subsequent reduction in the U.S. appropriations for IDA-6.

1983

January 11	New cofinancing instruments ("B-loans") were authorized by the executive directors. They assist Bank borrowers to increase and stabilize capital flows by linking part of commercial bank flows to IBRD operations.
February 22	The Special Action Program was established. This program was intended to accelerate disbursements to countries attempting to implement high-priority projects during periods of adverse external conditions.

1984

January– September	Negotiations began on IDA's seventh replenishment, and agreement was finally reached on $9,000 million.

1985

July 1   The Special Facility for Sub-Saharan Africa, to assist African governments undertaking reform programs, came into operation.

1986

January–   Negotiations began on IDA's eighth replenishment, and the
September   donors agreed on $11,500 million, with supplementary contributions from some countries.

July 1   Barber C. Conable became the Bank's seventh president.

1987

May 4   A Bankwide internal reorganization took place. The Bank's functions were rearranged into four complexes, each headed by a senior vice-president: Operations; Policy, Planning, and Research (which included a central Environment Department); Finance; and Administration. Within regions country departments were created that combined the functions previously divided between program and projects departments.

September   The Social Dimensions of Adjustment (SDA) Initiative was launched as a joint undertaking of the World Bank, the African Development Bank, and the United Nations Development Programme.

December 4   Donor countries agreed to establish the Special Program of Assistance to provide fast-disbursing aid to low-income indebted African countries undertaking reform programs.

1988

April 12   The convention establishing the Multilateral Investment Guarantee Agency (MIGA) came into effect.

April 27   The Bank's total authorized capital was increased to $171.4 billion.

1989

August 1   The Debt-Reduction Facility for IDA-only countries was established to ease their burden of external commercial debt.

December   IDa's ninth replenishment, totaling $15,500 million, was agreed.

1990

January 30   The IBRD's largest loan was approved. It was to Mexico for $1,260 million (in nominal terms) to support the country's debt reduction program.

June 30	Bank lending for education exceeded $1 billion for the first time in fiscal year 1990.
November 28	The Global Environment Facility (GEF) was launched as a three-year pilot program by the World Bank, the United Nations Development Programme, and the United Nations Environment Programme.

1991

June	IFC's board of directors approved an increase in the Corporation's capital to $2,300 million.
September 1	Lewis T. Preston became the Bank's eighth president.

1992

May 29	Switzerland became a member of the Bank.
June 16	The Russian Federation became a member of the IBRD and IDA.
July 6– September 22	Twelve republics of the former Soviet Union became members of the IBRD.
November 3	The report of the Task Force on Portfolio Management (the Wapenhans Report) was presented to the executive directors.
December	Agreement was reached on IDA's tenth replenishment, providing approximately $18,000 million.

1993

January 1	Three vice presidencies, dealing with the environment, human resources, and the private sector, were created.
September 22	The World Bank Inspection Panel was established.

1994

January 3	The Public Information Center at the Bank's headquarters in Washington, D.C. opened for business.
May 3	The Bank published a three-year, $1.2 billion program to assist the West Bank and Gaza in their transition to autonomous rule.
July 6	Eritrea joined the IBRD, bringing the Bank's total membership to 178.
September 8	The executive directors approved recommendations for mainstream guarantees as new operational tools for the Bank.
October	Negotiations began on IDA's eleventh replenishment.

1995

March 3	Korea became the first country to progress from being a concessional borrower from IDA to becoming an IDA donor and a "graduate" from the IBRD.
March 31	IDA's membership increased to 158.
May–June	Two $500 million loans were approved for Argentina to support the country's bank reform program.
	The Bank pledged to lend China approximately $3 billion a year for the next three years to improve infrastructure, reduce poverty, assist education, and protect the environment.
June 1	James D. Wolfensohn became the Bank's ninth president.
June 15	A $1.5 billion loan to Mexico was approved to strengthen the country's financial sector and ease the burden on the poor of post-devaluation problems.
June 30	World Bank commitments amounted to S22.5 billion in the fiscal year ending June 30, 1995.
	Action was pending on membership in the IBRD for Bosnia-Herzegovina, Brunei Darussalam, and the Federal Republic of Yugoslavia (Serbia/Montenegro).
July–December	World Bank commitments for the second half of 1995 amounted to $7.3 billion, compared with $7.9 billion for the same period in 1994.
	MIGA issued 23 investment guarantee contracts that amounted to more than $400 million and supported about $6.6 billion in foreign direct investment.
December	The Bank approved a Global Environment Trust Fund grant of $3.2 billion to finance an energy project in the Russian Federation to explore further development of the natural gas sector to reduce gas emissions.

Introduction

Background to the Bretton Woods Conference

In July 1944, while the world was still at war, delegations from forty-four Allied nations met at Bretton Woods, New Hampshire, to create a new international monetary and financial order for the postwar world. Agreement was reached in three weeks, and two new international organizations were established; the International Monetary Fund and the International Bank for Reconstruction and Development, commonly known as the World Bank.

A number of factors contributed to the success of the Bretton Woods Conference, officially named the United Nations Monetary and Financial Conference. In the period between the two world wars the breakdown of the gold exchange standard had been followed by exchange instability, competitive currency depreciation, and tariff discrimination, with individual countries attempting to emerge from depression at the expense of their neighbors. The unhappy state of the world during those years had brought many among the Allied nations to welcome the idea of new monetary, financial and trade arrangements, and their leaders were willing to support the United States and Britain in their efforts to achieve stability in the postwar world.

Preparing the Ground

The years of planning and discussion that preceded the actual conference at Bretton Woods played an important part in its success, as did the vision of two remarkable men: Harry Dexter White of the United States and John Maynard Keynes, afterward Lord Keynes, of Great Britain.

As early as 1941 both White and Keynes had begun work on plans for a new international monetary and financial system. By April 1942 White, then acting as special adviser to Henry Morgenthau, Secretary of the U.S. Treasury, had prepared his *Proposal for a United and Associated Nations Stabili-*

zation Fund and a Bank for Reconstruction and Development of the United and Associated Nations.

White's plans for the Bank were ambitious, and included some functions that were omitted from the Bank's Articles of Agreement, or charter, drawn up at Bretton Woods. As well as lending for postwar reconstruction and development in member countries, White also proposed that the Bank would guarantee private investments, stabilize international commodity prices, and issue its own currency. In addition, it would finance international relief efforts in areas devastated by war or natural disasters and would promote democratic institutions in member countries. Morgenthau was authorized by President Roosevelt to continue work on White's proposals, with assistance from a technical committee chaired by White. A memorandum was then prepared on a "United Nations Bank for Reconstruction and Development."

Keynes's plan for an International Clearing Union was presented to the U.S. in August 1942. Although he gave the proposed Union wider powers than White had assigned to his Stabilization Fund, including the issuing of an international currency (the bancor), Keynes did not at that time propose any plans for the future Bank. The White and Keynes plans were discussed by experts in several countries, a number of suggestions and counterproposals were put forward, and in November 1943, the U.S. Treasury published a modified version of White's original plan, which was intended to serve as the main text for the negotiations at Bretton Woods. In June 1944 a number of the delegates attended a preliminary conference in Atlantic City, New Jersey, during which the British delegation, led by Keynes, and delegates from other countries, presented draft proposals for the Bank, which had been drawn up during their voyage to the United States on the *Queen Mary*. Subsequently known as the "boat draft", these and other suggestions were combined with the American proposals for consideration at Bretton Woods.

Issues During the Bretton Woods Conference

Three commissions were established at Bretton Woods to carry out the work of the conference: Commission I, on the Fund, was chaired by White; Commission II, on the Bank, by Keynes; and Commission III, which considered other international financial issues, by Eduardo Suarez of Mexico. At first the delegates devoted most of their time to discussion of the proposed Fund; indeed, Commission II on the Bank did not begin its work until the second week of the conference. In his inaugural address as the Commission's chairman, Keynes stressed the importance of the Bank's future functions and took an active part in drawing up its Articles of Agreement, together with delegates from the United States, France, the Netherlands, Greece, and some of the Latin American countries. Although there had been some disagreement about the future constitution of the Fund, there was relatively little controversy concerning the Bank, and its Articles were approved with few changes.

Purposes of the Bank

Article I of the Bank's Articles, or charter, lists five purposes for the new institution. The first of these expresses the main objective of the Bank's founders: "To assist in the reconstruction and development of territories of members by facilitating the investment of capital for productive purposes, including the restoration of economies destroyed or disrupted by war, the reconversion of productive facilities, and the encouragement of the development of productive facilities and resources in less developed countries." A second purpose is to promote private foreign investment by means of guarantees or participations in loans and other investments and, when private capital is not available on reasonable terms, to provide, on suitable conditions, finance for productive purposes out of the Bank's own capital, funds raised by it, and its other resources. A third purpose is to encourage the long-range growth of international trade and the maintenance of equilibrium in balances of payments through supporting international investment for the development of the productive resources of members. The fourth purpose requires the Bank to arrange its loans in relation to loans through other channels, so that "the more useful and urgent projects" will be dealt with first. Finally, the Bank is urged "to conduct its operations with due regard to the effect of international investment on business conditions in the territories of members, and. . . . to assist in bringing about a smooth transition from a wartime to a peacetime economy."

The Beginnings of the Bank

After signature by twenty-nine governments, the Articles of the Bank and Fund entered into force on December 24, 1945. In March 1946, the inaugural meetings of the Boards of Governors of the two institutions were held in Savannah, Georgia, and certain issues were resolved that had not been settled at Bretton Woods, including the selection of Washington, D.C. as the headquarters for the Bank and the Fund, and the terms of service and salaries of the executive directors. Many of the participants would have chosen New York for the headquarters of the new institutions, but the United States preferred Washington, D.C. Lengthy discussions resulted in agreement that the executive directors should "function in continuous session," as laid down in the Articles. The subject of the directors' salaries was also hotly debated. Lord Keynes, who led the British delegation at Savannah, felt that they were too high at $17,000 per year. On June 18, 1946, Eugene Meyer was appointed as the Bank's first president, and the Bank opened for business one week later.

The Bank's Early Years

The Bank's first president, Eugene Meyer, was originally an investment banker in New York. He then held a number of U.S. government appointments, including membership of the Federal Reserve Board. Subsequently, he acquired the *Washington Post.* After assuming office in June 1946, Meyer established an organizational framework for the Bank, and approved appointments to the offices of Secretary, General Counsel, Treasurer, and Director of Personnel. The Bank's organization, as described in its first *Annual Report,* was very simple, consisting of the following offices and departments: Offices of the President, the Secretary, and the Treasurer; Legal Department; Loan Department; Research Department (afterwards Economic Department); Personnel Office; and Office Services. In August 1946 Meyer met a number of leading bankers in New York, and began the process of reassuring the financial community about the Bank's future policies. However, after difficulties with the Bank's executive directors concerning his authority as president, Meyer resigned after only six months in office.

John J. McCloy, the Bank's second president, was a lawyer who had been U.S. Assistant Secretary of War during the Second World War. He had close ties with a number of New York banking firms, and was well respected on Wall Street. He did not accept President Truman's invitation to succeed Meyer until he had received official assurances of support for his authority as Bank president. McCloy assumed office in March 1947, and in May of that year the Bank made its first loan, to France's Crédit National. Subsequently, other loans for reconstruction went to the Netherlands, Denmark, and Luxembourg.

McCloy considered that the major task of his presidency was to persuade American investors that Bank bonds were good investments. He worked closely with Robert Garner, the Bank's vice president, and Eugene Black, then U.S. executive director and afterwards the Bank's third president, to secure support for the Bank's first bond issue in the New York market. This took place in July 1947 and was very successful, being heavily oversubscribed.

A Bank mission went to Brazil in 1947, and was followed by missions to Chile, Egypt, India, Peru, the Philippines, and Turkey. Soon after, the Bank's first loan to a less developed country went to Chile in 1948. During 1949 loans were made for projects in Brazil, India, and Mexico. In May 1949 John J. McCloy resigned from the Bank to become U.S. High Commissioner in Germany.

Black's Bank

McCloy's successor, Eugene Black, had been a vice president of the Chase Bank in New York, and was widely respected as an expert in bonds and as a skilled negotiator. He had held office as U.S. executive director during McCloy's presidency and was well acquainted with the Bank and its staff. In July 1949 he was appointed president of the Bank, and held office for more than thirteen years. During that period it was often referred to as "Black's Bank." The new president made use of his negotiating skills to extend support for the Bank in the international financial markets. He supported the first public offerings of the Bank's bonds in England, and subsequent offerings in the Netherlands and Switzerland.

In 1952 an interdepartmental committee, chaired by Sir William Iliff, was established to examine the Bank's organization. It recommended the establishment of area departments, and the staffs of the Loan and Economic Departments were distributed among three area departments, a Technical Operations Department (TOD), and an Economic Staff. The new Technical Operations Department was organized on a functional basis, with subunits for agriculture, industry, transportation, etc. This organizational framework remained more or less unchanged for twenty years, and worked well while Bank lending was still comparatively small.

Black traveled extensively during his presidency, and helped to establish closer relations between the World Bank and its members. Lending to the developing countries increased, mainly for large irrigation projects, power systems or infrastructure. Black also acted as mediator in a number of economic disputes between Bank members, and played an active part, together with Sir William Iliff, a Bank vice president, in resolving the dispute between India and Pakistan concerning the division of the Indus waters. His negotiating skills were employed in obtaining large-scale international assistance for India and Pakistan, and he was actively involved in the establishment of aid consortia for both countries. During Black's presidency, the Bank's Economic Development Institute was established (1955), as were two of its affiliated institutions: the International Finance Corporation (1956) and the International Development Association (1960).

The Woods Era in the Bank

George Woods, the Bank's fourth president, continued and accelerated the process, begun under his predecessor, of transforming the Bank into a development institution. Woods, formerly chairman of the First Boston Corporation, was well known and respected in U.S. investment banking circles. He held office from January 1963 to March 1968.

Before his appointment as Bank president, Woods had advised Eugene Black on the marketing of Bank bonds, and had also participated as a consultant in a number of Bank missions. Consequently, he already had some experience with the problems of the developing countries, as well as prior knowledge of the Bank's activities and staff. From the beginning Woods supported IDA, emphasized the importance of IFC's operations, and asked for more Bank loans to assist agriculture and education in the developing countries. He also felt that the Bank needed more economists, and he asked Irving Friedman to direct the work of what eventually became a much larger economics staff.

During Woods's presidency, the Bank provided more technical assistance to the developing countries, introduced annual reviews of the economies of all borrowing countries, and made cooperative arrangements with OECD and the regional development banks to establish a system of international debt reporting. In 1964 Woods formally proposed that the Bank should be permitted to make loans to IFC of up to five times IFC's unimpaired subscribed capital and surplus. After changes in the Bank's and IFC's Articles of Agreement made this possible, IFC was able to increase its commitment to more than $50 million annually, compared with an average of $20 million in previous years. Woods strongly supported increased private foreign investment in the developing countries, and he took an active part in the negotiations leading to the establishment of the International Centre for Settlement of Investment Disputes (ICSID) in 1966. He also believed in more effective aid coordination, and during his presidency additional consultative aid groups were set up to assist member countries. There was also increased cooperation with the Food and Agriculture Organization of the United Nations (FAO), the United Nations Development Programme (UNDP), and the United Nations Educational, Scientific and Cultural Organization (UNESCO) in the identification and preparation of projects.

In the 1960s many of the newly independent African states became members of the Bank, their numbers increasing from eleven to thirty-two. Africa's share of Bank Group financing began to increase, and by 1967 it amounted to $86 million in Bank loans, $91 million in IDA credits, and $7 million from IFC.

Woods was asked to negotiate the second replenishment of IDA's funds in April 1965. He had become increasingly concerned about the problem of raising funds for IDA, and his advisers suggested that the Bank ask for $1 billion a year. However, Woods experienced difficulty, especially in the United States, in gaining support for such a large amount, and in spite of his efforts the second IDA replenishment was not agreed to during his presidency. Because of these problems, Woods was anxious to find a successor as soon as possible, favoring Robert McNamara. He had been impressed by McNamara's speech to the Association of American Newspaper Editors in 1966 and probably thought that the Bank would benefit from having a president who was close to the White House. Subsequently, it was announced that McNamara would assume office as the Bank's president in April 1968.

The McNamara Years

Robert S. McNamara, the fifth president of the World Bank, had previously served as president of the Ford Motor Company, and as Secretary of the U.S. Department of Defense. In April 1968, McNamara assumed office as the Bank's fifth president. He was surprised to find that there had been no recent Bank loans to such countries as Egypt and Indonesia, nor to the majority of the poorest African countries. During a meeting of senior Bank staff, he requested those present to prepare lists of all the projects and programs they would like the Bank and its affiliates to undertake if there were no financing constraints. It soon became clear that if all these proposals were accepted, their financing would amount to double the Bank's average rate of spending for the previous five years. The new president proposed this scale of expansion at the Bank's annual meeting in September 1968. McNamara had already begun to increase Bank borrowing, and he was able to announce that during the previous ninety days the Bank had borrowed more than in the whole of any previous year in its history. He also declared that there would be more Bank Group lending for programs and projects to remove the main constraints on development, which he considered to be increasing population growth, malnutrition, and illiteracy. To support this expansion of the Bank's activities, McNamara began to increase the number of Bank staff. This grew from about seven hundred and sixty professionals in fiscal year 1968 to more than two thousand five hundred by fiscal 1981. During this expansion, he took steps to make the staff as representative as possible of the Bank's membership.

From the beginning of his presidency, McNamara undertook a large number of personal visits, at least four a year, including many to developing countries. These took him to more than fifty countries, and involved discussions between McNamara and the country's finance minister and other high officials, followed by a meeting with the head of its government. In Africa, where Bank assistance was most needed and where McNamara made many of his visits, he established friendly relations with a number of national leaders. During such visits, McNamara also spent time in rural areas, coming to believe that poverty could only be reduced through direct action at the small farm level.

In late 1971 the Governors of the Bank began to consider the possibility of a second five-year term as president for McNamara. His achievements in assisting the developing countries were recognized, but there was some criticism of his poverty-oriented policies and of the increased size of the Bank. A consensus eventually emerged that McNamara should be reappointed, but at first this consensus did not include the United States. His years in office during the Vietnam war had left him with enemies in Congress, and there was opposition to his requests for increased foreign aid. American support for McNamara's second term finally came, but it has been described as "belated and grudging."

A comprehensive reorganization of the Bank took place in 1972. Five new regional offices were established at the Bank's headquarters in Washington, D.C.: (Eastern Africa; Western Africa; Europe, Middle East and North Africa; Asia; and Latin America and the Caribbean). Each office, headed by a regional vice president, was responsible for planning and supervising the Bank's assistance programs for the countries within the region, and employed most of the experts (economists, financial analysts, and loan officers) required for these operations. Country program departments, together with projects departments having their own sector specialists, were also established in each regional office. As part of the new organizational structure, further policy and operational support was provided through new central projects and development policy staffs, the former being responsible for projects in industry, population, nutrition, rural development, tourism, and urbanization, and the latter for global and countrywide policy issues, as well as the Bank's economic work, research program, and commodity analysis.

In September 1973, during the World Bank/IMF annual meeting in Nairobi (the first to be held in Africa), McNamara asked for more help for those living in "absolute poverty" and spoke of new Bank policies that were aimed at making the poor more productive. Loans would be made for integrated rural development projects, which would target small farmers, and include components to assist the very poor in rural areas. The Bank would also support projects involving family planning, health, nutrition, water supply and sanitation, housing, and urban development. McNamara's proposals were welcomed, and at the end of the meeting agreement was reached on a replenishment of IDA's funds at a higher level than before. This was regarded as an expression of confidence in McNamara and the Bank. Soon after the meeting, however, OPEC raised oil prices, and a crisis ensued that affected the industrialized countries as well as the developing countries. McNamara felt that the developing countries needed more external financing to maintain growth. Because the industrialized countries were facing difficulties, he believed that additional new financing could come only from the capital-surplus oil producers. Early in 1974 he went to Iran for discussions about an OPEC fund for development. Although agreement was reached, the United States was unwilling to cooperate, and the proposals came to nothing. In addition, McNamara had to face opposition from William Simon, Secretary of the Treasury from 1974 to 1977, who opposed any increase in the Bank's activities.

President Carter assumed office in 1977, and it was said that he intended to double U.S. foreign aid. However, many in Congress were opposed to this. In order to appease the critics, Carter's administration began to investigate the salaries paid to Bank and IMF staff, these being frequent targets of Congressional criticism. Although the investigation revealed that these salaries were no higher than banking salaries in other parts of the world, there was growing suspicion that the United States was trying to dominate or destroy the two institutions, especially when Congress subsequently tried to limit the use of IDA funds. McNamara insisted that under its Articles of Agreement the Bank could not accept "tied" funds. A compromise was reached, and it was agreed that the U.S. executive director would be instructed not to support such loans.

The Bank's activities continued to increase during McNamara's second term, but there were growing economic problems worldwide. In 1979 McNamara warned against the dangers of increased external debt in the less developed countries, and undertook to recommend consideration of requests for "structural adjustment" assistance. This new type of Bank aid was designed to supplement the relatively short-term financing provided by the International Monetary Fund and the commercial banks. It was intended to give medium-term assistance to countries endeavoring to reduce their current account deficits while maintaining programs of policy reform. Such loans differed from the Bank's traditional project loans because they were linked to reform programs rather than specific projects, and were for shorter periods. Although this form of lending was intended to be flexible, a borrowing country had to meet certain prerequisites, conditions were established, and a limit was placed on Bank and IDA loans and credits for adjustment. The first structural adjustment loans (SALs) were made in 1980, and sectoral adjustment loans (SECALs) were subsequently introduced.

McNamara's personal standing remained high, and the United States supported his reappointment for a third term as Bank president. However, during the negotiations for IDA's sixth replenishment, Vietnam invaded Cambodia, and McNamara was informed that the IDA replenishment bill would be defeated unless he assured Congress that the Bank would not proceed with some proposed loans to Vietnam. McNamara sent a letter to this effect to the appropriate House committee. This letter was subsequently published, and the Bank's Executive Board unanimously protested McNamara's action. Another problem arose when the OPEC countries requested that a representative of the Palestine Liberation Organization attend Bank/Fund meetings as an observer. It was clear that Congress would view a PLO presence unfavorably, and that this could affect the passage of appropriations for the Bank. McNamara obtained a vote from the Executive Board that postponed the issue for future consideration, but his action was criticized by many member countries. Such episodes, as well as continuing problems with the U.S. Congress, made McNamara's last years as Bank president very difficult. He decided not to complete his third term of office and retired in June 1981.

The Bank in the 1980s

Before his election as sixth president of the World Bank Group, Alden Winship Clausen had been the president and chief executive officer of the Bank of America. He assumed office in July 1981 and during his first months established a managing committee to provide overall guidance for the management of the Bank.

During Clausen's years in office, the Bank continued its policy of lending for structural and sectoral adjustment. These loans increased during the 1980s, and the Bank was able to assist heavily indebted countries in sub-Saharan Africa and Latin America. A number of special facilities and programs were introduced, especially for sub-Saharan Africa, and the Bank also supported debt and debt servicing reduction efforts by the indebted countries. In these years, the Bank's new involvement in its members' adjustment efforts came closer to the work of the International Monetary Fund, and the two institutions worked closely together to coordinate policy advice and financial help to their members.

There was increased support for agriculture in the 1980s, including agricultural research and extension, and more emphasis on the importance of resource management. A new issue for the Bank in the 1980s was the protection of the environment. Misgivings about the environmental effects of Bank projects had already been expressed in the 1970s, and at the beginning of the new decade the Bank established an environment department and stressed the need to prepare detailed environmental assessments during the early stages of project formulation.

In July 1986 Barber B. Conable, a lawyer and former member of the U.S. Congress, became the Bank's seventh president. He had represented a constituency in New York State for twenty years. Soon after Conable's appointment, an extensive organizational review of the Bank was announced. In 1987 the Bank's functions were rearranged into four broad areas: Operations; Finance; Administration; and Policy, Planning, and Research, each headed by a senior vice president. The regions within the Bank were reduced to four: Africa; Asia; Europe, the Middle East, and North Africa; and Latin America and the Caribbean. Each region, headed by a vice president, included a number of country departments, and a technical department, with several functional divisions for agriculture, industry, etc.

In his addresses as World Bank president, Conable stressed the need for careful consideration of the environmental effects of the Bank's projects, and supported Bank sponsorship of the Global Environment Facility. Poverty alleviation continued to be the Bank's major objective, and there was a new emphasis on an increased role for women in development. The Bank made more loans for family planning services, and Bank lending for education doubled. The convention establishing the Bank's fourth affiliated institution, the Multilateral Investment Guarantee Agency (MIGA), came into effect in 1988. In 1990, at the age of 68, Conable decided not to seek renewal of his term of office at the Bank.

New Challenges for the Bank in the 1990s

In September 1991, Lewis Thompson Preston, formerly board chairman and president of New York's Guaranty Trust Company, became the eighth president of the World Bank Group. He declared that poverty reduction was still the Bank's "overarching objective."

During Preston's years in office, all fifteen of the former Soviet republics became members of the Bank, and applied for financial and technical assistance from the Bank and its affiliated institutions. Bank-supported programs were initiated in the new South Africa, and banking relations with Vietnam were resumed. The Bank also encouraged peace efforts in the Middle East through its support for economic development in the West Bank and Gaza. There were new efforts to improve the efficiency of the Bank's operations, and an independent World Bank Inspection Panel was established in September 1993 to receive and investigate complaints that the Bank had not followed its own procedures concerning the design, appraisal, or implementation of Bank-supported projects. Pursuing a more open information policy about its operations, the Bank opened a Public Information Center at its headquarters in Washington, D.C. in January 1994. Because of ill-health, Mr. Preston decided to retire in 1995. He died after a brief illness in May 1995, shortly before his successor, James D. Wolfensohn, was to assume office.

Resources of the Bank

The IBRD's resources consist of its subscribed capital, reserves, surplus, and borrowed resources. Capital subscriptions paid to the IBRD comprise a paid-in portion and a larger callable portion, and the amount of each member's subscription is determined by its quota in the IMF, as laid down in the Bank's Articles of Agreement. The paid-in portion is paid to the Bank when a country becomes a member. The subscription consists of two parts, one initially paid in gold or U.S. dollars, and another paid in cash or noninterest-bearing demand obligations, denominated either in the member's currency or in U.S. dollars. The callable portion of the subscription cannot be used by the IBRD for disbursements or administrative costs. It can only be called for payments to the Bank's creditors arising out of its borrowings or loan guarantees and then only if the Bank is unable to meet its obligations in full out of its other assets. The Bank has not suffered losses on its loans or guarantees; rather, it has earned a net income every year since 1948.

Under the IBRD's Articles of Agreement, the total amount outstanding of disbursed loans, participations in loans, and callable guarantees cannot exceed the total value of the Bank's subscribed capital, reserves, and surplus. The adequacy of the IBRD's capital is reviewed every three years (more often if required), and increases are subject to negotiation and agreement by members. The IBRD's net income is calculated, and each year part of it is allocated to maintain the target level of its reserves (at present 13 to 14 percent of its lending) to provide for losses on its loans. The IBRD obtains much of its funds for lending to members through long-term borrowings in the international capital markets, and it also borrows at market rates from central banks and other government institutions. In addition to these borrowings, a significant part of the IBRD's resources is derived from its retained earnings, and from repayments on its loans.

The resources of the IBRD's affiliate, the International Development Association, are derived partly from its members' subscriptions, but mainly from "replenishments" provided by an agreement among donors every three years. IDA's other resources include repayments from past credits and transfers of net income from the IBRD. The resources of the International Finance Corporation are also derived partly from members' subscriptions, but the Corporation, like the IBRD, obtains funds through borrowings in the international markets. It also borrows from the IBRD.

Services

In addition to financial assistance, the Bank provides a variety of other services to its members, including technical assistance, training, and research. Technical assistance takes many different forms and can include feasibility studies, engineering design and construction, project supervision, research and development, and support for capacity- and institution-building. It is supplied through Bank-supported projects or project components, funds from outside sources but administered by the Bank, or directly through the Bank's administrative budget.

An important part of the Bank's technical assistance is provided through missions, comprised of Bank staff and expert consultants. At its request, a mission visits a member country to collect information about its economy or particular aspects of it, review government policies, and present reports with policy recommendations. These reports not only provide the information required for Bank assistance, but they are also useful to researchers, as they contain up-to-date statistics and other information probably unavailable elsewhere. The Bank also gives assistance through its economic and sector work (ESW), which provides policy-related and other detailed studies.

In recent years some Bank members have requested technical assistance to improve or reform their legal systems. Such assistance has been supplied through adjustment loans, components in investment loans, and freestanding technical assistance or capacity-building loans. Because many previously centralized economies in Central and Eastern Europe and the former Soviet Union are changing their institutions during the transition to market economies, the Bank is providing assistance for capacity- and institution-building. It is also one of the sponsors of the Joint Vienna Institute, which holds courses in market economics and financial analysis for officials from the transitional economies.

The Bank's Economic Development Institute (EDI) was established in 1955 to provide training for officials concerned with development programs and projects in the developing countries. Before 1962 EDI offered only general courses, lasting six months, in project preparation and sector planning, but as interest in these subjects grew, shorter two- and three-month courses were arranged in order to accommodate more participants. In the 1970s EDI held more training courses overseas, and increased its efforts to develop training capacity in the developing countries. By 1987, more than 85 percent of EDI's activities were taking place outside Washington, with emphasis on the smallest and poorest among the Bank's member countries, especially those in sub-Saharan Africa. EDI's courses now cover a wide range of subjects of current interest, including girls' education, gender issues, the environment, and macroeconomic and financial management. The Institute endeavors to provide basic skills training, much of it through training-of-trainers programs in cooperation with institutions in member countries. EDI also holds courses for countries in transition from centrally planned economies on such subjects as civil service reform, project management, decentralization of government, and privatization.

A research department was among the first of the offices and departments established in the Bank, and in 1946 its functions were described as "economic, statistical, and other research required in connection with the operations of the Bank." In 1971 the Bank's research program was formally established, and by 1980 more than one hundred research projects had been completed. Research projects are usually initiated within the Bank and often involve collaboration between Bank staff and the outside research community, especially institutions in the developing countries. It is the Bank's policy to support the development of indigenous research in these countries. The main center for research and research-related activities in the Bank is the Policy, Research, and External Affairs (PRE) complex, formerly Policy, Planning, and Research (PPR). Information on the Bank's current research is provided through an annual publication, *World Bank Research Program: Abstracts of Current Studies.*

During recent years Bank research has concentrated on the Bank's main operational activities, including adjustment, the decentralization and reduction of government activities, environmental protection, human resource development, natural resource management, poverty reduction, the private sector, public sector management, reform of centrally planned economies, and taxation. The Bank's research staff also provide comprehensive statistical information to assist operation staff in the development of programs and projects for developing and transitional economies. In addition, they are now assisting the countries of the former Soviet Union in their transition to market economies, with advice on policy reform and other issues, including agriculture, banking and finance, labor markets, privatization, and social safety nets.

The Bank publishes a large number of periodicals that deal with its work and related subjects. They include *Commodity Trade and Price Trends, Evaluation Results, Global Economic Prospects and the Developing Countries, Proceedings of the World Bank Annual Conference on Development Economics, Social Indicators of Development, Trends in Developing Economies, World Bank and the Environment, World Bank Annual Report, World Bank Atlas, World Debt Tables, World Development Indicators, World Development Report* (all annuals); *Commodity Markets and the Developing Countries, Finance & Development* (with the International Monetary Fund), *Financial Flows and the Developing Countries* (all quarterlies); *World Bank Economic Review* (three times a year); *World Bank Research Observer* (twice a year); *Bank's World* (every two months). In addition, the Bank issues press releases and other news material, books, pamphlets, and many publications in series (*see* the Bibliography).

Membership

In July 1944 delegates from 44 countries attended the United Nations Monetary and Financial Conference at Bretton Woods, New Hampshire, and participated in the establishment of the International Bank for Reconstruction and Development (BRD), informally called the World Bank, and the International Monetary Fund. With the exception of the Soviet Union, all the original participants in the conference became members of the Fund and the Bank, although New Zealand and Liberia did not join until the early 1960s. The U.S.S.R. had taken an active part in the conference and had even been assigned a large quota in the Fund, but it did not ratify the agreements, and never became a member of the two institutions. After the U.S.S.R. was officially dissolved in December 1991, the fifteen republics of the former Soviet Union applied for membership in the Fund and the Bank, all their membership procedures being completed by April 1993. Three original members of the Fund and Bank, Poland, Czechoslovakia, and Cuba withdrew, although Poland and Czechoslovakia eventually rejoined. In August 1952, Germany and Japan became members of the Fund and Bank; China joined in 1980 following a decision that the People's Republic of China would represent China in both institutions; and in May 1992 Switzerland, after a long association with both, became a member of the

Fund and the Bank. In December 1992, when Yugoslavia was no longer a unified country, the Fund agreed to reassign its quota among its former component states—Bosnia-Herzegovina, Croatia, Macedonia, Serbia/Montenegro, and Slovenia. When Czechoslovakia split into the Czech Republic and Slovakia, a similar procedure was adopted for membership by the two new states. Eritrea joined the IBRD in July 1994, bringing the total membership of the Bank to 178. At the end of June 1995, action was pending on membership in the Bank for Bosnia-Herzegovina, Brunei Darussalam, and the Federal Republic of Yugoslavia (Serbia/Montenegro). With the exception of Cuba, North Korea, and a few very small states, membership in the IBRD and the IMF is now almost universal.

Structure of the IBRD

The IBRD's Articles of Agreement state that "all the powers of the Bank shall be vested in the Board of Governors, consisting of a governor and an alternate appointed by each member in such manner as it may determine." A governor is usually the member country's minister of finance, a governor of its central bank, or an official of equivalent rank. The Board has a number of powers that cannot be delegated, including decisions on such matters as the admission or suspension of a member, an increase or decrease in the Bank's capital stock, suspension of the Bank's operations and distribution of its assets, and determination of the distribution of the Bank's net income.

All other powers of the Board of Governors have been delegated to the Bank's Executive Board, consisting of twenty-four executive directors "responsible for the conduct of the general operations of the Bank." Each executive director appoints an alternate who can attend meetings of the Board but is not permitted to vote if the executive director is present. The five countries with the largest number of shares in the IBRD's capital stock (the United States, Germany, Japan, France, and the United Kingdom) appoint their own executive directors. Of the remaining executive directors, one (Saudi Arabia) is appointed; China, Russia, and Switzerland have chosen to elect their own directors; and the other fifteen directors are elected by groups of countries. Originally, the Executive Board had only twelve members, but as the Bank's membership grew, so also did the number of executive directors.

The Bank's president is selected by the executive directors and is the chairman of the Executive Board, but has no vote except in the case of an equal division of votes. The president is chief of the operating staff of the Bank and, subject to the general control of the executive directors, is responsible for the organization, appointment, and dismissal of the Bank's officers and staff. During its first fifty years, the Bank has had nine presidents: Eugene Meyer (1946–47), John J. McCloy (1947–49), Eugene R. Black (1949–62), George D. Woods (1963–68), Robert S. McNamara (1968–81), A. W. Clausen (1981–86), Barber B. Conable (1986–91); Lewis T. Preston (1991–95), and James D. Wolfensohn (1995–   ). Traditionally, the president of the Bank has always been an American and the managing director of the Fund a European. The Articles of Agreement state that the president and staff of the Bank "owe their duty entirely to the Bank and to no other authority." The president, "subject to the paramount importance of securing the highest standards of efficiency and of technical competence," is required to "pay due regard to the importance of recruiting personnel on as wide a geographical basis as possible." Unlike the United Nations, the Bank does not have a system of quotas for determining staff recruitment. As of June 30, 1995, regular and fixed term staff of the Bank numbered 6,059, and of these 3,983 were higher-level staff. In addition, long-term consultants numbered 1,112.

It is stated in the Articles of Agreement that the Bank's principal office is to be located in the territory of the member holding the largest number of Bank shares. As the United States has more shares (255,590) than any other member, the Bank's headquarters are in Washington, D.C. The Bank also has offices in New York (World Bank Mission to the United Nations), Paris (European Office), London, and Tokyo; seven regional missions; fifty-nine resident missions; and a number of smaller offices.

In June 1995, the Bank's structure consisted of the president, three managing directors, two senior vice presidents (the General Counsel, and the senior vice president, Management and Personnel Services), and fourteen vice presidents (six responsible for the Bank's regions: Africa, East Asia and Pacific, South Asia, Europe and Central Asia, Middle East and North Africa, and Latin America and Caribbean); Cofinancing and Financial Advisory Services; the Controller: the Chief Economist, Development Economics; Environmentally Sustainable Development; Finance and Private Sector Development; Financial Policy and Resource Mobilization; Human Resources Development and Operations Policy; the Secretary; and the Treasurer), and the Director-General, Operations Evaluation. Each vice presidency also includes a number of departments.

Voting

Unlike the United Nations, which has a one country/one vote system, the World Bank has a system of weighted voting. Each member is entitled to 250 votes and receives one additional vote for each share held in the

Bank's capital stock. The number of shares allocated is based on the member's quota in the International Monetary Fund, so that the richer countries subscribe to more shares than the developing countries. This system recognizes the differences among members' holdings, and is intended to protect the interests of the countries that make more substantial contributions to the Bank's resources. If a country's economic situation changes over time, its quota is adjusted and its allocation of shares and votes changes accordingly. This has occurred in the cases of Japan and Germany, now second and third after the United States in their subscriptions to the Bank's capital stock and their voting power.

Certain policy decisions by the Board of Governors require a approval by 85 percent of the total votes, but in most other cases a simple majority is sufficient. The Board normally meets only once a year at the annual meeting, and conducts most of its voting by mail. The Executive Board rarely votes, preferring to reach decisions by consensus.

The Bank's Affiliated Institutions and their Contribution to Development

Until 1956 the IBRD acted alone. Subsequently, increased involvement with the developing countries and limitations on lending imposed by its Articles made it necessary to create four affiliated institutions to meet all the needs of its members. The Bank and these institutions form the World Bank Group.

The International Finance Corporation (IFC)

The first of the Bank's affiliates, the International Finance Corporation (IFC), was created in 1956 to "further economic development by encouraging the growth of productive private enterprise in member countries, particularly in the less developed areas." Unlike the Bank, IFC is not required by its Articles to obtain "guarantee of repayment by the member government concerned." Although the Corporation's operations are closely coordinated with and complement the activities of the other institutions in the World Bank Group, it is legally separate and has its own Articles of Agreement, management, and financial structure. However, the president of the Bank is also the president of IFC, and the members of the Bank's Board of Governors and Board of Executive Directors can serve IFC in the same capacity if the countries they represent are also members of IFC. The Corporation draws on the Bank for administrative and other services, but it has its own legal and operational staff. In 1961, IFC's Articles were amended to permit it to make equity investments, and in 1965, the IBRD's

Articles were amended to enable the Bank to make loans to IFC of up to four times IFC's unimpaired subscribed capital and surplus. Before 1966 the Corporation's investments averaged only about $30 million annually. This rate more or less doubled between 1966 and 1968, doubled again when Robert McNamara became president of the Bank, and has continued to rise steadily since then, amounting to nearly $3 billion in fiscal year 1995.

The International Finance Corporation has been described as a combination of a multilateral development bank and a private merchant bank. It is the largest source of direct financing for private sector projects in the developing countries. Its share capital is provided by its members, but IFC raises most of its funds for financing through its bond issues, which have a triple A rating in the international markets. The Corporation makes direct investments in the form of loans or equity investments (or a combination of both), undertakes stand-by and underwriting operations, and assists in the establishment and support of local capital markets. It charges market rates for its loans and seeks profitable returns on its investments. Because IFC is skilled in risk management and project appraisal, the projects that it supports are usually successful. As a result, the Corporation is able to play an important catalytic role in obtaining additional funding for its projects from other sources, either through cofinancing or through loan syndications, underwritings, or guarantees. In addition to these activities, IFC offers a number of advisory services to business and governments, and provides technical assistance. In recent years it has played an important part in providing assistance to countries in Central and Eastern Europe and the former members of the Soviet Union, in their transition to market economies.

The International Development Association (IDA)

The Bank's second affiliated institution, the International Development Association (IDA), was established in 1960. Officially, the World Bank consists of the IBRD and IDA, although the IBRD alone is often referred to as the World Bank. By the mid-1950s, it was becoming clear that the world's poorest countries would not be able to borrow from the IBRD at its near market rates for loans and that there was an urgent need for a lender providing loans on concessional terms. Proposals were put forward to change the Bank's Articles and establish a "soft window" for lending within the Bank itself, but it was felt that this might jeopardize the Bank's high rating in the markets and make it more difficult for the Bank to borrow at favorable rates, so a new institution was preferred.

Although the Association was established as a separate entity, the Bank and IDA are more or less inseparable. They have the same staff, the same headquarters in Washington, D.C., the same president, and both institutions use the same criteria for evaluating their projects. The main difference is in their financing, since IDA cannot borrow funds in the international markets, and is dependent on its members' subscriptions, on repayments of its credits, and on periodical "replenishments" by the donor countries. IDA's loans, called credits, go to governments, and they, together with other donors, match IDA's lending. As a result, the Association plays an important catalyzing role in generating funds to assist the poorest countries.

Since 1960 IDA has provided more than $75 billion to promote development. About seventy countries are eligible to borrow from IDA, and many of its credits go to those with per capita annual incomes of $635 or less. Almost half of these credits go to Africa, and most of the remainder to poor countries in Asia, including Bangladesh, China, India, Nepal, and Pakistan. The Association has provided financing for a wide variety of projects, including rail and road improvements, energy resources, telecommunication, and water supply. In recent years IDA has increased its support for projects in the social sector, with emphasis on primary education, basic health care, nutrition, and family planning. During the 1980s, IDA assisted its members to institute policy reforms for sustainable growth and made a number of loans for adjustment programs that include safety nets to protect the poor.

IDA's lending is determined by a country's commitment to poverty reduction, economic adjustment and growth, and environmental sustainability, assessments of performance in these areas being made each year in IDA-eligible countries. As part of its continuing efforts to reduce poverty, the Association has prepared detailed poverty assessments with all its borrowing countries and has provided assistance to meet each country's specific needs. IDA is also concerned with the role of women in development, and has completed assessments of their situation in some twenty-five developing countries, including studies of women's education, reproductive health, and special roles in agriculture and the work force. Since 1992 IDA has provided $2.5 billion for projects involving the environment that are designed to conserve natural resources, improve the urban environment, and reduce pollution.

The International Centre for Settlement of Investment Disputes (ICSID)

In October 1966, the Bank's third affiliate, the International Centre for Settlement of Investment Disputes (ICSID), was established by the

Convention on the Settlement of Investment Disputes between States and Nationals of other States. The Convention was drawn up by the Bank's executive directors, with assistance from Bank staff and a number of legal experts from member countries. It came into effect after ratification by twenty of the contracting states that had signed the Convention.

ICSID attempts to promote increased flows of international investment by providing facilities for resolving disputes through conciliation and/or arbitration between a contracting state and a foreign investor. The Centre's governing body is its administrative council, consisting of a representative from each contracting state. The Bank's president is the non-voting chairman of the council. ICSID's secretariat is in the Bank's headquarters in Washington, D.C., and its overhead expenses are borne by the Bank. The Centre's activities include the administration of its arbitration and conciliation functions, and arbitration, conciliation, and fact-finding proceedings. ICSID also undertakes research and publication activities in connection with international investment law. As of June 30, 1995, 119 countries were members of ICSID, and 15 additional countries were in the process of becoming members.

The Multilateral Investment Guarantee Agency (MIGA)

The Bank's fourth affiliate, the Multilateral Investment Guarantee Agency (MIGA), was established in April 1988, when the Convention establishing the Agency had been ratified by twenty-nine countries. Membership in MIGA is open to all members of the Bank. By July 1995, 128 countries had become members, and 24 developing countries and countries in transition were in the process of fulfilling membership requirements.

MIGA is an autonomous institution within the World Bank Group, with a council of governors and a board of directors. The president of the Bank is ex officio the Agency's president, and serves as the non-voting chairman of its board of directors, and the Bank's governors and directors also serve as governors and directors of MIGA. MIGA's purpose is to encourage investment flows for productive purposes to developing countries by providing insurance against political risks for private investors, by promoting investment activity, and by assisting developing countries to create attractive investment climates. Investments are normally covered for fifteen years, with possible extension up to twenty years. The Agency's Guarantees Program protects investors agains losses from currency transfer, expropriation, war and civil disturbance, and investment-related breach of contract by host governments. Its Policy and Advisory Services (PAS) promote investment opportunities in developing member countries through investment promotion conferences and other advisory activities.

Conclusion

It is now more than half a century since the delegates of 44 nations met in conference at Bretton Woods, New Hampshire, and created two institutions, the International Monetary Fund and the World Bank, to promote financial stability, to support reconstruction after the Second World War, and to encourage development in their member countries. In July 1944 the world was still at war, the world economy was dominated by the United States, the economies of Europe and Japan were in ruins, Africa was still dominated by the colonial powers, and much of Asia was just beginning to emerge from colonialism.

Since Bretton Woods, substantial economic and social progress has been achieved. The restoration of war-damaged economies was quickly completed, world trade dramatically increased, and there was a general trend toward more open economies. In the developing countries, average life expectancy increased by about 50 percent, the numbers of children attending school grew considerably, and since 1960 the average per capita income has more than doubled. Many developing countries, especially those in East Asia, have succeeded in reducing poverty. The Bank has made a significant contribution to this progress in development through its support for over six thousand operations with financing of more than $300 billion in some 140 countries. Over the years it has created affiliates to meet all the needs of its members: IDA to assist the poorest countries; IFC to promote the private sector in the developing countries; ICSID to settle investment disputes; and MIGA to promote foreign investment. Until 1980 most Bank loans were for investment projects such as roads and dams. In response, however, to the balance-of-payments crises in many of its developing country members the Bank then introduced adjustment lending to support programs of policy reform. As well as lending directly, the Bank has played an important part in catalyzing financial support from other sources, and in coordinating international aid flows. After more than 50 years of experience in working with its members on development issues, it has evolved from its original role of providing financial assistance to a much wider advisory role.

In spite of all their efforts, and all the progress that has been made, many challenges still remain for the Bank and its affiliates. More than a billion people in the developing countries struggle to live on less than one dollar per day, and two out of five people lack clean water and basic sanitation. Because of high population growth and slow economic progress, half the people in sub-Saharan Africa are still trapped in poverty. The World Bank and the International Monetary Fund are currently working on a new initiative to assist forty-one countries, many of them in Africa, that are facing overwhelming debt burdens. Although both institutions are assisting the countries of Central and Eastern Europe and the former Soviet Union, serious problems have been encountered during their transition to market economies. Post-apartheid South Africa and the West Bank and Gaza also present new challenges.

Today, the Group is operating in a world that is very different from the one envisaged by its founders. Its approach to development has been reshaped by the lessons of experience, as well as by new thinking about development and about the environment. The development process has been described as "a difficult and risky endeavor." The World Bank Group, like many of those involved in this endeavor, has made mistakes and has received its share of criticism. On balance, however, the Bank and its affiliates have reduced poverty and raised living standards in many countries. For the future, the World Bank Group, the world's largest development agency, will continue its efforts to meet the needs of its members, with poverty reduction continuing to be the Group's "overarching" objective.

The Dictionary

A

Acquired Immunodeficiency Syndrome (AIDS). See AIDS (Acquired Immunodeficiency Syndrome).

Adjustment and the World Bank. In the Bank's view, macroeconomic stabilization and structural adjustment are separate but complementary aspects of the adjustment process, the former being achieved through budgetary discipline and control of inflation, and the latter through measures designed to put the economy on a growth path for the long term.

Between 1980 and 1993 the Bank supported one hundred and fourteen adjustment operations in fifty-three countries. Two-thirds of these countries were relatively successful in implementing the policies agreed with the Bank, and were able to reduce price distortion and inflation, to stabilize their foreign exchange reserves, and to achieve per capita income growth. They also succeeded in reducing the number of people in poverty and in maintaining or increasing expenditure in such areas as health, eduction, and social security/welfare programs. Few of the Bank's early adjustment loans included provisions for safety net programs, but subsequently targeted safety net measures were attached to adjustment loans or formed part of sectoral interventions.

Africa (Sub-Saharan) and the World Bank. Bank assistance to sub-Saharan Africa (SSA) began in 1960, when the Bank approved a loan to Ethiopia. The first IDA credit went to the Sudan in 1961. Since then, the World Bank Group has provided more than $21 billion for development in the region, with large increases in Bank and IDA assistance occurring after Robert S. McNamara became president of the Bank in 1968. Most of the countries in sub-Saharan Africa have received help from IDA, as many African countries cannot afford to borrow on IBRD terms and are eligible for concessional assistance. Between 1960 and

1964 only four African countries received IDA credits, but since then Africa's share of these credits has steadily increased. Major African borrowers from IDA include Ethiopia, Ghana, Madagascar, Sudan, and Zaïre. Nigeria was one of the few African borrowers from the IBRD, receiving 1.1 percent of total IBRD loans between 1955 and 1959. From 1965 to 1969, Nigeria's share of IBRD lending increased to 2.7 percent after it graduated from IDA-eligible status, rose to 3.5 percent between 1970 and 1974, and fell to 1.8 percent between 1975 and 1979 when Nigeria was close to graduation from IBRD borrower status. Owing to instability in world oil prices, Nigeria's economy suffered a sharp decline in the 1980s, and the country received sector adjustment loans from the Bank in 1984 and 1987. Côte d'Ivoire graduated from IDA borrowing in 1973, and its share of Bank lending was 1.3 to 1.7 percent between 1975 and 1979. From 1982 to 1986, the Bank supported the country's structural adjustment efforts with three structural adjustment loans. Other IBRD borrowers in Africa have included Kenya, South Africa, Tanzania, and Zambia.

Agriculture, rural development, and infrastructure have been major areas for Bank and IDA assistance to sub-Saharan Africa, with much of IDA's assistance going to infrastructure, especially transportation. Because agriculture is an important element in African economies, about one-third of the Bank's total lending to the region has gone to agriculture, in the form of support for single crop projects, area or regional agricultural and rural development projects, and national agricultural programs. In the mid-1970s the single crop approach was found to have serious disadvantages, and there was a shift in project design to address the needs of African farmers as a whole through area or regional development projects. Such projects were successful in Malawi and Ethiopia but enjoyed less success in other countries, as they had relatively high costs per beneficiary and required skilled management. Rural development projects received Bank support in Tanzania, Sudan, and Zambia, but had similar disadvantages. In contrast, a national agricultural program in Ethiopia, intended to increase fertilizer use and extend the rural road network, was very successful. Experience in Bank-supported agricultural extension was mixed, with good results being obtained in Ethiopia, Kenya, and Zimbabwe. In the area of agricultural research, the Bank supports efforts by the Consultative Group on International Agricultural Research (q.v.) to improve African farming methods and technologies. It also sponsors the Special Program for African Agricultural Research (SPAAR), which coordinates donors' contributions, disseminates information on new technologies, and assists African national and regional research.

Many sub-Saharan African countries achieved independence in the early 1960s, but they depended on mineral or agricultural exports, and had very small manufacturing sectors. Their governments believed that industrialization would bring about rapid economic growth, and requested Bank aid for industrial development. In the immediate post-independence period, the Bank's assistance to African industry was largely indirect, but subsequently loans were approved for specific investment projects, mainly in mining and resource-based industry. The International Finance Corporation (q.v.) has also been involved in Africa's industrial sector. Present Bank assistance to African industry is directed toward the rehabilitation or privatization of existing large industrial enterprises, the promotion of medium-sized and small-scale industry, and the reform of financial institutions supporting development in the industrial sector.

In 1979 the Bank's African governors asked for a special report on the problems of the region and the solutions proposed by the Bank. Two years later, the Bank published *Accelerated Development in Sub-Saharan Africa: An Agenda for Action.* Known as the Berg report, after its coordinator, Elliot Berg, the findings and recommendations of the report were widely criticized. The Bank responded with a series of publications on its policies in Africa. A new approach was proposed in its *Toward Sustained Development in Sub-Saharan Africa: A Joint Program of Action* (1984), which called for a collaborative effort between African governments and the international community.

To assist member countries in adjusting their economies in the 1980s, the Bank introduced structural adjustment loans (SALs) to support programs of policy and institutional change. Other fast-disbursing instruments for adjustment included sector adjustment loans (SECALs), and industrial sector adjustment loans (ISALs). In Kenya, because of serious short-term problems, the performance of the SAL program was mixed, but between 1981 and 1985 Malawi successfully implemented three Bank-financed structural operations.

The Bank has found that one of the main causes of project failure in sub-Saharan Africa has been the limited administrative and institutional capacity of borrowers. In cooperation with governments, the Bank has endeavored to improve public management at the national level, to introduce reforms in the management of state enterprises, to strengthen institutions at the sectoral level, and to improve delivery of local services in such areas as agricultural extension and health care. The Bank is also one of the sponsors of the African Capacity Building Initiative (q.v.).

During recent years the flow of resources to sub-Saharan Africa has been reduced, owing to deteriorating terms of trade, limited absorptive capacity in traditional areas of investment, and large debt-servicing burdens. The Bank has attempted to revive assistance to the region by reporting to donors on priority needs, improving aid coordination, and seeking additional cofinancing. More than half of Bank-financed projects in Africa during the 1980s included cofinancing, which was obtained mainly from official sources and was more or less equal to the funds provided by the Bank. In 1985 the Bank reached agreement with fourteen donor countries to establish a Special Facility for Africa (q.v.) This assists IDA-eligible countries in sub-Saharan Africa that are undertaking appropriate medium-term programs of policy reform.

A recent Bank publication, *Adjustment in Africa: Reforms, Results, and the Road Ahead* (1994) attempts to answer three questions: How much did adjusting African countries change their policies? Did their policy reforms restore growth? What is the road ahead for adjustment? The answers suggest that although many African countries have made progress in improving their policies and restoring growth, they still have a long way to go.

In fiscal year 1995 the Bank introduced the broad sector approach to investment lending in Africa because traditional investment operations, financed project-by-project and donor-by-donor, had been unsatisfactory. As part of the new approach, local stakeholders are involved from the beginning in order to ensure ownership and sustainability; the program is sector-wide, and covers all policies and projects; the sector policy framework is developed in close collaboration with the country's private sector, NGOs, and project beneficiaries; and long-term external technical assistance is minimized, with emphasis on local capacity-building. Operations of this type have been approved for Mozambique and Zambia, and their number is expected to rise to about 20 percent of total lending in the next three years.

Current priorities for the Bank in Africa include: poverty reduction through environmentally sustainable development; development of human resources; action against land degradation and desertification; working with its major partners to implement the objectives of the Special Program of Assistance (q.v.); and getting better results through improved quality of projects and their implementation. Since the recent parity change, assistance to the CFA countries has included about $1 billion from IDA in quick-disbursing credits and adjustment operations. The Bank has funded post-devaluation programs for the short term and increased expenditures on labor-intensive civil works programs, rural infrastructure, education, and health for the longer term.

African Agricultural Services Initiative. Introduced by the Bank in 1988, this initiative was designed to improve African agricultural performance through better use of existing technology and the development and dissemination of new technology. Substantial foreign exchange resources were provided under the initiative, and Bank technical staff were stationed in African countries to assist in implementation. Important new features comprise the whole range of agricultural services, including inputs, credit, and marketing; emphasis on national rather than on project levels; management of services by local staff; direct contact with farmers; commitments by donors to long-term objectives; and improved aid coordination.

African Capacity-Building Initiative (ACBI). Co-sponsored by the World Bank, the United Nations Development Programme, and the African Development Bank (qq.v.), the ACBI was launched in February 1991. Its objective is to strengthen African skills and institutions for economic policy analysis and macroeconomic management. During a four-year pilot phase, the ACBI will draw on a fund of about $100 million, pledged by international agencies, donor nations, African governments, and private sources. The Bank's contribution will not exceed 15 percent of the pledged fund.

Through an African Capacity Building Foundation, to be based in Harare, Zimbabwe, grants will be provided for policy analysis and development management programs in institutions of higher learning. Fellowships will be established for African civil servants, business leaders, and academics. An international executive board, comprising experts in public policy and development from Africa and elsewhere, and representatives from the three sponsoring agencies, will guide ACBI's program.

African Development Bank (AfDB). The African Development Bank was established in September 1964 and began operations in July 1966 at its headquarters in Abidjan, Côte d'Ivoire. Cooperation between the AfDB and the World Bank began in 1967. Both institutions take part in economic missions to member countries and participate in consultative group meetings chaired by the Bank. They jointly support structural adjustment programs under the Special Program of Assistance (q.v.), and also work together in the Social Dimensions of Adjustment Program (q.v.), the Energy Sector Program, the Water Supply and Sanitation Program, and the African Capacity Building Initiative (q.v.). The World Bank has been the leading cofinancing partner of the AfDB since the two institutions cofinanced their first project in 1969.

In 1986 relations between the AfDB and the World Bank were formally defined in two cooperation agreements. The first agreement is mainly concerned with consultation involving public investment programs, consultative groups, economic missions, policy-based lending, and cooperation in the field. The second agreement deals with cooperation in policy-based lending operations. Relations between the senior managers in both institutions are good, and semi-annual consultations are held at this level. Cooperation between the two banks has been strengthened by the World Bank's appointment of a representative from its office in Abidjan to coordinate operational activities. Currently, the Bank and the AfDB continue to work closely together, and the AfDB's cofinancing of Bank-assisted projects has grown from about $170 million in 1985 to more than $525 million in 1991.

As an African institution, the AfDB is sensitive to African politics and problems, and this has sometimes caused policy differences with the World Bank. As an example, in recent years the World Bank was dissatisfied with Zaïre's utilization of funds provided by the Bank, and ceased making new loans to that country, while the AfDB continued to lend. Because the AfDb represents the interests of African countries, and sometimes rallies to the defence of those thought to be treated unfairly by the developed nations, it is said to have approved projects that were previously turned down by the World Bank. However, both the AfDB and the World Bank share common goals concerning Africa's development, and their differences are small in comparison with what has been achieved by their years of successful cooperation.

Agricultural Extension and the World Bank. The Bank began to support agricultural extension in 1964, when part of a $2.8 million IDA credit to the Kenya Tea Development Authority was devoted to training and salaries for the agricultural instructors who replaced departing expatriates. Three years later, the Bank started to promote the training and visit (T & V) system of agricultural extension. As part of a national extension system, the T & V system includes trained village-level extension workers. These workers are informed about new developments in agricultural research and are trained to pass on information useful to farmers. Because they are unable to have personal contact with all the farmers in their areas, these extension workers hold regular meetings with organized networks of farmers to pass on the information they have received. Through these networks information is shared with other farmers and feedback on its usefulness is passed back to the village-level extension workers, and by them to the research community.

Between 1965 and 1969, the Bank supported extension components in only six projects, of which four were in Africa. During the next five years, the Bank's interest in agricultural extension grew considerably, and by 1974 the Bank was supporting fifty-one projects with extension components of $122 million. This growth trend has continued, making the Bank the largest international supporter of agricultural extension. Although Western Africa has had the largest number of projects with extension components, the Bank's investment in agricultural extension has been highest in Latin America and South Asia. There have been relatively few borrowers for extension, with ten countries (India, Nigeria, Mexico, Indonesia, Turkey, Thailand, Bangladesh, the Philippines, and Malaysia) accounting for nearly 70 percent of Bank support. India, which has received more than $279 million in Bank investments for extension, has been involved since 1974 when, with assistance from IDA, the T & V system was introduced in Rajasthan. Subsequently, the system was adopted by other Indian states, and by 1986, as part of the Third National Agricultural Extension Project, IDA credits for extension had been provided to seventeen states. In many of these states, yield increases and changes in cropping patterns have been attributed to extension. For the years 1990–94 the Bank expects to invest about $150 million a year in projects involving agricultural extension in twenty-seven countries, sixteen of them in Africa.

The Bank's support for the T & V system has influenced extension work throughout the developing world. The system has been adopted in more than forty countries, and in a number of cases, it has been credited with increased agricultural production. The T & V system has been criticized by some experts who accuse the Bank of "selling the methodology as *the* universal extension system" without sufficiently considering the needs of individual countries. In reply, supporters of the system argue that the Bank has always adapted T & V to local conditions. The Bank's involvement in agricultural extension has also included support for international conferences on the subject, and for the publication of studies and reports on extension methodology and evaluation.

Agricultural Research and the World Bank. The Bank's support for agricultural research began relatively late, in the mid-1960s, and its first investment for a national agricultural research project went to Spain in 1970. When borrowing countries indicate their willingness to adopt mutually acceptable agricultural research strategies combined with related national policies, the Bank provides technical and financial support for a ten to fifteen year program, possibly involving one or more phases. The first phase includes national research planning and preparation, staff recruitment and training, and support for ongoing research activities; the second, and possibly a third phase, covers planning for future research. Institution-building, including the training of management and staff, is an important element in the Bank's support for national agricultural research systems and emphasizes the employment of staff from the country involved. A Bank project for agricultural research also includes annual workshops to review progress, internal reviews performed at the project's headquarters, periodical reviews by visiting specialists, and the employment of consultants on a short-time basis to review and evaluate the project. In fiscal year 1990 the Bank was supporting twelve national agricultural research projects in various stages of preparation and implementation. Several new projects of this kind will be undertaken during the next five years.

Research components in Bank agricultural and rural development projects are intended to develop knowledge or techniques for specific areas in agriculture, or to raise the level of national research capacity through training and technical assistance. Similar components in education projects are intended to expand existing agricultural research facilities in universities, to upgrade the quality of research and teaching staff, and to create or improve teaching programs for undergraduates. Since 1981, the Bank has also provided financing for agricultural research reform and reorganization through components in policy-based loans (structural and sectoral adjustment loans).

Eleven hundred and forty-six agricultural sector projects, including irrigation and drainage sub-sector projects, were approved during fiscal years 1974–90. Of these projects, four hundred and eighty-eight had agricultural research components that were designed to develop knowledge and techniques for specific agro-ecological areas or to improve national research capabilities. Most of the projects were in Africa (thirty countries), followed by Asia and the Pacific (seventeen countries); Europe, Middle East and North Africa (twelve countries), and Latin America and the Caribbean (nine countries). Although delays in implementation often occurred, all completed projects were classified as satisfactory, and most of their objectives were achieved. Of the projects with agricultural research components, a few, such as the Mexican Rainfed Agricultural Development Project and the Brazil North-East Rural Development Project I, included substantial investments for agricultural research, but most research components were relatively small and went to institution-building, individual research programs, technical assistance, and staff training.

Through its Economic Development Institute (q.v.), the Bank is providing agriculture-related courses for mid- and high-level staff from the developing countries. The Bank continues to support the efforts of the Consultative Group on International Agricultural Research (q.v.), and since 1984 has made a limited number of grants to international agricultural research institutions that are not associated with the Group. Bank support for CGIAR and the non-CGIAR centers is expected to remain constant during the 1990s.

Agriculture and the World Bank. The Bank's first loan for agriculture went to Chile in 1948, providing $2.5 million for agricultural machinery. Although Bank lending to the developing countries began to grow in the 1950s, the relatively small amount that went to agriculture was mainly directed to capital-intensive projects in irrigation and flood control. After 1960, Bank support for agriculture in the developing countries was greatly increased by the creation of IDA because many of these countries, ineligible for Bank loans, were able to borrow on concessional terms from the new institution. In its early days, however, IDA had only limited financial resources, and most of its available funds went to countries in South Asia, including India and Pakistan. Forty percent of this assistance was directed to agricultural development.

During the 1960s population growth and crop failures added to the growing pressure for increased agricultural investment. In 1964, Bank president George Woods called for more projects to assist agriculture, and the Bank began to include components in its large irrigation projects that provided extension and credit to farmers. A large number of Bank loans were made to national credit institutions, particularly in India and Mexico, for on-lending through local intermediaries to groups of farmers to finance infrastructure, and to individual farmers to acquire equipment and livestock. It has been estimated that these Bank-supported credit programs assisted at least twenty million farmers, many with small or medium-sized holdings.

When Robert McNamara became president of the Bank in 1968, his emphasis on poverty alleviation, especially in the rural areas, brought about a dramatic increase in the Bank's lending for agriculture, with annual lending growing from $400 million in the early 1970s to more than $3 billion each year by the early 1980s. The number of agricultural projects also grew considerably, and more than doubled by the end of the McNamara era. During these years Bank lending for agriculture was influenced by the concept of integrated rural development, with projects designed to raise the productivity and income of small-scale producers by combining directly productive agricultural components with the provision of social services. Assistance was also provided to introduce new, high-yielding varieties of rice and wheat, and to increase the use of fertilizers.

As part of its support for agriculture, the Bank directed about 75 percent of its loans to projects for irrigation, credit, and area and rural development. The remainder were approved for agricultural extension and research (qq.v), agroindustries, fisheries, forestry (q.v.), land settlement, livestock, and tree crops. Irrigation accounted for 33 percent of agricultural investment, and this increased the irrigation capacity of developing countries by about 25 percent, resulting in significantly higher rice and wheat production, mainly in Asia. Area development programs used multisectoral approaches as part of the effort to assist small farmers, and projects of this type were supported in Indonesia, Brazil, Nigeria, and Central Africa. More recently, the Bank has tended to reduce the scope of such projects, concentrating more directly on raising agricultural productivity and output.

During the years 1974–84 the Bank provided two-thirds of multilateral aid, and nearly one-third of all official assistance to agriculture. In the same period it invested about $33 billion in agricultural projects that attracted total investments of $90 to $100 billion. India was the largest borrower for agriculture from the Bank, followed by Mexico, Indonesia, Brazil, Romania, and Yugoslavia. India was also the largest borrower from IDA. By 1984 China had become the eighth largest borrower for agriculture from the Bank and was second only to India in borrowing from IDA.

In general, during the 1980s, the number of projects in the agricultural sector declined, although total lending increased. In fiscal year 1983, nearly 20 percent of agricultural projects were below $10 million, although 20 percent amounted to $100 million or more. Of the sixty-eight projects financed, thirteen accounted for more than half of the $3.8

billion loaned. Nearly all the loans below $10 million were made to Africa, while those above $100 million went mainly to the Bank's regions of Europe, Middle East and North Africa, Latin America and the Caribbean, and South Asia. During the same year the Bank and IDA financed a record amount of the local costs of agricultural projects, with 45 percent of IDA credits going to such costs. About a quarter of the loans included financing for agricultural sector policy adjustments, reflecting the changing nature of the Bank's involvement in agricultural development.

Critics have questioned the nature of the Bank's contribution to agriculture, and have doubted the effectiveness of its loans and credits. Some countries, such as India, would probably not have achieved all their objectives in agriculture without the Bank's assistance. In sub-Saharan Africa, however, where the Bank has been the largest single lender for agricultural development, production has stagnated in some countries, or even declined. The success of Bank agricultural projects in Africa has been limited by external and internal factors, including bad weather, political instability, overvalued exchange rates, high taxes on agriculture, and low prices for farmers. By the 1980s, however, lending for agriculture and rural development had grown to 33 percent of Bank lending to Africa, as compared with about 6 percent in the early 1960s.

There have complaints that in some cases the Bank's designs for agricultural projects have been too complex, and that governments in many developing countries lack the budgetary capacity and institutional flexibility to implement projects successfully. In the wake of failures in earlier agricultural projects, the Bank is now encouraging more participation by local communities in project design and implementation, and is increasing its support for capacity- and institution-building. The Bank has also found that policies to assist the small farmer are successful when the government is supportive and the institutional environment effective. Bank-supported projects are now designed differently and contain components that promote continued cooperation and efficient management after the project has been completed.

AIDS (Acquired Immunodeficiency Syndrome) and the World Bank. The first Bank support for AIDS control went to the Africa region in 1987 as a component in the Zimbabwe Family Health Project. Because grant financing for national AIDS programs was available from the World Health Organization's Global Programme on AIDS (q.v.) and from bilateral donors, Bank loans and credits were initially used to support health systems that included AIDS programs. The first Bank credit for a freestanding AIDS project went to Zaïre in 1989, and health projects in Burundi, Lesotho, and Malawi also included funding for large parts of their AIDS control programs.

In Latin America and the Caribbean, two AIDS components were included in a Bank project approved in fiscal 1988 in response to a severe AIDS epidemic in Brazil. Bank funding also supported an AIDS control program in Haiti. The Bank's second freestanding AIDS control project, for India, was approved in fiscal 1992, and discussions are now in progress on programs for Indonesia and the Philippines. In Central and Eastern Europe and in the Middle East and North Africa the Bank's involvement in AIDS control programs has been limited because countries in these areas have had alternative sources of financing. Recently, however, discussions have begun between the Bank and the countries of the former Soviet Union on possible research and project preparation activities in connection with AIDS.

Albania and the World Bank. Between the end of World War II and 1990, Albania suffered under an authoritarian and isolationist regime, led by Enver Hoxha, which blocked the country's economic and social development. For some years after the Second World War, Albania had close relations with Yugoslavia, the Soviet Union, and China. When these relationships ended, Albania remained isolated from the rest of the world until after Hoxha's death in April 1985. By the end of the decade, the country's economy had deteriorated to such an extent that Hoxha's successor abandoned Albania's former doctrine of self-reliance and established economic and political relations with some Western countries. In 1990 the first multi-party elections were held, and in October 1991 Albania applied for membership in the Bank. Following the March 1992 elections, Albania's Democratic Party was able to form a government with a strong mandate for social and economic reform, and negotiations were reopened with the Fund and the Bank. These were successfully concluded in June 1992, when Albania also became eligible for assistance from IDA.

The Bank's first operation in Albania, the Critical Imports project, provided loans for the import of machinery and equipment to restore roads and ports, repair irrigation and electric power systems, and improve agricultural production. With further help from the Bank, the government established a three-year public investment program to rehabilitate existing facilities, and to finance new investments. More than half the roads in Albania were repaired or improved through a Bank-supported transport project, and the port facilities of Durrës, Albania's second largest city, were restored and extended with additional financing from a Kuwait government fund. A Bank project for improving the city's water supply will restore full service to consumers, repair the sewage system, and strengthen the management of the institutions supplying these services.

Albania's power system is in urgent need of improvement, and the Power Loss Reduction project, with financing by the government and the Bank, will reduce the present widespread unbilled use of electricity. Another Bank project will rehabilitate and expand Albania's electric transmission and distribution systems. To assist the Albanian government to deal with these problems, the Bank has financed a study of the country's energy sector, and projects that are based on the study's findings are already in preparation.

Traditionally, agriculture is the most important sector in Albania's economy, but since 1990 farming and livestock production have been depressed. The Bank has contributed to the revitalization of this sector through an agriculture adjustment credit that supports the government's reforms and provides rapidly disbursing credit to finance imports. It also includes a credit line for farmers and farmers' associations and provides technical assistance to the agricultural banking system. Because, in some parts of Albania, irrigation is essential for agricultural production an irrigation rehabilitation project is being considered for possible IDA financing.

The Bank is now directing aid toward Albania's social sector, and in September 1993 the executive directors approved projects for labor development and the establishment of a social safety net. Other projects under consideration are intended to improve the schools and restore Albania's primary health care system.

Alternate Executive Directors. Each Bank executive director (q.v.) appoints an alternate, who has full power to act in his or her absence. Alternates may participate in Executive Board meetings but cannot vote unless the executive directors who appointed them are absent.

Annual Meetings. The annual meetings of the Bank's Board of Governors (q.v.) are held jointly with the governors of the International Monetary Fund (q.v.). An inaugural meeting was held in Savannah, Georgia, in March 1946, and the first annual meeting took place in Washington, D.C. in September/October 1946. Subsequent annual meetings were held in London, England, in 1947; in Washington, D.C., in 1948–51, and in Mexico City in 1952. It then became customary to hold consecutive meetings in Washington, D.C., with the following meeting being held in a member country that is in a different geographical region. In 1955 the annual meeting was held in Istanbul, Turkey; in 1958 in Delhi, India; in 1961 in Vienna, Austria; in 1964 in Tokyo, Japan; in 1967 in Rio de Janeiro, Brazil; in 1970 in Copenhagen, Denmark; in 1973 in Nairobi, Kenya; in 1976 in Manila, the Philippines; in 1979 in Belgrade, Yugoslavia; in 1982 in Toronto, Canada; in 1985 in Seoul, Korea; in 1988 in Berlin, Germany; in 1991 in Bangkok, Thailand; and in 1994 in Madrid, Spain.

The Bank-Fund annual meetings are regarded as the world's largest international financial conference. Although relatively little official business is transacted during the meetings, they are attended by several thousand participants, including officials, financial experts, economists, observers, and journalists, and provide a unique opportunity for the exchange of official and unofficial views on the world's financial and economic situation. The annual meetings are preceded by meetings of the Group of Ten, the Group of Twenty-Four, the Development Committee, and the Interim Committee (qq.v.).

Arab Development Assistance and the World Bank. Since 1973 there has been a substantial increase in Arab financial support for the World Bank. This has taken various forms, including increases in the Arab countries' shareholding in the IBRD, sustained borrowing by the Bank, contributions to IDA's replenishments, cofinancing of Bank projects by Arab national and regional development institutions, and financial aid to such programs as the Bank's Special Program of Assistance (q.v.) to countries in sub-Saharan Africa.

Much of the Arab support has come from Saudi Arabia, followed by Kuwait. By mid-1993 Bank borrowing transactions with the Saudi Arabian Monetary Authority (SAMA), including direct private placements in various currencies, and subscriptions by SAMA to the Bank's existing arrangements, had amounted to about $6.7 billion. Saudi Arabia contributed $150 million to IDA's tenth replenishment, and its total contribution to IDA over the years has exceeded $2 billion. The International Finance Corporation (q.v.) has borrowed $35 million from SAMA and has a line of credit of $100 million to support its activities in the developing world. About 70 percent of the assistance received from the Saudi Fund for Development (SFD) has been cofinanced with the Bank.

Kuwait's assistance to the Bank has been mainly in the form of contributions to IDA, and so far these have amounted to more than $650 million.

Argentina and the World Bank. Argentina became a member of the Bank in September 1956. A Bank mission visited Argentina in February 1957 to study the country's general economic situation, with emphasis on agriculture, transportation, and electric power, In 1958 and 1960 the Bank acted as executing agency for studies financed by the United Nations Special Fund and Argentina's government to examine the country's transport and power needs. The Bank made its first loan to Argentina (for a highway project) in June 1961, and during the next twenty years it supported projects for electric power, livestock development, industry, railways, and roads.

Following unsuccessful programs of adjustment during the 1980s, Argentina introduced new reform measures for restructuring the public sector, liberalizing trade, and privatizing many public enterprises. In fiscal year 1990/91 Bank lending to Argentina included $300 million for public enterprise reform, $33.5 million for strengthening agricultural services, $300 million to support the privatization or restructuring of public enterprises in the telecommunication, railway, and hydrocarbon sectors, $23 million to strengthen administration of the public sector reform program, and $200 million to assist Argentina's provinces in their own structural reform programs. The Bank continued to play an important part in Argentina's adjustment process, and in fiscal 1991/92 it lent $325 million for further support of Argentina's public sector reform program, $28 million to assist in the privatization of the country's state oil company, and $20 million to strengthen tax administration.

In fiscal 1992/93 Argentina borrowed $300 million to complete the large Yacyreta hydroelectric project, $340 million for road construction and maintenance, $170 million for flood reconstruction work, and $300 million for privatizing or restructuring public industrial enterprises. An additional loan for $450 million went to finance the interest and principal collateral for the par bonds to be issued by Argentina in exchange for eligible debt, and to support the implementation of the agreement between Argentina and its commercial bank creditors. During fiscal 1993/94 the country's economy grew at a rate of more then 5 percent, and the government was able to progress from loans to support adjustment to longer-term loans for human resources development, environmentally sustainable development, and private sector development. Bank lending to Argentina during these years included a $500 million loan for capital market development, and $100 million for a project to expand basic health care, nutrition, and child development services for the poor. In fiscal 1994/95 Argentina's loans from the Bank included $190 million to finance investments in secondary education, $300 million to support fiscal reform in the country's provinces, $500 million for assistance toward the costs of privatizing or closing weak provincial banks, $210 million for public sector management at the provincial and municipal levels, and $225 million to assist public sector reform in the provinces.

Articles of Agreement. The Articles of Agreement that govern the International Bank for Reconstruction and Development, informally called the World Bank, were drawn up at the United Nations Monetary and Financial Conference, which was held at Bretton Woods, New Hampshire, July 1–22, 1944. The conference, generally known as the Bretton Woods Conference (q.v.), was attended by delegates representing forty-four nations, as well as a number of international organizations. Commissions were established to consider all the proposals that had been made regarding the two institutions. John Maynard Keynes, afterward Lord Keynes, was chairman of Commission II on the Bank, and was actively involved in drawing up the Bank's Articles. The conference's Final Act, which included the Articles of Agreement of the International Monetary Fund and the International Bank for Reconstruction and Development, was signed by all the delegates on July 22, 1944.

Article 1 of the Bank's Articles of Agreement lists its purposes; Article 2 covers membership in and capital of the Bank; Article 3 contains general provisions relating to loans and guarantees; Article 4 covers its operations; Article 5 is devoted to organization and management; Article 6 covers withdrawal and suspension of membership and suspension of operations; Article 7 describes the Bank's status, immunities and privileges; Article 8 includes procedures for amendments to the Articles; Article 9 is devoted to interpretation of the Articles; Article 10 contains "Approval Deemed Given"; and Article 11 includes final provisions.

The Bank's Articles of Agreement have been amended twice. On December 17, 1965, Article 3, covering the Bank's loans and guarantees, was amended to enable the Bank to "make, participate in, or guarantee loans" to the International Finance Corporation (q.v.) of up to four times IFC's unimpaired subscribed capital and surplus. Subsequently, on February 16, 1989, Article 8, which contains procedures for amendments to the Articles, was amended, and the total voting power required for approval of a proposed amendment was changed from "four-fifths of the total voting power" to "eighty-five per cent of the total voting power."

The Articles of Agreement that govern the International Development Association (IDA) were drawn up by the Bank's executive directors, and came into effect September 24, 1960. Article 1 lists IDA's purposes; Article 2 covers membership and initial subscriptions; Article 3 includes additions to resources; Article 4 covers currencies; Article 5 contains operations; Article 6 describes organization and management; Article 7 lists withdrawal, suspension of membership, and suspension of operations; Article 8 contains status, immunities, and privileges; Article 9 covers amendments; Article 10 includes interpretation and arbitration; and Article 11 lists final provisions.

IDA's Articles are very similar to those of the International Bank for Reconstruction and Development. The main difference is in Article 2, covering membership and initial subscriptions. Unlike members of the IBRD and IFC, IDA's member countries are divided into two categories: Part 1 (the richer countries) and Part 2 (developing countries). These are set out in Schedule A of the Articles, and the membership and subscription requirements for each category are listed in Article 2 of IDA's Articles. According to Article 3 of these Articles, IDA's resources include "replenishments," which are reviewed at regular intervals (currently every three years) and are provided by the Part 1 countries.

The Articles of Agreement that govern the International Finance Corporation (IFC) were drawn up by the Bank's executive directors, and came into effect July 20, 1956. Article 1 describes IFC's purpose; Article 2 covers membership and capital; Article 3 describes operations; Article 4 covers organization and management; Article 5 includes withdrawal, suspension of membership, and suspension of operations; Article 6 lists status, immunities, and privileges; Article 7 covers amendments; Article 8 includes interpretation and arbitration; and Article 9 contains final provisions.

IFC's Articles of Agreement have been amended three times. Article 3 of the original Articles stated that "the Corporation's financing shall not take the form of investments in capital stock." On September 21, 1961, this was changed to "the Corporation may make investments of its funds in such form or forms as it may deem appropriate in the circumstances." On the same date, the clause in Article 3 which states that "the Corporation shall not assume responsibility for managing any enterprise in which it has invested" was extended to limit IFC's exercise of voting rights in such companies. On September 1, 1965, Article 3 and Article 4 were amended to permit IFC to borrow from the Bank up to four times its unimpaired subscribed capital and surplus. Finally, on April 28, 1993, Article 2 and Article 7 were amended to change the voting majority required for increasing IFC's capital stock and for amending its Articles of Agreement.

Asian Development Bank (AsDB). Sponsored by the UN Economic Commission for Asia and the Far East, the Asian Development Bank (AsDB) was established in November 1966, with headquarters in Manila. Eugene Black, after leaving office as president of the World Bank, acted as adviser to the preparatory committee of the Asian Development Bank. The AsDB's first president and vice-president were previously executive directors of the World Bank. The charter of the Asian Development Bank is very similar to the Articles of Agreement, or charter, of the World Bank. It provides funds, encourages investment, supplies technical assistance to its developing member countries, and promotes economic growth and cooperation in the Asian and Pacific regions.

At the senior management level, there is an active commitment to collaboration between the World Bank and the AsDB, and annual policy coordination meetings have been held since the 1970s. Collaboration on the operational level includes exchange of information on current work programs, lending allocations, planned missions, and policy papers. Both the World Bank and the AsDB participate in consortia and consultative group meetings for various Asian nations. They also work together, sometimes with other donors, on an increasing number of projects, and the World Bank has cofinanced many AsDB loans. Cofinancing by the AsDB for Bank projects usually consists of parallel financing of separate projects within a sector, except for unusually large projects or for projects in the Pacific islands in which the AsDB usually takes the lead role in preparing, processing, and supervising projects. In fiscal year 1992/93 the AsDB worked with the Bank on initial economic work and analyses for Cambodia, and it also provided cofinancing for projects in Fiji and Indonesia.

B

Basic Needs. The term "basic needs" has been defined as "comprising minimum quantities of such items as food, clothing, shelter, water, and sanitation that are necessary to prevent ill health and under-nourishment." Early in 1978 a Bankwide work program was launched to study the operational implications of meeting basic needs within a short period, possibly in one generation, as a principal objective of national development efforts. The program, which was enthusiatically supported by Bank president Robert S. McNamara, included general studies to explore the concept of basic needs; country and cross-country studies to determine the extent of unmet basic needs and to review policy options for improvement; and sector studies to analyze methods of meeting basic needs in a number of key sectors. The studies forming part of the work program were widely discussed at the staff level, and some studies were also reviewed by the Bank's senior management.

The main conclusion of the program's general studies was that satisfying basic needs should be one of the main objectives of development, but should not be regarded as a strategy in itself. Country studies on conditions in Brazil, Egypt, the Gambia, Indonesia, Mali, Somalia, and Sri Lanka focused on the extent of unmet basic needs in these countries, and demonstrated that the most urgent of these could be met without sacrificing economic growth. The program's sector studies emphasized that human attitudes and motivation, as well as social institutions and organization, were as important as adequate financial resources in achieving successful implementation of a basic needs program. The ultimate test of such a program was the country's commitment to it.

A comparison of World Bank lending in the fiscal years 1970 and 1980 shows a large increase in loans for basic needs programs. Those covering education, population, health, housing sites and services, and water supply rose from $340 million in 1970 to $1,299 million in 1980. During the 1980s, in response to the debt crisis, Bank policies emphasized lending for adjustment and subsequently focused on the alleviation of poverty, in which efforts to meet basic needs continued to play an important part.

Black, Eugene R. (1898–1992). Eugene Black, the Bank's third president, had formerly served as a vice president of the Chase Bank in New York. He was respected in banking circles as an expert in bonds and a skilled negotiator. When John J. McCloy succeeded Eugene Meyer as president of the Bank, Black was appointed U.S. executive director. He worked closely with McCloy on marketing the Bank's first bonds and making its first loans. In 1949 McCloy resigned to become U.S. High Commissioner in Germany, and Black succeeded him as Bank president, serving in that capacity until 1962.

Black's negotiating ability helped the Bank to gain the confidence of the financial markets in the developed world. He also established friendly working relations with the Bank's executive directors and staff. In addition, Black acted as mediator in several economic disputes between Bank members and played a leading part, together with Sir William Iliff (a Bank vice president) in resolving the dispute between India and Pakistan concerning the division of the Indus waters. Black also made an important contribution to the Bank's future through his active support for the creation of the International Development Association and the International Finance Corporation (qq.v.). See *also* Mediation and the World Bank.

Board of Governors. According to the Bank's Articles of Agreement (q.v.), "All the powers of the Bank shall be vested in the Board of Governors," and as such it is the Bank's senior decision-making body. The Board consists of one governor and one alternate governor appointed by each member country. The office is usually held by the country's minister of finance, governor of its central bank, or a senior official of similar rank. Subject to the decision of their member countries, governors and alternates serve for terms of five years and can be reappointed. An alternate can vote only when his principal is absent. One of the governors is selected by the Board to act as chairman.

The Board has delegated its powers involving the conduct of the Bank's business to the executive directors (q.v.). However, the Articles of Agreement state that the Board cannot delegate certain of its powers. These include deciding on the admission of new members; increasing or decreasing the Bank's capital stock; suspending a country's membership; settling appeals from interpretations of the Articles of Agreement by the executive directors; making permanent arrangements to cooperate with other international organizations; deciding to suspend permanently the operations of the Bank and to distribute its assets; and determining the distribution of the net income of the Bank.

Most Board decisions require approval by a simple majority vote; a few require special voting majorities. Usually, the Board of Governors meets only at the annual meetings, which are held jointly with the International Monetary Fund (qq.v.). The Boards of the two institutions have established the practice of holding the meetings in consecutive years in Washington, D.C., and every third year in a member country other than the United States. The Articles state that additional Board meetings can be held whenever required by the Board, or called by the executive directors. Meetings of the Board can be called by the directors when requested by five members, or by members having one-third of the total voting power. A procedure exists, however, by which the executive directors may obtain a vote by the governors on a specific question without calling a meeting of the Board, so that many votes taken by the Board are actually recorded by mail. Governors and alternates "serve as such without compensation from the Bank," but they are paid "reasonable expenses" by the Bank when they attend meetings. The Board of Governors determines "the remuneration to be paid to the executive directors and the salary and terms of the contract of service of the president."

Borrowing by the IBRD. In contrast to many commercial banks, whose risk assets often exceed 15 to 20 times their equity base, the Bank's founders restricted its borrowing to a very conservative 1:1 ratio. Because of the Bank's prudent borrowing policies, and its preferred creditor status, Bank bonds have received a triple A rating from the bond rating services. The Bank's financial strength ensures its continuing access to the international capital markets, enabling it to borrow on favorable terms, and to make loans to its members at the lowest possible cost.

In the Bank's early years, it was necessary to convince the U.S. markets that Bank bonds were good investments. Two of its presidents, John J. McCloy and Eugene Black, both well-known in the U.S. investment world, were successful in their efforts to establish the Bank in the financial markets. The IBRD's first bond offer, in the New York market in July 1947, was successful, being heavily over-subscribed. Between 1950 and 1955, the Bank borrowed regularly in that market, but for relatively small amounts. The IBRD's first issue in a currency other than the U.S. dollar was a Swiss franc private placement with the Bank for International Settlements (BIS) in 1948, and its first public issue outside the United Sates was a £5 million sterling issue in London in 1951. The Bank's first Canadian dollar issue was offered in 1952, and its first bonds in Dutch guilders in 1954. Between 1965 and 1968, the Bank borrowed a total of $2.35 billion, nearly $600 million annually, about 50 percent more than in the previous four years. The IBRD then began borrowing in German marks, and it borrowed for the first time in the Middle East with a $15 million issue taken up by the Saudi Arabian Monetary Authority.

After Robert McNamara became president of the Bank, its borrowing increased considerably, and amounted to $6.65 billion ($4.9 billion after debt retirement) in the years 1969–74, seventy percent more than the Bank's total net borrowing in the previous eighteen years. This increase in borrowing was intended to finance expanded lending to members and to increase the Bank's liquid assets for future flexibility in lending. In 1970–71 Japan emerged as a major source of financing for the Bank. There were five placements with the Bank of Japan, amounting to 151 billion yen, which were the first public issues of Bank bonds denominated in yen. The Bank's net annual borrowings tripled between 1975 and 1981, with aggregate borrowings of more than $31 billion. The Organization of Petroleum Exporting Countries (OPEC) became an important new source of financing. After other sources dried up, Germany, Japan, and Switzerland provided most of the Bank's funds.

By the end of the 1980s the IBRD had borrowed in more than twenty currencies and had adopted a policy of diversifying its borrowing by country and by currency in order to draw on the world's accumulated savings. The Bank had begun to use currency swaps in 1982 and interest swaps in 1986. By 1993 it had engaged in the equivalent of $15 billion in these transactions.

The Bank does not take currency risks in its borrowing, so its assets are maintained in amounts to match the its liabilities in each currency. Lending rates for Bank loans are determined by the Bank's own cost of borrowing, and interest rate risks are passed on to borrowers through variable-rate Bank loans. In order to reduce the cost of borrowed funds, the IBRD uses currency swaps, short-term and variable rate instruments, and prepayments or market repurchases of its borrowings. During fiscal year 1995, the IBRD raised $9 billion through medium-and long-term borrowing in seven currencies. Short-term borrowings outstanding were $3.9 billion before and after swaps.

Brady Plan. In March 1989 Nicholas Brady, then Secretary of the U.S. Treasury, proposed that countries with sound adjustment policies should have access to debt and debt service reduction facilities supported by international institutions and official creditors. This proposal represented a change in the existing debt strategy, from support for adjustment with new loans to support for adjustment with debt and debt service reduction. The Bank's executive directors subsequently approved guidelines and procedures for an operation to support debt and debt service reduction for heavily indebted middle-income countries, with the stipulation that IBRD lending for the operation would not exceed $6 billion for the fiscal years 1990–92. *See also* Debt and Debt Service Reduction (DDSR).

Brazil and the World Bank. In 1949 the Bank made its first loan to Brazil, which over the years has become one of the Bank's main clients, receiving more than $16 billion in Bank loans. Almost half of these loans have been for energy, transport, and heavy industry, with the remainder going to agriculture and rural development, banking and credit, and social programs, including education, health, water supply, and urban services. From the 1980s Bank assistance to Brazil has also included loans for adjustment and policy reforms. Much of the dialogue and cooperation with Brazil is conducted through the Brazil Department in the Bank's Latin America and Caribbean (LAC) region. The Department has five divisions covering country operations; agriculture operations; industry and energy operations; infrastructure operations; and population and human resources operations. The Bank maintains a resident mission in Brasilia, and also has offices in Mato Grosso and Recife.

Until the 1970s Bank loans to Brazil's energy sector were mainly for the construction of hydro-generation and transmission systems. More recent Bank lending to this sector has supported rehabilitation, conservation, and environmental management of existing systems and it has been extended into the hydrocarbon field, with emphasis on increased utilization of natural gas. In Brazil's transport sector Bank loans have gone to highways, rural roads, railways, ports, and urban transport. The Bank has aided Brazil's industrial development with loans of about $1.3 billion, mainly for heavy industry. Brazil's efforts to deal with rapid urbanization have also received Bank assistance, and loans for this sector total more than $1.8 billion. Between 1970 and 1980, the Bank provided financing for basic water supply and sewerage with twelve projects amounting to about $1.4 billion.

More than fifty agricultural projects in Brazil have been financed by the Bank, with a total loan commitment of more than $4.5 billion. They cover irrigation, livestock, forestry, agricultural credit and marketing, land settlement, research and extension, and management of natural resources. In 1985 a National Irrigation Plan was launched to irrigate one million hectares over five years, with priority for the Northeast. The Bank and the Brazilian government completed an irrigation sub-sector review in 1990, and a project was approved to assist small farmers by providing infrastructure for irrigation.

A number of Bank projects have supported basic education, and others have been designed to strengthen secondary and technical education, higher education, and scientific research. Bank assistance to Brazil has included efforts to address rural poverty, especially in northeastern Brazil, through a regional development program comprising ten Bank-supported projects in eight states, with a total loan commitment of about $500 million. The projects did not achieve all their objectives, and the Bank was criticized by environmentalists for its failure to consider the possible effects of these projects on Brazil's tropical forests and their indigenous inhabitants.

Much has been achieved in over four decades of collaboration between Brazil and the Bank. However, much still remains to be done. In the 1990s the Bank continues to support Brazil's efforts to achieve adjustment and to restore growth, collaborating with the government in programs that increase productivity, improve conditions for the poor, protect the environment, and conserve the country's natural resources.

Bretton Woods Commission. Established at the initiative of the Bretton Woods Committee (q.v.), the Commission is a private independent group of senior individuals with experience in international finance, development, economics, and related areas of public policy. On the occasion of the fiftieth anniversary of the Bretton Woods Conference, the Commission issued a detailed report and recommendations in a publication entitled *Bretton Woods: Looking to the Future* (Washington, D.C., 1994). This publication examines the present state of the international monetary system, development finance, the International Monetary Fund (q.v.), and the World Bank and its affiliates. A number of recommendations for the future are included.

Bretton Woods Committee. This nonprofit, bipartisan group in the United States was organized to increase public understanding of the World Bank, the International Monetary Fund, and the African, Asian, and Inter-American Development Banks (qq.v.). The Committee supplied the initiative for establishing the Bretton Woods Commission (q.v.).

Bretton Woods Conference. The United Nations Monetary and Financial Conference, better known as the Bretton Woods Conference, was held at Bretton Woods, New Hampshire, July 1–22, 1944. It was attended by delegates from forty-four nations, who generally agreed on the need for international economic cooperation in the postwar world. The years of planning and discussion that preceded the actual conference, laid the foundation for its success. The negotiations were dominated by the United States and the United Kingdom, both anxious to reach agreement, and their lead was followed by the other countries.

In order to complete their work as quickly as possible, the participants in the conference established three technical commissions: the first, chaired by Harry D. White (q.v.) of the United States, worked on the IMF's Articles of Agreement; the second, chaired by Lord Keynes, undertook a similar function for the International Bank for Reconstruction and Development, and the third, chaired by Eduardo Suarez of Mexico, considered other forms of international financial cooperation. Each commission established committees and subcommittees to work on the various proposals for the Bank and the Fund. The "Preliminary Draft of Proposals for the Establishment of a Bank for Reconstruction and Development" was submitted on July 10, 1944, together with alternative and supplementary texts. After further discussion, the draft proposals for the Bank's Articles of Agreement, or charter, were approved by the delegates and were included in the Conference's Final Act.

Broches, Aron. An international lawyer and arbitrator, Aron Broches acted as secretary to the Netherlands delegation during the Bretton Woods Conference (q.v.). He joined the Bank in 1946, became Assistant General Counsel in 1951, and director of the Bank's Legal Department and Associate General Counsel in 1956. Broches held office as the Bank's General Counsel in the years 1959 to 1979, and during 1967 to 1980 was also general secretary of the International Centre for Settlement of Investment Disputes (ICSID). As a leading member of the Bank's legal staff for more than 30 years, he played a major part in the development of its law and operations.

By-Laws (International Bank for Reconstruction and Development). The By-Laws are adopted under the authority of, and are intended to be complementary to, the Bank's Articles of Agreement (q.v.). In the event of a conflict between anything in the By-Laws and any "provision or requirement" of the Articles, "the Articles shall prevail." The By-Laws have been amended from time to time since they were first issued in 1946; the most recent version, published in 1991, is "as amended through September 26, 1980." They deal with the meetings of the Board of Governors and the Exeutive Board (qq.v.), as well as other matters involving the Bank's organization.

C

Capital Increases (IBRD). According to the Bank's Articles of Agreement, the original authorized capital stock of the Bank was fixed at $10 billion, divided into 100,000 shares with a par value of $100,000 each in 1944 U.S. dollars. On April 27, 1988, resolutions authorizing a general capital increase (GCI) of $74.8 billion in the Bank's authorized capital were adopted by the Board of Governors, bringing the Bank's total authorized capital to $184 billion. The paid-in part of the subscription was set at 3 percent, with 97 percent callable. Previously, there had been two general capital increases. The first increase, in 1959, doubled the original authorized capital from $10 billion to $20 billion, and the second, in 1979, increased the Bank's capital from $41 billion to $81 billion. There have also been a number of selective capital increases. Such increases may either provide shares selectively to certain members, to adjust their relative shareholdings in the Bank in line with their changing positions in the world economy, or they may provide shares for new members. *See also* Financial Resources (IBRD).

Caribbean Development Bank (CDB). Established in 1970, the CDB has directed much of its development assistance to the Commonwealth Caribbean countries, especially the small states forming the Organisation of Eastern Caribbean States (OECS). The CDB's headquarters are in Barbados.

During the 1970s, the World Bank provided financing for projects in the region's agricultural, transport, power, and education sectors, but since 1980 Bank lending has mainly gone to support structural adjustment. Between 1970 and 1990, the World Bank made five loans to the Caribbean Development Bank, amounting to about $96.6 million, for on-lending to finance projects in IBRD/IDA eligible countries at interest rates reflecting its own costs. In some cases IDA funds have been blended with IBRD funds for loans to eligible countries; other countries, like Guyana, receive only IDA resources.

In 1990, a *Memorandum of Understanding* between the two institutions stated that "the CDB will complement and eventually supplant some current Bank roles in the region in areas where the CDB has a comparative advantage over the Bank." In future, the CDB will undertake adjustment lending in association with the World Bank and will be responsible for investment lending in the U.K.-dependent territories and the OECS. The administrative costs of World Bank lending to the region are relatively high owing to the large number of countries, their size, the relative smallness of projects, and the extensive economic work required of the Bank in its capacity as chair of the aid advisory group to the region. Closer cooperation with the CDB and lending through it will enable the World Bank to support small projects that would otherwise be very costly to administer.

Although relations between the World Bank and the CDB are good, some CDB members have suggested that certain Bank policies should be reviewed and possibly modified. For example, as the Bank lends to the CDB at market rates, the CDB has to add a mark-up to its own lending rates. As a result, many of its borrowers find the CDB rates too high, and look for alternative financing. Bank procedures for loan approval have also been criticized as being too lengthy and too cumbersome.

Central Bank Facility. The Bank uses this facility to offer to central banks and other government organizations a one-year U.S. dollar-denominated variable rate instrument, with the interest rate adjusted monthly on the yield of the one-year U.S. Treasury bill plus a spread.

China and the World Bank. China's decision to participate in the International Monetary Fund (q.v.) and the World Bank came after an extended period of consideration and preparation. Following the death of Mao Zhedong, the Chinese government decided to introduce economic reforms, change the country's agricultural system, and expand exports. In January 1979 the United States and the Chinese government established formal diplomatic relations. After Congress ratified the United States trade agreement with China in February 1980, the Chinese ambassador in Washington indicated that his country wished to seek membership in the Fund and the Bank.

In March 1980, an IMF mission went to China, and the Fund's Executive Board subsequently decided that the People's Republic of China would represent China in the Fund. A Bank delegation, led by Robert McNamara, went to China in April 1980 for discussions about Chinese entry to the Bank. It was agreed that China would be a single-state constituency, with sufficient votes to elect its own executive director. The Chinese expressed hopes that they would receive technical help and advice on development issues, as well as project assistance from the Bank. In May 1980, China's application for membership was approved by the Bank's Executive Board. In preparation for China's entry, the Bank established a China division, which became a department after the large-scale reorganization of the Bank in 1987. This is now one of the Bank's largest departments.

A Bank mission led by Shahid Husain went to China in July 1980, and it was agreed that the country's first project would be submitted to the Bank's Executive Board within a year. Agreement was also reached on the first five projects for Bank consideration. These covered higher education, improvement of port facilities, soil drainage, agricultural extension and research, and assistance to the China Investment Bank. In June 1981 China's first project, for higher education, was approved by the Executive Board, and the loan of $200 million was financed by a blend of IBRD and IDA lending. Bank lending to China was temporarily halted because of retrenchment efforts by the Chinese government in 1981–82. The Bank renewed its activities in China after visits in 1982–83 by its senior vice president, Ernest Stern, and by Bank president A.W. Clausen. Bank missions resumed their visits, and a number of sectoral studies were published covering many aspects of the country's economy. Each study involved extensive fieldwork by Bank staff, and discussions with Chinese officials.

The Bank's investments in China increased from $600 million in 1983 to $1 billion in 1984. Between 1985 and 1986, they amounted to a little over $1 billion each year, including approximately $420 million annually from IDA; in 1987 they reached $1.4 billion, and stood at just under $1.7 billion in 1988. When China's growth rate rose to 11 percent, the economy began to experience inflation. The first structural adjustment loan to China, amounting to $300 million for rural development, was approved in 1988. Bank lending to China was reduced during the next two years, but by the end of 1990 inflation had been reduced, investment was resumed, and projects approved for IBRD and IDA assistance in 1990–91 totaled $1,579.3 million. In 1992 Bank loans amounted to $2,526.3 million and went to projects in agriculture, education, industry, population, health and nutrition, and ports and waterways. During 1993–94 Bank and IDA loans and credits totaled more than $3 billion annually and included large amounts for energy, irrigation, and transportation.

In 1995, the Bank was working with China on reforms in state-owned enterprises and the financial sector. A large part of the Bank's agricultural and almost all of its social sector operations have shifted to China's poorer provinces, and the country has introduced its first comprehensive plan to fight poverty. Known as the 7–8 plan, it has been designed to eliminate poverty in seven years among the 80 million people that China considers poor.

Clausen, Alden Winship (1923–   ). Before his election as sixth president of the World Bank Group in July 1981, A.W. Clausen was the president and chief executive officer of the Bank of America. Soon after assuming office in the World Bank, Mr. Clausen established a managing committee to provide overall guidance for the Bank's management. Subsequently, he presided over an extensive reorganization of the Bank's economic analysis, research, and policy activities, as well as of its Central Projects staff.

During his years in office, Mr. Clausen strongly supported Bank assistance for structural adjustment, and agricultural and rural development. He also advocated additional aid for agricultural extension and research, and for programs to increase food supply and to develop energy resources. He constantly emphasized the need for additional assistance to sub-Saharan Africa, and stressed the importance of resource management and environmental issues in the design of Bank projects. He decided not to seek a renewal of his term of office in the Bank, and was succeeded as the Bank's president by Barber B. Conable (q.v.) in July 1986.

Cofinancing. Because the Bank can provide only part of the resources needed to assist its member countries, it encourages borrowers to supplement the Bank's resources with additional external investment finance. This form of collaborative finance, known as cofinancing, is derived from the following sources: agencies or government departments administering bilateral development programs; multilateral agencies such as regional development banks; export credit agencies, which either lend directly or provide guarantees to commercial banks extending export credit; and commercial banks.

Over the years lenders have found that cofinancing, especially in connection with multilateral development agencies, offers certain advantages, and substantially reduces the risks in lending to developing countries. In the early 1970s only about 60 Bank projects each year were cofinanced. By 1993, however, cofinancing in the Bank's operations was estimated at $11.6 billion, and more than half of all Bank projects and programs attracted some form of cofinancing.

In January 1983 the executive directors approved the establishment of a new set of cofinancing instruments, comprising the B-loan program, to increase and stabilize flows of private capital on approved terms by linking part of the flows from commercial banks to IBRD operations. These instruments offered three options: direct Bank participation in the late maturities of a B-loan; Bank guarantee of the late maturities, with the possibility of release from all or part of its share; and Bank acceptance of a contingent obligation to finance an element of deferred principal at final maturity of a loan with level debt-service payments and variable amounts of principal repayment. A fourth option was subsequently approved, which covered the prearranged sale of participations in Bank loans arranged on commercial terms.

In July 1989 the Bank's cofinancing and financial intermediation functions were combined into a single vice presidency, the Vice Presidency for Cofinancing and Financial Advisory Services (CFS), to promote the flow of financial resources to developing countries from non-Bank sources and to act as general coordinator of official and private sector cofinancing of Bank projects. The Expanded Cofinancing Operations (ECO) program was also established to assist eligible borrowers seeking to gain access to capital markets and to medium-term credit facilities. As part of the Special Program of Assistance (q.v.), which supports adjustment programs in low-income, debt-distressed countries in sub-Saharan Africa, funds are provided through cofinancing of IDA operations.

Japan, through its Overseas Economic Cooperation Fund and the Export-Import Bank of Japan, now accounts for the largest share of official cofinancing in support of Bank operations. Substantial cofinancing contributions also come from Germany and the United States. Recent years have seen increased cofinancing of Bank-assisted projects and programs by a number of multilateral institutions, including the African Development Bank (q.v.), the Arab Fund for Economic and Social Development, the Asian Development Bank, the European Bank for Reconstruction and Development, and the Inter-American Development Bank (qq.v.). The World Bank has also increased its efforts to catalyze private cofinancing for a broader range of its projects.

Colombia and the World Bank Group. In the period between August 1949 and July 1971 Colombia received forty-nine loans and credits from the World Bank Group, totaling almost $900 million. Although both the International Development Association and the International Finance Corporation (qq.v.) have made investments in Colombia, most operations of the World Bank Group up to the 1970s were in the form of IBRD loans for projects, mainly for electric power and roads. The Bank also supported projects for the rehabilitation and expansion of Colombia's railroads and assisted industrial development through loans to the Banco de la República for on-lending by development finance companies. IFC had equity participations in the development finance companies established with Bank assistance, and these continued to be an important source of financing for private industry in Colombia.

In 1962 a Bank mission visited Colombia and evaluated the country's development plan. Certain protectionist elements in the plan were rejected, and a new four-year plan was proposed, which included measures to encourage foreign investment in Colombia, and recommended a number of financial, monetary, and trade reforms. At the government's request, the Bank established a Consultative Group for Colombia to coordinate external aid. The participating countries and agencies committed more than $2 billion in loans for Colombia's development. An outward-looking strategy was subsequently adopted that, combined with a general recovery in the world economy, contributed to the country's recovery.

By the end of the 1980s falling coffee prices, deteriorating exchange rates, and the international recession combined to produce serious trade deficits and an economic crisis. Colombia borrowed from the Bank for a variety of purposes, including an adjustment loan ($304 million) for public sector reform. In the 1990s Colombia has received Bank assistance for agriculture, energy, export development, health services, highways and rural roads, natural resources management, the private sector, and rural development. Projects were approved in fiscal year 1995 for the development of agricultural technology, and technical assistance to Colombia's energy sector.

Committee of the Whole. This committee, comprising all the Bank's executive directors, serves as a forum for preliminary discussion of issues before these are presented to the Executive Board (q.v.). In addition, the Committee acts as a preparatory body for the Board's work in connection with the Development Committee (q.v.).

Committee of Twenty. Formally known as the Committee of the Board of Governors on Reform of the International Monetary System and Related Issues, the Committee of Twenty was established by the IMF in 1972 to prepare a draft for a reformed international monetary system, after the United States had announced in August 1971 that it was suspending the convertibility of the dollar into gold. Despite two years of discussion, the Committee was unable to reach agreement on a new system and submitted its final report to the Fund's Board of Governors in 1974. An Outline of Reform was attached to this report in which the Committee pointed out weaknesses in the Bretton Woods system and made some recommendations for improvement, including special measures for the developing countries. These recommendations were put into effect by the establishment of the Development Committee (q.v.).

Conable, Barber B. (1922–   ). Barber B. Conable, the Bank's seventh president, was previously a U.S. Congressman, representing Rochester, New York, from 1965 to 1984. He served on the House Ways and Means Committee, as well as on other congressional committees, and was a member of four presidential commissions. Before entering public service, Mr. Conable practised law in New York State.

Shortly after assuming office in 1986, Mr. Conable announced an organizational review of the Bank, and an extensive reorganization was put into effect in 1987. During his presidency, he stressed the need for careful consideration of the environmental effects of the Bank's projects, and supported the establishment of the Global Environment Facility (q.v.). Mr. Conable identified the alleviation of poverty as a major Bank objective, promised more Bank loans for the delivery of effective family planning services, supported an increased role for women in development, and pledged that the Bank would double its lending for education. Having reached the age of 68, Mr. Conable decided not to seek renewal of his term of office at the World Bank.

Conditionality and the World Bank. The Bank's Articles of Agreement state that, except in exceptional circumstances, Bank loans should be only for specific projects, that the Bank should ensure that the proceeds of loans are used only for the purposes specified in the loan, and that the borrower ahould be able to draw on the account established for the project "only to meet expenses in connection with the project as they are actually incurred."

Because the Bank is prevented by its charter from making unconditional loans, even when nearly all Bank loans were for specific projects, conditions were attached that the borrower had to accept. Some of these conditions involved policy changes, such as when the Bank refused to lend to governments that had defaulted on obligations to foreign bondholders or were unwilling to control inflation. In the 1960s the Bank employed a form of program lending in India with policy reform conditions. For other countries, indicators of economic performance were used as determinants of aid flows.

In April 1979 Robert McNamara (q.v.) announced the Bank's proposed move to make nonproject assistance available to countries prepared to adopt policies considered by the Bank as necessary for development. Structural adjustment lending was formally introduced in early 1980. Initially, there was some skepticism in the Bank, especially among members of the Executive Board, about the desirability of this type of lending, as a condition was attached to such loans that the borrowing country should also have a program approved by the IMF. This was not a very popular requirement, and many borrowers preferred the Bank's sectoral adjustment loans, which did not include this requirement.

These two forms of policy-based lending now account for about 25 percent of Bank loan disbursement. The amount of conditionality attached to this type of loan is related to the size of the loan and covers a wide range of policy areas. Apart from the question of leverage, an additional complication was the relationship between the Bank and the International Monetary Fund (q.v.), in which Bank conditionality was introduced into a situation in which IMF conditionality might already be operating. There were also questions about possible IMF/World Bank cross-conditionality, possible differences in the nature of the two conditionalities, and the need to reconcile them. These issues were settled in the late 1980s by the introduction of policy framework papers (q.v.) and a joint memorandum concerning relations between the Bank and the Fund.

Consortia, Consultative Groups, and Aid Groups. Established under Bank auspices at the request of a member country, consortia and consultative groups are designed to coordinate development assistance programs and policies for the country involved. Consortia for India and Pakistan were established between 1958 and 1960. Consultative groups and aid groups were established for fifteen member countries in the years 1962 to 1971, and added subsequently for other countries. At present, there are about forty of these groups. Although they are country-focused, these groups often meet in Paris or Washington, D.C., rather than in the capital of the country involved. Sometimes their activities are supplemented by coordinating groups at the country level that do meet in the country involved.

In making an agreement concerning future aid, the recipient country negotiates with each donor individually, not with the consortium or consultative group as a whole. Originally, the members of such aid groups consisted of representatives from Canada, France, Germany, Italy, Japan, the United Kingdom, and the United States. More recently, membership has expanded to include a number of the smaller European countries (Austria, Belgium, Finland, the Netherlands, Spain and Switzerland), and some other countries, including Australia, India, and Kuwait.

India and Pakistan are the only two countries for which the Bank has organized consortia. Originally, consortia differed from consultative groups in that their members made specific pledges of aid during meetings to meet the targets specified in the recipient country's development plan. Today this no longer occurs, although the principal donors are usually willing to make fairly definite statements about their intentions. During consultative group meetings, on the other hand, the Bank and the other participants usually describe their aid plans in more general terms.

Consultants. In addition to its regular staff, the Bank employs a number of consultants and outside experts on contract. At the end of June 1995 there were 1,112 higher-level, long-term consultants (those with contracts for six months or more) working for the Bank.

The use of consultants by Bank borrowers and by the Bank as executing agency for the United Nations Development Program (q.v.) has been described in various Bank publications, the most detailed being *Guidelines for the Use of Consultants by World Bank Borrowers and by the Bank as Executing Agency* (1984).

Bank borrowers employ both individual consultants and consulting firms to provide such services as preinvestment studies, preparation and implementation services, and technical assistance. Consulting firms can include private companies, public companies or corporations, government enterprises, nonprofit organizations, and universities. Their contracts are directly with the borrower, or with an agency designated by the borrower. The Bank encourages borrowers to employ domestic consultants or consulting firms in connection with Bank-financed projects.

Information on a large number of consulting firms is stored in the Data on Consulting Firms (DACON) system that is shared by the Bank and other international agencies. This system may be consulted by the representatives of Bank borrowers and member governments. The performance of consulting firms is recorded in connection with Bank- and UNDP-financed contracts where the Bank is executing agency. Although Bank staff are prepared to advise and assist the borrower during all stages of the selection process, they do not participate in making short lists of firms, evaluating proposals, or negotiating contracts.

Consultative Group on International Agricultural Research (CGIAR). Co-sponsored by the World Bank, the Food and Agriculture Organization of the United Nations, and the United Nations Development Programme (qq.v.), the CGIAR system was established in 1971. It is an informal association of some forty public and private donors currently supporting a network of eighteen international agricultural research centers, with the headquarters of all except four in the developing countries. Most of the donors come from the industrial countries. Some developing countries, however, also contribute to CGIAR, and a number of nondonor developing countries participate in its meetings. The Bank provides up to 15 percent of CGIAR's funding, subject to a fixed ceiling. The group's chairman is a vice president of the Bank, and its executive secretary and secretariat have offices in the Bank's headquarters in Washington, D.C. CGIAR's Technical Advisory Committee gives advice on scientific matters and recommends budgets for the various research centers.

Since its establishment, CGIAR has endeavored to assist developing countries to solve problems in agriculture, fisheries, food production, and forestry, and it has supported efforts to improve and expand agricultural research in these countries. The Group has been associated with the achievements of the "green revolution," which introduced high-yielding varieties of rice and wheat into developing countries in Asia, Latin America, and the Middle East, enabling many poor countries to reduce their food-deficits and achieve surpluses in food production.

In recent years the growing complexity of CGIAR's operations, together with declines in donor support, have caused difficulties in the Group's financing and governance. A program of renewal and re-dedication was launched in 1994.

Consultative Group to Assist the Poorest (CGAP). In March 1995 the executive directors approved the Bank's participation in a consultative group whose purpose is to increase the resources available to the very poor. Financing for the Group included $30 million from the Bank and contributions from other donors amounting to $70 million. The CGAP was formally constituted in June 1995, with participation by Canada, France, the Netherlands, the United States, the Asian Development Bank, the Inter-American Development Bank, the International Fund for Agricultural Development, the United Nations Development Programme, and the World Bank. CGAP has a small secretariat, housed within the World Bank, which will seek proposals from participating institutions and governments, and will approve funding within the framework approved by the Group.

Convention Establishing the Multilateral Investment Guarantee Agency. The idea of establishing a Multilateral Investment Guarantee Agency (q.v.) emerged during the 1950s. It was discussed in the Bank on various occasions from 1962 to 1972, but no decision was reached about creating the agency. In 1981 Bank president Clausen revived the concept in his address to the Bank's Board of Governors during the annual meeting. Detailed studies by Bank staff and discussions with the executive directors resulted in a proposal that was presented to the Executive Board in May 1984. The proposal was subsequently embodied in a *Draft Outline of the Convention Establishing the Multilateral Investment Guarantee Agency,* which was circulated in October 1984. Further consultations with governments followed. The final version of the Convention was prepared in September 1985 and it was opened for signature by members. The Convention came into effect in April 1988, and MIGA was formally inaugurated on June 8, 1988.

Chapter 1 of the Convention covers MIGA's establishment, status, purposes, and definitions; chapter 2 includes membership and capital; chapter 3 describes operations; chapter 4 is devoted to financial provisions; chapter 5 lists organization and management; chapter 6 contains voting, adjustments of subscriptions, and representation; chapter 7 includes privileges and immunities; chapter 8 lists withdrawal, suspension of membership, and cessation of operations; chapter 9 covers settlement of disputes; chapter 10 covers amendments; and chapter 11 includes final provisions. Like the members of the International Development Association (q.v.), MIGA's members are divided into two categories, listed in Schedule A of the Agency's Articles. Category 1 contains MIGA's high-income members, and category 2 the middle- and low-income countries. *See also* Multilateral Investment Guarantee Agency (MIGA).

Convention on the Settlement of Investment Disputes between States and Nationals of Other States. The desirability of institutional facilities for the settlement through conciliation and arbitration of disputes between states and foreign investors, was first discussed by the Bank's Board of Governors during their annual meeting in 1962. The executive directors were then asked to study the matter. They held a series of informal discussions and then proposed that the Bank should convene meetings of legal experts to consider the subject in more detail. Meetings attended by legal experts from eighty-six countries, were held in Addis Ababa, Santiago de Chile, Geneva, and Bangkok. In September 1964 the executive directors agreed to undertake the formulation of a convention, which was submitted to the Bank's members in March 1965. The Convention came into effect in October, 1966.

Chapter 1 covers establishment and organization; chapter 2 describes the Centre's jurisdiction; chapter 3 covers conciliation; chapter 4 is devoted to arbitration; chapter 5 includes replacement and disqualification of conciliators and arbitrators; chapter 6 covers cost of proceedings; chapter 7 describes place of proceedings; chapter 8 is devoted to disputes between contracting states; chapter 9 includes amendment procedures; and chapter 10 contains final provisions. *See also* International Centre for Settlement of Investment Disputes (ICSID).

Country Assistance Strategy Statement (CAS). This statement has become the most important summary of the Bank's assistance program to a particular country. It assesses progress in reducing poverty and improving social conditions, and indicates how policies aimed at poverty reduction are included in the overall country assistance strategy. The CAS statement should be supported by the findings of the country's poverty assessment (q.v.) if one has been prepared.

During fiscal year 1994 the Executive Board reviewed these statements for sixty IBRD and IDA borrowers, and set new guidelines for their preparation. In 1995, after further review, the Board suggested that the quality of these papers still needed improvement, especially in their coverage of social and poverty-related concerns and in their examination of problems related to the external environment.

Cross-Border Initiative (CBI). Cosponsored by the African Development Bank (q.v.), the European Commission for the European Union, the International Monetary Fund, and the World Bank, the CBI was endorsed by thirteen countries at a meeting in Uganda in August 1993. Nine of these countries have since confirmed their intention to participate. The CBI is based on a new integration concept that promotes mobility of factors, goods, and services across national boundaries. It is intended to facilitate private investment, trade, and payments in Eastern and Southern Africa and in the Indian Ocean countries. The reform agenda supported by the CBI includes exchange and trade liberalization, strengthening of financial intermediation, deregulation of cross-border investment, and the movement of goods and services among participating countries.

Currency Swaps. Used by the Bank as a liability management tool, swaps involve the exchange of a stream of principal and interest payments in one currency for a similar stream in another currency. They are used to borrow in the ultimately desired target currency at below the cost of a market borrowing in that currency.

D

Dams and the World Bank. The World Bank is the largest single funding agency for major dams in the world. Since 1970 it has provided funds to more than one hundred countries for more than four hundred projects involving dams. By regions, most financing for dams has gone to South Asia, followed by Europe, the Middle East and North Africa, Sub-Saharan Africa, and Latin America and the Caribbean. Of the forty-five major dams under construction in 1988, the Bank was directly involved in eight, either for part of the dam construction or for additions to hydropower installations, irrigation systems, or water supply facilities. In India the Bank has provided financing for about 131 dams, in some cases for dam construction, and in others for the irrigated areas downstream of existing dams.

The Bank's involvement in dam construction has been criticized by groups and individuals concerned with the environmental, ecological and social costs of dam projects. Others have expressed doubts about the safety of large dams. In response to these concerns, the Bank has produced guidelines to incorporate safety and environmental concerns into the design of dams. For Bank-supported dam projects, the project's concept and design must be reviewed by an independent panel of experts; experienced engineers, selected according to the procedures laid down in the Bank's guidelines for the use of consultants, are required for project construction and supervision; and after construction periodical inspections have to be carried out by qualified, independent experts. The Bank also recommends the use of local professionals for regular inspections and monitoring, with additional training, if necessary, in dam safety.

Debt and Debt Service Reduction (DDSR). In April 1989 the IMF's Interim Committee and the World Bank/IMF Development Committee (qq.v.) recommended that both the Bank and the Fund should provide support for voluntary, market-based debt reduction. Although it was expected that the two institutions would provide roughly equal resources, it was agreed that each would determine the amount of its own contribution.

The Bank's executive directors subsequently approved initial guidelines and procedures for an operation to support debt and debt-service reduction for heavily indebted middle-income countries, with the stipulation that IBRD lending for the operation would not exceed $6 billion in fiscal years 1990–92. Member countries would be eligible for assistance if they had adopted sound economic policies but required debt and debt-service reduction to achieve reasonable medium-term growth objectives. Under the approved procedures, the Bank's support would involve about 25 percent of a country's adjustment lending program over a three-year period, or around 10 percent of its overall lending program in cases where Bank lending was for investment. In certain circumstances additional resources of up to 15 percent of an overall three-year lending program would be made available. Loans for the DDSR operation would be made on regular IBRD terms, through direct lending arrangements that the borrower could use for debt-reduction and credit-enhancement programs approved by the Bank. Because the Bank's resources for this program would be limited, the executive directors recommended that efforts should be made to mobilize additional support from other sources. Also, as DDSR would be a new program for the Bank, they suggested that it should be reviewed annually.

In June 1991 debt and debt-service reduction programs were initiated for Mexico and Venezuela. The following year, Nigeria and the Philippines restructured almost $10 billion in commercial debt. Brazil reached an agreement in principle with its creditor banks, and Argentina, supported by a Bank commitment of $450 million, came to an agreement with the banks in April 1993 that reduced the face value of its debt by almost $3.3 billion. In December 1993, Jordan successfully negotiated with its commercial creditors to restructure an estimated $900 million in principal and arrears. Bulgaria and the Dominican Republic continued to make progress toward agreement with their creditor banks. Following the third review of the DDSR program, the executive directors agreed that the program should be extended beyond the three-year period originally envisaged.

Debt Reduction Facility for IDA-Only Countries. Owing to the lack of adequate mechanisms for easing the burden of external commercial debt owed by IDA-eligible countries, the Bank's executive directors approved operational guidelines and procedures for a debt reduction facility in 1990. Countries eligible for this assistance are those with gross national product (GNP) per capita of $685 or less for which no IBRD lending is projected over the next few years. All such countries with heavy commercial debt burdens are eligible for assistance from the facility if they have undertaken a medium-term adjustment program and a strategy for debt management, and if both are satisfactory to IDA.

Funding for the facility was provided by the Bank through the transfer to IDA of $100 million of fiscal year 1989 IBRD net income. It was agreed that the resources of the facility would be available for three years, and any funds not disbursed would be returned to IDA for use in its general operations. Because the resources of this facility were limited and were made available on a grant basis, the extent of help to any one country was limited to $10 million, except in very exceptional circumstances. Participating countries were expected to make every effort to mobilize additional resources for debt-management from other donors.

Five operations under the facility, amounting to $45 million, were completed for Mozambique and Niger in fiscal 1991, and for Bolivia, Guyana, and Uganda in fiscal 1993. In fiscal 1994, operations were in progress for Albania, Nicaragua, Sao Tomé and Principe, Sierra Leone, Tanzania, and Zambia. At an average cost of $0.12 per dollar of debt, the facility's operations eliminated 89 percent of the commercial debt of these countries. In 1992 the Bank's Executive Board agreed to extend the facility's operation, and an increasing number of severely indebted, low-income countries have expressed interest in gaining access to its resources.

Developing Countries. Although this term was not included in the IBRD's Articles of Agreement (q.v.), Article I, which lists its purposes, includes among them "the encouragement of the development of productive facilities and resources in less developed countries."

Development Committee. The Joint Ministerial Committee of the Boards of Governors of the World Bank and the International Monetary Fund on the Transfer of Real Resources to Developing Countries, generally known as the Development Committee, was established in October 1974, on the recommendation of the Committee of Twenty (q.v.). The Committee's proposal was subsequently approved under a parallel resolution adopted by the Boards of Governors of the Bank and the Fund.

Members of the Development Committee are designated by each Bank or Fund member country that appoints an executive director, or by a group of countries that elects an executive director. They are governors of the Bank or Fund, ministers, or other high-ranking officials. Committee members are appointed for two years. Each member country and group may also appoint seven "associates," so that countries not represented on the Development Committee are able to attend its meetings. The chairman of the Committee is elected by its members, normally for a term of two years. Traditionally, the chairman is a national of a developing country, and the executive secretary, who is responsible for planning, organizing, and reporting on the Committee's work under the general direction of the chairman, is from one of the developed countries.

Meetings of the Development Committee are held twice a year, in spring to coincide with meetings of the IMF's Interim Committee, and in autumn during the Bank/Fund annual meetings (qq.v.). The president of the Bank (q.v.) and the managing director of the Fund participate in the Committee's meetings and present reports on the issues under consideration. Representatives from other economic or financial organizations may attend meetings as observers. It is now customary for the chairman of the Group of Twenty-Four (q.v.) to address Development Committee meetings.

The Committee's activities include support for international cooperation in development activities; coordination of international efforts to finance development; and advice to the Boards of Governors of the Bank and the Fund on all aspects of the transfer of real resources to the developing countries. Staff from both institutions provide papers and progress reports for items on the Committee's agenda. A steering committee, chaired by the executive secretary and including Bank and Fund representatives, meets regularly to coordinate institutional support for the Development Committee. The executive directors of the Bank and the Fund review all documentation prepared for the Committee's meetings, and present issues for consideration by their representatives. It should be emphasized that the Committee is an advisory body, and as such its functions do not conflict with those of the Executive Boards of both institutions, which are responsible for policy formulation.

During the 1970s the Committee examined the problems of the developing countries with serious balance of payments difficulties. It recommended more official development assistance to these countries, and discussed ways of improving their access to capital markets, stabilizing their export earnings, and reducing poverty. Adjustment issues and problems of external debt in the developing countries engaged the Committee's attention at the beginning of the 1980s, and it strongly supported efforts by the Bank to expand lending for structural and sectoral reforms in the highly indebted countries. Subsequently, the Committee urged the Bank to give high priority to private sector development and took an active part in encouraging international support for Bank and Fund policies to deal with the desperate economic situation of sub-Saharan Africa. In the 1990s the Committee's meetings continue to provide opportunities for constructive international discussion of issues affecting both developed and developing countries.

Documents and Information. As part of its operations, including project work and the assessment of progress in its member countries, the Bank is in a unique position to collect economic and social data. In the past, the Bank considered that much of this material, such as discussions with member countries, reports on the state of their economies, and information about Bank-supported assistance programs, should remain confidential. There is no limitation on the Bank's period of confidentiality, and, according to Article 7 of its Articles "the archives of the Bank shall remain inviolable."

In August 1993 the Bank's executive directors approved a more open information policy, which allowed access by the public to a number of operational documents previously available only for official use. They include project information documents (PIDs) for Bank (IBRD, IDA, and IFC) projects, country and economic sector work reports, sectoral policy papers, staff appraisal reports, operations evaluation material, and various papers relating to the environment. Information about these documents may be obtained from the Bank's Public Information Center (q.v.), which opened in January 1994 at Bank headquarters in Washington, D.C. Similar services are available from Bank offices in London, Paris, and Tokyo, and from Bank resident missions. A catalog of available documents, as well as the text of available PIDs, is accessible through the Internet.

E

Economic Development Institute (EDI). Established in 1955 with headquarters in Washington, D.C., the Institute's objective is to provide training for officials concerned with development programs and projects in developing countries. EDI's full-time teaching staff includes experts from Bank departments, other international organizations, government agencies, universities, and private companies. Before 1962 EDI offered only general courses, lasting six months. As interest in project preparation and sector planning began to grow, the Institute added shorter, two- to three-month courses on these subjects. At first EDI's courses were conducted in English only, but since 1962 its courses have also been offered in French and Spanish, and subsequently in many other languages.

Six months before an EDI course is scheduled to begin, announcements are sent to agencies in the developing countries. Either directly or through their central banks or planning offices, the agencies nominate candidates for the courses, which are usually limited to twenty-five participants.

Selection is made by an admissions committee of senior Bank officials. Participants who successfully complete their courses become Fellows of EDI.

During the 1970s the Institute attempted to meet the rapidly growing demand for its courses by holding more of them overseas, and by associating EDI activities with the institutions and governments of member countries. In 1974 the Institute's work was reviewed by the Bank's Executive Board, which recommended that the Institute should organize more overseas training programs, and increase its efforts to develop training capacity in developing countries. Subsequently, EDI's programs included more support for institutes in developing countries, more national and regional courses (especially in sub-Saharan Africa), more courses and seminars on subjects of current interest in the Institute's Washington program, and a substantial increase in the production and distribution of EDI's training materials. A number of EDI's books, course notes, case studies, and exercises were published, and work began on teaching modules and audio-visual packages.

The Institute introduced its first courses for China in 1981, and extended its training efforts for Arabic-speaking countries. In 1983 a report on "The Future of the EDI" was prepared. This recommended that the Institute should arrange more policy-oriented training for upper-level staff from the developing countries, produce additional policy-oriented training materials, broaden its support to training institutions in developing countries, and seek additional financial assistance for training. By 1987 more than 85 percent of the Institute's activities were taking place outside Washington, and the poorest or smallest countries (many in sub-Saharan Africa) were selected for special attention. During these years, many participants in EDI's courses came from sub-Saharan Africa, and a little less than half of its budget was allocated to its activities in this area.

Cofinancing of the Institute's activities increased to about 25 percent of total expenditures, the main contributors being the United Nations Development Programme (q.v.), the Canadian International Development Agency (CIDA), and the International Fund for Agricultural Development (IFAD). In 1987, with grant funding from the government of Japan, the Bank established the World Bank Graduate Scholarship Program, which is administered by EDI. Intended to finance graduate studies leading to a higher degree in development-related social sciences, this program is open to applicants from member countries.

During the years 1988 and 1989, EDI improved its seminars for trainers and expanded its support for training institutes in developing countries. In response to the Bank's increased emphasis on the role of women in development, it launched a program of activities to enhance trainers' and policymakers' understanding of these issues. A new system of classifying EDI's training materials has made a large volume of informal materials more readily available. EDI's formal materials are listed in the Bank's *Index of Publications* and the EDI catalog. These materials may be obtained through the Bank's commercial outlets.

For the 1990s, the Institute is strengthening local training facilities, emphasizing sector-related adjustment concerns in its courses, moving from *ad hoc* cofinancing of its activities to multiyear programs, making more systematic evaluations of its work, and publishing annual reports on its activities. It has introduced a new program for training institutions in Portuguese-speaking Africa. Progress has been made on the UNEDIL project, which is sponsored by the United Nations Development Programme (q.v.), the Institute, and the International Labour Organization (ILO). Its purpose is to support African management-training institutions and associations. In response to requests for training programs from the former republics of the Soviet Union and countries in Central and Eastern Europe, EDI is holding courses for senior officials who are dealing with privatization, the restructuring of state enterprises, and the management of commercial banks. It also works closely with Russian universities, designs seminars, and produces teaching materials in local languages. In June 1994 EDI launched a program in the West Bank and Gaza.

To assist in South Africa's transition from apartheid, EDI is organizing training programs for future civil servants, local government officials, and personnel in non-governmental organizations. The Institute's Grassroots Management Training Program, begun as a pilot project in Tanzania and Malawi, has been extended to Burkina Faso, India, Nigeria, and Senegal. This program trains local trainers to pass on grassroots management practices to women who operate very small businesses.

Education and the World Bank. The Bank began lending for education in 1963, when it approved a loan for building secondary schools in Tunisia. Since then the Bank has become the largest single supplier of external finance for educational development, now providing about 15 percent of all official external aid to education. Bank loans for education during the past thirty years through fiscal year 1994 have amounted to $19.2 billion for more than five hundred projects in some one hundred countries. In addition to loans, Bank support for education includes technical assistance, dissemination of information, and the mobilization and coordination of external aid. Because of its long experience in the educational field, the Bank is also a major source of advice in such areas as educational finance and school management.

Bank investment in education and training can be direct or indirect. It can be for education projects that lend directly for general and technical education at various levels, vocational education, and training in specific occupational categories, or for project-related training, in which lending for education is indirect. Before the Bank approves a loan connected with education, a mission composed of educators, economists, and administrators visits the borrowing country and works with its officials to prepare an in-depth analysis of its education sector. This analysis forms the basis for a continuing dialogue between the Bank and the borrower, and serves as a framework for the design of future educational development strategies.

In the early days of Bank lending for education, more than half of its loans were for the construction of schools, colleges, and administrative buildings, and the remainder went to secondary schooling, technical and vocational education, and teacher training. After the Pearson Commission's report was published in 1969, the Bank reviewed and expanded its lending for education. Its projects were enlarged to support improvements in the quality of education and in the effectiveness of educational institutions.

Bank lending for education and project-related training has been reviewed each year since 1976, and the Operations Evaluation Department (OED) has conducted project performance evaluations for more than 160 completed education projects. OED has also prepared impact evaluation reports on projects in Colombia, Thailand, and the Philippines, and has reviewed sectoral operations in the formal education sector(1978), the project-related training sector (1982), and the effects of fifteen years of Bank-supported educational investment in Korea.

There are four main types of Bank loans for education.

1. Specific Investment Loan (SIL). Loans of this type finance projects that create new educational and training capacity, or improve the quality of existing programs. Such loans are appraised and supervised by Bank staff, and are disbursed over a period of five to seven years for specific works, products, and services.
2. Sector Investment Loan (SIM). This type of loan focuses on policy and institutional objectives. Responsibility for projects financed by a SIM is

more with the borrower than with the Bank. Typically, these loans finance part of a country's broad investment program for education, and project appraisal and implementation are sometimes delegated to an intermediary institution. The disbursement period for SIMs is three to seven years.

3. Sector Adjustment Loan (SECAL). Loans of this type, recently introduced in the education sector, support comprehensive reform of the borrowing country's education system. They are approved for countries that are experiencing great economic difficulties but are willing to adjust their educational policies to reflect their economic situation. Such loans are disbursed quite quickly.

4. Hybrid Loan. This is a new lending instrument that includes adjustment and investment features. It is intended to assist poorer countries requiring investment in educational infrastructure as well as sector adjustment.

Lending for education has increased significantly since 1980 and now amounts to about $2 billion a year. Previously, it was concentrated in Africa, East Asia, and the Middle East, but it is now important in all the Bank's regions. The education of females is receiving more attention in Bank projects, its share increasing from 15 percent of projects in the 1980s to 22 percent since 1990. In fiscal years 1990–94 a third of all Bank lending for education was for primary education, and future plans for the sector indicate that this trend will continue. Lending for non-formal education has increased, and (in the years up to 1989) more than ninety Bank education projects contained non-formal elements, including basic skills and literacy programs. Loans for secondary education declined between 1980 and 1990, but have increased since then, with 30 percent of education projects now including a secondary education component. In fiscal year 1994 the International Finance Corporation made its first education loan to a private secondary school in Uganda.

Since it began lending for education, the Bank has supported more than two hundred projects involving vocational and technical schools and institutions. Loans for this type of education have declined in the 1990s because many countries now believe that on-the-job training by employers is often more effective than formal education. In recent years, the Bank and its borrowers have studied a number of alternatives to formal vocational education, including pre-employment training in countries where enterprises have little training capacity, and informal firm-based short courses.

The Bank has lent more than $3 billion to assist higher education, about 27 percent of its total investment in the education sector. Nearly 60 percent of this lending has gone to Asia. Many Bank projects for higher education now support capacity development in such fields as agriculture, engineering, research, and mid- and high-level science, the Bank's objective being to narrow the gap between the industrial and developing countries in their research ability and their capacity to acquire and adapt new technologies. Some developing countries, such as Brazil, have received assistance in building up their science and technology subsectors. In other cases support has been given to staff training. Increasingly, such loans focus on the development of national capacity in order to reduce dependency on external training experts.

As part of its effort to raise educational standards in the developing world, the Bank has increased its own research in education, and has shared information about its results through books, journal articles, and working papers. Subjects of current research include educational finance, education for women, the demand for education, and the cost-effectiveness of various investments in education. The Bank plays a leading role in the international educational community through its contribution to education worldwide. It works closely with the United Nations Development Programme (q.v.), the United Nations Children's Fund, and the United Nations Educational, Scientific, and Cultural Organization. The Bank also takes an active part at the regional and international level in the coordination of educational investment by other donors. An example of the Bank's work in this area is a new group, Donors to African Education, which was created in 1987 after the Bank published *Education in Sub-Saharan Africa: Policies for Adjustment, Revitalization, and Expansion*. The group, which consists of international agencies and a number of foundations, meets every two years with ministers of education from sub-Saharan Africa to coordinate assistance efforts.

For the 1990s and beyond, the Bank continues to encourage its low- and middle-income country members to give higher priority to education and educational reform in their economic reform programs. An increased share of Bank lending for education is going to the poorest countries, especially to those receiving IDA assistance in Africa and South Asia. Other Bank objectives in education include expanding present systems of training, increasing higher education's contribution to development, and supporting more project-related training.

Electric Power and the Bank. The Bank has been actively involved in the electric power sector since its earliest days. Its first loan for power went to Empresa Nacional de Electricidad (ENDESA), Chile's principal power utility, in 1948. Bank lending for electric power includes loans for specific projects, program loans, technical assistance loans, and sector and subsector policy loans. In addition, power sector components have been included in multisectoral lending instruments, such as structural adjustment loans (SALs) and public enterprise restructuring loans (PERLs).

From the start of World Bank operations until June 1982, Bank/ IDA lending and credits for electric power amounted to $17.8 billion, exceeded only by agriculture ($26.5 billion) and transportation ($18.7 billion). As "agriculture" and "transportation" are general terms covering many different types of projects, Bank lending for electric power possibly represents the largest single purpose for which its funds have been used. As of June 1982, loans for electric power had been made to eighty-six countries and had financed more than four hundred projects. Most of this lending went to Latin America (37 percent), followed by South Asia (20 percent), East Asia (19 percent), Europe, the Middle East, and North Africa (15 percent), and sub-Saharan Africa (9 percent). Six countries (India, Brazil, Colombia, Indonesia, Mexico, and Thailand) accounted for about half of all Bank/IDA commitments in the electric power sector and about 30 percent of all the projects.

India has been the largest single borrower of Bank and IDA funds for electric power, and during the years 1949–75 it received loans for projects to support hydropower development, transmission and distribution networks, and rural electrification. Since then the Bank has approved more credits for rural electrification and has participated in financing for several large thermal plants.

Between 1949 and 1959, the Bank made several loans, totaling $240 million, for electric power in Brazil. Until the early 1970s most Bank lending supported the construction of hydro generation and transmission facilities in south and southeastern Brazil. Subsequent projects have been directed toward improving power supplies for the whole country, and there has been more emphasis on reaching low-income groups and rural areas. Since 1986 the Bank has supported financial rehabilitation, conservation, and environmental management in the power system as a whole. It has encouraged governments to increase real tariff levels, in order to restore the sector's profitability and to provide funds for expansion.

The Bank has committed more funds for electric power in Colombia than in all other countries except Brazil and India. The first loan was made in 1950, and by the early 1960s the Bank had made loans to three of Colombia's major utilities. It was clear that electric power in the central part of Colombia would be more effectively developed if the three systems were linked, and a Bank loan for this purpose was approved in 1968. Connection was completed by 1971, but various issues, including organization, least-cost operation, and finance were unresolved through most of the 1970s. A compromise solution to these problems was not reached until 1978.

Bank and IDA lending to Indonesia began in 1968, the first credits for electric power being approved in 1969, 1972 and 1973. All these credits and loans were part of a technical assistance program for Indonesia's state power agency, Perusahaan Lestrik Negara (PLN). The Bank, the government, and PLN worked out a financial recovery program for the agency that resulted in a substantial improvement in its financial and operating situation.

Mexico, the fifth largest borrower from the Bank for electric power, received its first loan in 1949 for the Mexican Light and Power Company (Mexlight). In connection with this loan, as well as another in 1950, the government agreed that Mexlight would be permitted to increase its tariffs, allowing "a reasonable rate of return." A similar agreement about tariffs was made in connection with a loan to Mexico's Comisión Federal de Electricidad (CFE). The Bank made more loans to CFE in the years 1955–71 and requested further tariff increases, to which the government reluctantly agreed. Up to 1970 there was some improvement in CFE's financial situation, but subsequently it was unable to meet the targets for the Bank's loans. As a result, the Bank made no loans to Mexico for electric power from 1972 to 1988.

The Bank's first loans to Thailand's power sector were made between 1957 and 1967 for the Yanhee project, a multipurpose power and irrigation project. The Bank insisted that a separate authority should be created in connection with the project, and the Yanhee Electricity Authority (EGAT) developed into a highly efficient organization. Beginning in 1975, the Bank also made a number of loans for rural electrification projects in Thailand. All these projects were successfully implemented. During the 1980s the Bank supported moves to increase private participation in Thailand's power sector.

In many developing countries, Bank loans for electric power have gone to enterprises operating within the framework of state ownership and public control. Before the mid-1970s the financial situation of such enterprises was generally satisfactory, but in later years power sector finances, efficiency, and institutions were adversely affected by rising oil prices, currency devaluations, and inflation. In addition, public control of the sector was often subject to political pressures, making governments reluctant to implement financial and operating agreements and to introduce market-based tariff rates. Responding to this situation, Bank projects in recent years have expanded from traditional lending for electric power supply and now include components dealing with such issues as pricing, institutional strengthening, and investment planning. Today, most Bank power loans contain revenue and capital structure covenants to ensure the financial viability of projects in the electric power sector. The former are intended to control operating costs, including depreciation and debt servicing, while the latter limit borrowing to prudent levels, subject to consultation with the Bank. To make power suppliers more efficient, the Bank is supporting efforts to increase local manpower skills and institutional capacity.

In order to encourage private sector participation in the power sectors of developing countries, the credit support programs developed by the Bank, the International Finance Corporation, and the Multilateral Investment Guarantee Agency cover some risks to private investors through guarantees. "Build, Own, Operate" (BOO) and "Build, Own, Operate, Transfer" (BOOT) schemes are also used to support private participation in the power sector. Under a BOO scheme, a private company, or a joint venture with minority public participation, is established to plan, finance, construct, and operate power generation facilities. In a BOOT arrangement, ownership of the power facility is transferred to another entity after a specified period of operation.

Emergency Assistance and the Bank. Although the Bank usually provides advice and finance in connection with the long-term development plans of its member countries, it also supplies financial and technical assistance in response to major emergencies. Bank procedures for handling emergency lending have evolved over the years, and now usually take the form of reconstruction loans following natural or man-made emergencies.

During the period 1960 to 1988, the Bank approved fifty-seven emergency loans and credits. The emergencies were nearly always the result of major natural disasters (hurricanes, earthquakes, droughts, etc.), but they also included emergencies caused by war or civil disturbances. Since those years, the design of emergency operations has been simplified, and they are now more closely linked to the restoration of particular facilities or services. Changes have also been made in the design of multisector reconstruction loans. Today, funds are not allocated in advance to specific subprojects, so that these can proceed when ready, and delays in disbursement are minimized.

In 1994 the Bank helped to prepare and finance an emergency recovery program (ERP) for Burundi that addressed priority needs in health, primary and secondary education, agriculture, infrastructure, and the private sector. A donor consortium committed $53 million toward the cost of the ERP, which included $14.6 million in IDA funds. After receiving an appeal from the United Nations, the Bank approved an emergency grant for Rwanda of $20 million to assist the relief activities of various United Nations agencies. The Bank subsequently helped to prepare a $200 million emergency recovery program, which included a $50 million IDA credit. An emergency economic recovery credit was approved for Haiti in December 1994.

Early in 1995 the Russian government urgently requested the Bank for assistance in containing one of the world's largest oil spills, which had occurred in the Komi Republic in northern Russia. The Bank agreed to prepare an emergency loan, provided that the Russian government would finance containment and clean-up operations until Bank funds were available. Within three months a $140 million project was approved, with $99 million in IBRD funds, $25 million from the European Bank for Reconstruction and Development (q.v.), and $16 million from the pipeline operator. Canada and the United States also provided financing for consultant services in the preparation of the project.

Experience has shown that certain factors have contributed to the success of Bank emergency operations: strong government commitment; prompt involvement of Bank staff during the early post-disaster stage; limited objectives and realistic time frames for achieving them; a strong prior relationship between the Bank and the agencies involved; and institutional arrangements that are kept as simple as possible. The design of Bank emergency operations now includes procedures for possible reallocation of existing loans; flexibility with regard to conditionality; and efforts to mitigate the effects of disasters, especially in disaster-prone countries, through the allocation of resources for future relief.

Energy Sector and the Bank. By the early 1970s many countries had experienced years of low energy prices and plentiful fuel supplies, with growing per capita use of energy. After the first oil shock, rapidly rising oil prices and interruptions in supplies forced governments to seek alternative sources of energy and to introduce policies aimed at conservation and efficiency.

In response to the changed world energy situation, the Bank began to assist member countries with petroleum development. Between 1979 and 1981, Bank lending for petroleum amounted to $1.35 billion. Of the projects financed, half were for predevelopment activities, including technical assistance, geological surveys, and exploratory or appraisal drilling. Assistance was also given to member countries on the formulation of exploration policies, the choice of technologies, market surveys, training, contracts with foreign companies, and other legal matters. Because of the high costs of exploration and production, the Bank tried to increase participation by private companies, and in some cases participated in financing exploration programs undertaken jointly by national and private oil companies.

Many developing countries lack the technical skills to investigate the increased use of coal, so the Bank has provided assistance in carrying out utilization studies, exploring export opportunities, and analyzing the possibilities of fuel substitution in the industrial sector. Bank missions in the years 1979–81 reviewed the coal sector in ten developing countries, and this work led to follow-up projects in several countries. Bank lending for the generation and transmission of electric power (q.v.) also increased, with new emphasis on hydropower and coal-fired thermal plants.

Renewable energy holds considerable promise for the developing countries and plays an important part in the Bank's energy program. One objective of this program is to expand fuelwood production. Other types of renewable energy include solar and thermal technologies, hydro power and wind power from small units, and applications of biomass and biogas technologies. The Bank has attempted to gain operational experience with the most promising of these new technologies, and efforts have been made to build local capacity in developing countries for the design and implementation of future programs.

Since 1980 the Bank has funded more than forty projects entirely devoted to energy efficiency. Many of these projects have introduced technical changes and improvements, rehabilitated power and industrial facilities, and encouraged conservation in all sectors. In 1983, in cooperation with UNDP and a number of donor countries, the Bank established the Energy Sector Management Assistance Program (q.v.). Recent Bank projects have included energy efficiency improvements in the fertilizer industry (China, Indonesia, Turkey, and Yugoslavia), the pulp and paper industry (Turkey), the textile industry (Philippines and Turkey), the cement industry (India), and the metals industry (Egypt and Guyana). In the power sector, the Bank has supported the rehabilitation of old plants, the upgrading of transmission and distribution systems, the use of energy audits to reduce wastage, and the establishment of institutions to promote energy efficiency. It has also supported current projects in the oil and gas industries containing energy efficiency components.

As part of its sector and project work, the Bank actively monitors, reviews, and disseminates information about new energy-efficient and pollution-abating technologies, and assists in financing their application. Current Bank policies to promote energy efficiency emphasize the integration of energy issues into country policy dialogues; the restructuring and regulation of the energy sector; careful consideration of energy pricing issues; private sector involvement in the sector; and pollution-abating components in loans to enterprises supplying energy.

Energy Sector Management Assistance Programme (ESMAP). Established in 1983 in cooperation with the United Nations Development Programme (q.v.) and a number of donor countries, this program was originally designed to assess the effects of changes in energy prices on the developing countries. Today, ESMAP focuses on sector restructuring, energy efficiency and regulation, household fuels, institution-building, and policy advice. Its activities, now integrated into the Bank's Industry and Energy Department, complement Bank operations and bilateral aid programs.

In fiscal year 1994 ESMAP assisted developing countries with their energy strategies, often as part of reform programs. Its work in the areas of household and rural energy continued in such countries as Bolivia, Chad, India, Jamaica, Mali, Rwanda, and Vietnam, while training and local capacity-building efforts were supported in Brazil, China, Pakistan, Tanzania, and Zimbabwe. In other countries, including Morocco and Mozambique, work on oil and gas continued, with emphasis on the development and use of natural gas.

Environment and the World Bank Group. Since the late 1960s the Bank has been criticized by environmentalists for failing to consider all the environmental effects of the projects it supports. In 1970, during the presidency of Robert S. McNamara, the Bank became the first multilateral development agency to appoint an environmental adviser. Three years later the Bank's Office of Environmental Affairs was established. In 1987 it became the Environment Department, with responsibility for general environmental policy and research. The Department is also responsible for informing Bank staff about the application of environmental principles to the Bank's lending operations and for preparing working papers on natural resource management, environmental quality and health, and environmental economics.

In fiscal year 1986 the Bank introduced a number of initiatives to improve the environmental aspects of Bank assistance to developing countries. These included a program of natural resource management that was designed to extend and improve the Bank's country economic and sector work on environmental issues, the creation of a global data base on environmental conditions in developing countries, the development of new guidelines and policies for wildland management (q.v.) and the handling of archaeological sites, and the establishment of pesticide evaluation and testing centers in East and West Africa.

According to Bank project procedures, environmental issues are identified during the project's preparation stage as part of the initial executive project summary (IEPS). This recommends a category for the project, and suggests an environmental impact assessment (EIA), if one is needed. Projects fall into the following categories: those that require a normal EIA, those requiring a limited EIA, those that do not normally require EIAs; and those that do not need a separate EIA because the environment is the main focus of the project. Normally, EIAs are required for projects involving dams and reservoirs, irrigation and drainage, power resources, industrial plants, mines, pipelines, ports and harbors, transportation, reclamation or development of new lands, and resettlement. Projects in such areas as reforestation or pollution abatement normally do not need separate EIAs.

After an appropriate category has been assigned to the project, Bank staff and the borrower discuss the terms of reference for the environmental impact assessment, and a field visit is made by the Bank's environmental staff. The EIA is prepared by the borrower, often assisted by Bank staff from the country department involved and the regional environment division, with support from the Bank's Environment Department. An EIA for a major project may require six to eighteen months to prepare, and forms part of the project's overall feasibility study, and its findings are included in the project design. The Bank's project appraisal team then reviews the EIA with the borrower, assesses the adequacy of the institutions responsible for environmental planning and management, and determines whether the EIA's recommendations have been properly addressed in the project design. After summarizing the main findings of the assessment, the team's report covers the alternatives considered, possible mitigating or compensatory actions, efficiency of the local environmental staff, environmental monitoring arrangements, and the borrower's consultations with affected groups. Formal clearance has to be given by the regional environmental division before the regional vice president can authorize further negotiations with the prospective borrower. The project may have to be redesigned if unexpected environmental problems arise during its supervision stage. After project completion, the Bank's Operations Evaluation Department receives a report that evaluates the anticipated, as well as the unanticipated, effects of the project and the results of any corrective actions.

In recent years the Bank has made a number of loans to support environmental objectives or to correct the possible adverse effects of projects on the environment. For example, a loan to Algeria for integrated pest management was intended to reduce the use of agrochemicals. Loans to Malawi and Pakistan were designed, in part, to achieve more efficient use of forest resources through conserving fuelwood and protecting indigenous forests. During 1995 the Bank prepared environmental strategies for several key regions and countries, expanded research on a broad range of subjects concerned with the environment, and integrated environmental issues into country policy dialogues, economic and sector work, and lending operations.

The International Finance Corporation (q.v.) has stated that the projects it supports have to satisfy the same environmental standards as those applied to Bank and IDA projects, and that an EIA must form part of the project appraisal process. In 1989 IFC appointed an environmental specialist to ensure that its projects conform with local environmental requirements as well as with Bank guidelines and policies.

Environmentally Sustainable Development (ESD). In January 1993 the Bank established a central vice presidency for environmentally sustainable development (ESD). This recognizes that development can be achieved and sustained only through the integration of economic, social, technical, and ecological dimensions. Since its establishment, ESD has played an important part in promoting integrative approaches to development that include natural resources and ecosystem management, urbanization, food security, and institutional and physical infrastructure. It has also provided direct operational support through participation in activities in new areas, production and dissemination of "best practice" papers, and review of sector work and best practices prepared in other parts of the Bank. ESD's vice president consults with environmental nongovernmental organizations on a bimonthly basis. ESD has become increasingly involved in the social aspects of development by providing technical support on social issues and promoting participatory approaches in Bank operations. During 1995 it held sixty-nine training courses that covered the full range of its activities. Efforts were also made to build partnerships with others, both inside and outside the Bank.

Europe (Central and Eastern) and the World Bank Group. In recent years the countries of Central and Eastern Europe (CEE) have replaced authoritarian regimes with democracies and have been moving from more or less centrally planned economies to market economies. The Bank's involvement with these countries goes back, in some cases, to the Bretton Woods Conference (q.v.), where Poland, Czechoslovakia, and Yugoslavia were founding members of the Bank and the International Monetary Fund (q.v.). After a few years Czechoslovakia and Poland ceased to be members. Romania joined the two institutions in 1972, Hungary in 1982, and Poland rejoined in 1986. Czechoslovakia, later the Czech Republic and Slovakia, rejoined in 1990, and in the same year Bulgaria joined the Fund and the Bank. In January 1991 Albania (q.v.) applied for membership in the Fund, the Bank, and IFC.

Before 1990 most Bank lending to Central and Eastern Europe was for projects, the majority for agriculture, industry, and infrastructure, and total Bank lending commitments to the region up to 1992 were a little more than $10 billion. Yugoslavia had received ninety-nine Bank loans during this period, amounting to $5.3 billion. Romania stopped borrowing from the Bank in 1982, and repaid its debt by 1989. In 1990 it restored full relations with the Bank and also became a member of IFC. After reaching agreement with the IMF on a standby arrangement, Hungary received a structural adjustment loan from the Bank that supported further structural and social reforms, as well as the privatization of some state enterprises. In February 1990 Poland's stabilization efforts were supported by an IMF standby arrrangement and by debt rescheduling with Paris Club creditors. These arrangements made Bank lending to Poland possible, and led to a commitment of $781 million for agroprocessing, export industries, transport, energy, and pollution abatement. Also in 1990 the Bank established a resident mission in Warsaw.

The International Finance Corporation (q.v.) has been active in Central and Eastern Europe since 1968, its commitments to Yugoslavia alone amounting to about $700 million. In Hungary, IFC has been involved in five joint ventures in the productive sector, in a joint venture bank, and in an internationally distributed investment fund. The Corporation has also provided credit for small- and medium-sized private enterprises in cooperation with a local Hungarian bank. IFC has undertaken three operations in Poland with a total commitment of about $55 million. It has recently advised the Polish government concerning privatization, capital market development, and methods of attracting foreign private investment.

In the 1990s Bank Group assistance to the CEE countries has included support for efforts to promote the private sector and encourage a competitive environment, progressive privatization of the existing productive base, development of small- and medium-sized enterprises, improvements in infrastructure, more efficient use of energy resources, development of environmental policies, modernization and restructuring of the banking and financial sectors, redeployment of labor, the establishment of a new human resources base, and the provision of social safety nets.

To support its lending operations in Central and Eastern Europe, the Bank Group has also undertaken substantial economic and sector work (ESW), including country economic memoranda, trade analyses, financial sector assessments and industrial sector work in Hungary and Yugoslavia, and studies of environmental and social sector issues in Hungary and Poland. The Economic Development Institute (q.v.) has expanded its activities in the region, with courses covering macroeconomic and public sector management, industrial restructuring, labor and social protection, and environmental issues.

The International Finance Corporation (q.v.) opened offices in Warsaw, Budapest, and Prague in 1991. IFC's Capital Markets Group has assisted in the creation of new financial sector institutions, and its Corporate Services Group has advised on restructuring and privatization in Poland, Hungary, and the Czech Federal Republic. The Multilateral Investment Guarantee Agency (q.v.) has undertaken a $30 million reinsurance transaction for an investment project in Hungary, and a number of projects in other CEE countries are under consideration. For the immediate future, the Bank proposes to lend an estimated $7–8 billion, covering all CEE countries, to assist in their transition to market economies.

European Bank for Reconstruction and Development (EBRD). The EBRD was established in May 1990, and began operations in April 1991. The members of the European Union, together with the Commission of the European Communities and the European Investment Bank, hold 51 percent of EBRD's shares. The United States is the largest single shareholder with 10 percent of the shares, Japan holds 8.5 percent, and the countries of Eastern Europe 11.9 percent. At the end of December

1993 the EBRD's authorized capital was ECU 10,000 million (approximately US$13,980 million).

The EBRD's objective is to support the progress and economic reconstruction of those countries in Central and Eastern Europe that undertake to put into practice the principles of multiparty democracy, the rule of law, respect for human rights, and a market economy. According to the agreement establishing the EBRD, 60 percent of its lending is to go to the private sector. Together with the World Bank and other agencies and institutions, the EBRD is one of the sponsors of the Joint Vienna Institute (q.v.). During fiscal year 1992 the EBRD cofinanced a Bank project in Hungary for telecommunication, and one in Poland for housing, and jointly appraised with the IBRD and the European Investment Bank a telecommunication project in Czechoslovakia. Cooperation between the Bank and EBRD in the former Soviet Union includes technical assistance for privatization.

Executive Board. Except for certain powers specifically reserved to them by the Articles of Agreement, the Bank's governors have delegated their powers for the conduct of the general operations of the Bank to a board of executive directors that performs its duties on a full-time basis at the Bank's headquarters in Washington, D.C. Originally, the Bank's Articles of Agreement provided for twelve executive directors (q.v.), but by 1995 their number had increased to twenty-four, reflecting the growth in the Bank's size. Five of the executive directors are appointed by the five member countries that hold the largest number of shares in the Bank's capital stock (United States, Japan, Germany, France, and the United Kingdom). Saudi Arabia also appoints its own director. China, the Russian Federation, and Switzerland have sufficient votes to appoint their own executive directors. The other executive directors are elected, and represent groups of member countries. The number of countries in each group varies from four or five up to twenty or more. Each executive director appoints an alternate (q.v.) who is empowered to act in his absence. Appointed executive directors hold office until their successors are appointed; elections for elected executive directors are held every two years, or as necessary.

The president of the Bank is, *ex officio*, the chairman of the Executive Board, but he has no vote at Board meetings except a deciding vote in the case of an equal division. The Board functions "in continuous session at the principal office of the Bank" and meets "as often as the business of the Bank may require." The quorum for a meeting is a majority of the directors, exercising not less than half of the total voting power. For formal meetings of the Board, an agenda is prepared and circulated before the meeting is held. Although the executive directors can ask for a formal vote, decisions are usually made by consensus. In the rare cases when a vote is called for, an appointed executive director casts the number of eligible votes held by the country appointing him or her, and an elected executive director casts the total votes of the group of countries he or she represents. *See also* Voting.

Executive Board Committees. The executive directors are assisted by a number of committees, and some additional ad hoc committees, as required. These committees usually have only six or eight members, and all executive directors can attend their meetings. They include the following:

1. Joint Audit Committee (JAC). Established in 1970, this committee, consisting of eight executive directors, represents the Bank's shareholders in overseeing the soundness of Bank financial practices and the adequacy of the work of its Operations Evaluation and Internal Audit departments (qq.v). Each year, the JAC nominates a firm of private, internationally established accountants to conduct the Bank's annual audit. It is also briefed on the status of the Bank's current loan portfolio, it reviews the situation of countries in arrears to the Bank, and it receives reports on recent developments in non-accrual countries.

2. Committee on Cost Effectiveness and Budget Policies. This committee, established in 1986, examines those aspects of the Bank's business processes, administrative policies, and budget practices that significantly affect the cost-effectiveness of Bank operations.

3. Committee on Personnel Policy Issues. Established in 1980, this committee advises the executive directors on staff compensation and other significant personnel policy issues. It also maintains close liaison with the IMF's executive directors on these issues.

4. Committee on Directors' Administrative Matters. This committee, established in 1968, considers administrative matters relating to the executive directors and to their alternates, advisers, and staffs. It coordinates many of its recommendations with a similar committee in the IMF.

5. Ad Hoc Committee on Review of Board Committees. Established in December 1993 to review the function, structure, and terms of reference of the standing committees of the executive directors, the Committee completed its work in April 1994. Its conclusions and recommendations were approved by the executive directors in May 1994.

6. Executive Directors' Steering Committee. This is an informal advisory body of executive directors, composed of the dean and co-dean of the

Board, and the chairpersons of the other standing Board committees. It meets monthly to review the executive directors' work program.

Executive Board Procedures. Within the framework of the Articles of Agreement, the Executive Board decides on Bank policy and approves all credit and loan proposals put forward by the Bank's president (q.v.), who is the chief of the operating staff of the Bank, and conducts, under the general direction of the executive directors, the ordinary business of the Bank. The Executive Board is also responsible for presenting to the Board of Governors (q.v.) an audit of accounts, an administrative budget, the *Annual Report* on the Bank's operations and policies, and any other matters that should, in their judgment, be submitted to the Board of Governors at its annual meetings, or at any time during the year.

The authority of the Executive Board is exercised in the following areas:

1. Through its annual examination of the Bank's financial and operating programs and administrative budgets, the Board determines the allocation of staff and financial resources for the coming year.
2. Through its review of evaluations of completed projects and the Bank's experience in individual sectors and with particular policies, and also through its participation in the annual review of portfolio performance, the Board is actively involved in auditing the Bank's development effectiveness.
3. Through its review of specific policy proposals, the Board determines Bank policies.
4. Through its approval of lending operations, and through its review of strategies for country assistance, the Board oversees the Bank's lending program.

Policy decisions made by the Executive Board cover the Bank's lending rate, the allocation of its income, staff compensation, and the Bank's research program (q.v.). Annual reports reviewed by the Board include project supervision and implementation, the activities of the Joint Audit Committee (q.v.), the financial statements of the Bank and the International Development Association, and the staff retirement plan. Particular attention is devoted to the Operations Evaluation Department (q.v.), which, under the management of its director general, is linked administratively to the Bank's president, but is directly responsible to the Executive Board. The Board is also actively involved in the work of the Development Committee (q.v.).

In addition to the formal regular Board meetings, with their fixed agenda, the executive directors also meet as the Committee of the Whole (q.v.). From time to time, the Board holds seminars with Bank management, in which informal discussions take place. Minutes of the regular Board meetings are detailed and carefully checked. A summary of the discussion is read to the meeting and subsequently circulated to the offices of the executive directors and selected staff members. Minutes of other meetings are shorter and summarize the main points of the discussion. All minutes become part of the Bank's archives and are not made public.

Executive Directors. Executive directors are full-time officers of the Bank, appointed or elected by member countries, and their salaries are paid by the Bank. They have a dual responsibility, as they represent the interests and concerns of their country, or group of countries, to the Executive Board and the Bank's management, as well as the interest and concerns of the Bank to the country or groups of countries that appointed or elected them. Because they serve as an important channel of communication between the Bank and its members, the dual role of the executive directors necessitates frequent communication and consultation with governments.

The question of whether the executive directors should serve the Bank and the Fund on a full-time basis was discussed during the Bretton Woods Conference (q.v.), and the question was raised again during the inaugural meeting of the Boards of Governors of the Bank and the Fund, held in Savannah, Georgia, in March 1946. This was an issue that divided the U.S. and British delegations, and Lord Keynes (q.v.), leader of the British delegation, strongly supported the proposal that the executive directors would be available for meetings but would not be expected to serve full-time. The U.S. representatives felt equally strongly that they should serve full-time, and their views eventually prevailed. During the Savannah meeting, the salaries of executive directors and their alternates were set at $17,000 for an executive director and $11,000 for an alternate. Many of the participants, including Lord Keynes, felt that these salaries were too high, compared with the salaries of other government officials, but they were eventually approved. In the Bank's early years, executive directors were often senior officials in their home governments, but more recently, governments have tended to appoint less senior members of their administrations. However, membership of the Board continues to be very highly regarded.

F

"Fifth Dimension" Program (International Development Association). This program, which is financed out of IDA reflows, provides additional resources to countries that have outstanding debt to the IBRD, are current in their debt-servicing payments to the IBRD or IDA, and are implementing IDA-supported adjustment programs. In fiscal year 1995 the program provided supplemental IDA allocations, totaling $185.8 million, to fourteen countries.

Financial Resources (IBRD). The IBRD's financial resources consist of its subscribed capital, reserves, and surplus. Its subscribed capital, which forms the larger part of its equity, consists of "paid-in" and "callable" capital. On June 30, 1995, the total subscribed capital of the IBRD was $176.4 billion, or 96 percent of its authorized capital of $184 billion. Capital subscriptions to the IBRD comprise two portions: a paid-in portion and a larger callable portion. The paid-in portion is paid to the IBRD when a country becomes a member, and consists of two parts: one initially paid in gold or U.S. dollars, and another paid in cash or noninterest-bearing demand obligations, denominated either in the currency of the member or in U.S. dollars. Members are required to maintain the value of the amounts paid in their own currencies. If their currencies depreciate significantly against the standard of value of the IBRD's capital, which is based on the 1974 SDR, they are required to make additional payments to the IBRD. The callable portion of the subscription cannot be used by the Bank for disbursements or administrative costs; it can only be called for payments to the Bank's creditors arising out of its borrowings or loan guarantees, and only then if the Bank is unable to meet its obligations in full out of its other assets.

Under the IBRD's Articles of Agreement, the total amount outstanding of disbursed loans, participations in loans, and callable guarantees cannot exceed the total value of the Bank's subscribed capital, reserves, and surplus. The difference between that limit and the actual total of disbursed loans, participations, and callable guarantees is called "headroom." The adequacy of the IBRD's capital is reviewed every three years (more often if necessary), and increases are subject to negotiation and agreement by members. In order to determine when a capital increase is necessary, and the amount required, two indicators are used: the amount of headroom available and the period when it might reasonably be exhausted; and consideration of the Bank's sustainable level of lending.

The IBRD's overall country-portfolio risk is reviewed regularly, and this determines the annual allocations for current and longer-term lending, as well as the level of loan-loss provisions and required reserves. The Bank's net income is calculated, and a portion of this is allocated each year to maintain the target level of its reserves, at present 13 to 14 percent of its lending, to provide for possible losses on its loans.

In the 1990s Bank members continue to subscribe to the $74.8 billion general capital increase (GCI) approved in 1988. It was then arranged that the executive directors would review the adequacy of the Bank's capital every three years. The second triennial review was performed in June 1994, and it was agreed that the Bank's capital was expected to remain sufficient to support the projected level of lending for the remainder of the decade.

The IBRD obtains most of its funds for lending to members through medium-term and long-term (MLT) borrowings in the international capital markets, and it also borrows at market rates from central banks and other government institutions. At the end of fiscal year 1995, the IBRD's liquidity totaled $18.4 billion. The Bank's liquid assets are invested in fixed-income markets. In addition to its borrowings, a significant part of the IBRD's resources is derived from retained earnings, and the repayments on its loans.

Food and Agriculture Organization of the United Nations (FAO). The activities of the FAO began at a meeting of forty-four nations in 1943. Its first conference was held in Quebec in 1945, and its permanent headquarters were established in Rome in 1951. FAO's objectives are to raise nutrition levels and improve the production and distribution of food and agricultural products for all the peoples of the world.

Since April 1964 FAO has operated a cooperative program with the World Bank that is intended to further agricultural progress in developing countries by combining the staff resources and experience of the two organizations for certain operations. The program seeks to expand investment in agriculture by assisting governments to identify and prepare investment projects for Bank and IDA financing. FAO designates a team of staff members to be employed full-time on World Bank-oriented activities. Project identification and preparation missions are normally the responsibility of FAO, and all other missions are undertaken by the Bank. Both institutions have found these cooperative arrangements mutually useful, and have renewed them several times.

Foreign Investment Advisory Service (FIAS). FIAS was created in 1986 by the International Finance Corporation (q.v.) in response to the growing interest by governments in attracting foreign direct investment. It provides advice on improving the climate for productive foreign investment to more than forty member countries, including a number of former centrally planned governments. FIAS informs its members about laws, regulations and procedures, and assists them to create effective institutional frameworks for interacting with investors, developing investment promotion strategies, and meeting long-term development needs through the transfer of capital, technology, and management skills. It also performs research on issues arising from its advisory work, and organizes seminars and conferences for officials and foreign investors.

FIAS was operated by the International Finance Corporation (q.v.), the Bank, and the Multilateral Investment Guarantee Agency (q.v.), through mid-1994. MIGA then severed its relationship with FIAS in order to conserve its resources and build up reserves. In 1995 FIAS completed twenty-six advisory projects, assisted Gambia to restructure its foreign investment policies, advised Zimbabwe's investment promotion agency, proposed restructuring changes for agencies in Bolivia and Peru, and evaluated Kazakhstan's foreign investment laws. Among its current activities FIAS is advising China on policies for foreign investment in infrastructure, and is promoting linkages between foreign investors and domestic firms in Indonesia and the Philippines.

Forest Sector and the World Bank. The first Bank loans for forestry went to Finland ($2.3 million) and Yugoslavia ($2.7 million) in 1949. Early Bank lending to this sector was mainly for forest-based industries and extraction of raw material, but after the Bank adopted a wider development agenda, new concerns influenced its policies for forestry. The Bank's current objectives for the sector include efforts to reduce deforestation, the planting of sufficient new trees, and the management of forest resources in ways that will satisfy the growing demand by the rural poor for forest products and services.

Before 1978 the Bank's total commitments to the forest sector amounted to only $199 million, but since then Bank loans have supported more than eighty-four free-standing forestry projects, mainly in Africa and Asia, with total commitments of more than $2,225 million. In addition, there have been significant forestry components in many agricultural and rural development projects, including some that have involved experiments with soil and moisture conservation, and others that have assisted marginal agriculture that could otherwise infringe on forest areas.

A recent report by the Bank's Operations Evaluation Department (q.v.) analyzed Bank experience in the forest sector from 1949 to 1990 and concluded that the Bank needed to strengthen its work in this sector, and to improve the technical performance of its forest projects. The report also recommended that the design of social forestry projects should be based on better understanding of local structures and motivations in tree-planting and management, and that local institutions, such as property rights and possible land use conflicts, should be more carefully considered during project preparation.

The Bank holds regular consultations on forest issues with the regional development banks, the Food and Agriculture Organization of the United Nations (FAO), the United Nations Environment Programme (UNEP), and nongovernmental organizations (qq.v.). It is closely involved with the Global Environment Facility and the Consultative Group on International Agricultural Research (qq.v.), both active in the forest sector. In 1986 the Bank, together with FAO, the United Nations Development Programme, and the World Resources Institute, sponsored the Tropical Forestry Action Plan (q.v.). The Bank is also assisting governments to prepare forest resource inventories, to establish systems for resource assessment, and to improve the performance of agencies dealing with forestry.

In projects involving tropical moist forests, the Bank has adopted, and encourages governments to adopt, a precautionary policy. It has been found that some Bank-supported projects, especially those concerned with agricultural settlements or infrastructure, have had undesirable effects on tropical forests and their inhabitants. Consequently, the financing of projects that could lead to the loss of such forests is now subject to rigorous environmental assessment and to careful evaluation of the social issues involved. In the twenty countries that contain 85 percent of tropical forests, the Bank has made special efforts to support economic development in poor areas near the forests in order to limit encroachment and eventual loss.

As part of its continuing effort to address new challenges in the forest sector, the Bank is encouraging its members to adopt innovative and experimental measures. Recent examples include: the involvement of forest-user groups in forest management in Nepal; the establishment of a unit to enforce environmental guidelines in national forest programs in Sri Lanka; the strengthening of property rights around two forest areas in New Guinea; assistance for women's groups in tree-planting and wood-lot management in Zimbabwe; and the development of environmental guidelines for plantation management in China. Other Bank-financed programs are attempting to meet the fuelwood needs of poor rural communities and low-income urban families, to support tree-planting programs for small farmers and the landless, and to assist women through social forestry schemes.

Current Bank lending to the forest sector now distinguishes between projects that are environmentally protective and those oriented toward small farmers, and all other forestry operations, including commercial plantations. Projects in the first two categories are considered on the basis of their economic, social, and environmental merits, while approval for other projects is conditional on government commitment to sustainable and conservation-directed forestry.

G

Garner, Robert Livingston (1894–1975). After holding office as financial vice president of the Guaranty Trust Company and subsequently of the General Foods Corporation, Robert L. Garner became vice president of the IBRD in February 1947. He considered that his main mission was to create an efficient staff for the Bank, and he actively supported the Bank's first informal training programs, and the establishment of the Economic Development Institute (q.v.). It was Garner's "firm conviction that the most promising future for the less developed countries was the establishing of good private industry," and he felt that the Bank should develop a new approach to ensure "the spread of private industry and business." In May 1952 he presented a memorandum on the proposed new organization to Bank president Eugene Black, who was sympathetic to the idea. Garner then set up a committee to draft a charter for the organization, which was provisionally named the International Finance Corporation. It took several years to build up interest in Garner's proposals, but finally Black was able to persuade the U.S. to support them. IFC was officially established in July 1956, and Garner resigned from the Bank to become president of the new corporation. He retired from IFC in October 1961.

General Arrangements to Borrow (GAB). In October 1962 the International Monetary Fund (q.v.) made arrangements to borrow, in special circumstances, specified amounts from eleven industrial countries (Belgium, Canada, France, Germany, Italy, Japan, the Netherlands, Sweden, Switzerland, the United Kingdom, and the United States). Except Switzerland, which did not join the Bank and the Fund until 1992, all these countries were members of the Fund. They subsequently became known as the Group of Ten (q.v.). The GAB made it possible for the Fund to borrow up to $6 billion in the participants' currencies to help in financing large drawings by members during a crisis or when it seemed that the Fund might not have sufficient resources to meet such needs. The arrangements were activated on a small number of occasions in the years between 1964 and 1978. In response to the debt crisis, major reforms in the GAB were introduced in 1983.

Global Environment Facility (GEF). The GEF was established in 1991 as a three-year pilot project sponsored by the United Nations Development Programme, the United Nations Environment Programme (qq.v.) and the World Bank. It consists of a council, an assembly, and an independent secretariat headed by a chief executive officer. The Bank is the trustee of the GEF trust fund, it acts as one of GEF's implementing agencies, and it provides administrative support for the Facility's secretariat.

The Global Environment Facility provides grants to developing countries for projects and activities to protect the global environment in ways consistent with their national development objectives, focusing on such areas as climate change, biodiversity, protection of international waters, and depletion of the ozone layer. All countries with per capita incomes below $4,000 qualify for grants from the Facility. GEF's funds, which are administered by the Bank, are in addition to the financing for national environmental assistance provided by the Bank and other international development agencies. At the United Nations Conference on Environment and Development (q.v.), held in Rio de Janeiro, Brazil, in June 1992, GEF was designated in the Conference's Agenda 21 as a source of funds for achieving global environmental benefits.

In March 1994 seventy-three participating governments concluded negotiations to restructure GEF and to replenish its core fund with more than $2 billion for a three-year period. Up to the end of fiscal year 1995, 148 projects totaling $869 million were approved by GEF's participants. Of these, sixty-three projects (for $558 million) were allocated for World Bank/GEF investment projects. Under the new arrangements, the Bank's Executive Board is now reviewing and approving Bank-implemented GEF projects in the same way as Bank projects, and GEF processing procedures have been aligned with Bank investment processing procedures.

Global Programme on AIDS (GPA). Established in 1987 and sponsored by the World Health Organization (q.v.), the GPA is designed to coordinate research, develop methods, and implement plans to control AIDS (q.v.). In fiscal year 1989, and subsequently, the program has received a special grant of $1 million from the Bank, to support operational research.

Governance and the World Bank. Governance has been defined by the Bank as "the manner in which power is exercised in the management of a country's economic and social resources for development." For the Bank, good governance is synonymous with sound development management. The four areas of governance that are consistent with the Bank's definition and are within its mandate are public sector management, accountability, the legal framework for development, and information and transparency.

Until the 1980s the Bank's involvement in public sector management (PSM) was mainly with the agencies implementing Bank-financed projects. When adjustment lending was introduced, the Bank began to expand its approach to PSM with broad-based sector adjustment loans, and with lending for improved financial management and civil service reform. Support was also given to the establishment of social safety nets, to the divestiture and privatization of public enterprises, to tax reform, and to decentralization. Bank loans for institution-building have gone to Armenia, Belarus, Georgia, Kazakhstan, Ukraine, and other former Soviet republics. In East Asia and the Pacific the Bank has assisted Indonesia with PSM reform, and China with efforts to decentralize public administration. Because public sector capacity has collapsed in some countries in Sub-Saharan Africa, Bank assistance to PSM in these countries has focused on rebuilding capacity and on addressing the systemic failures that contributed to the collapse. In the special case of the West Bank and Gaza, the Bank is cooperating in the establishment of a Palestinian entity to manage the emergency development program, and will provide support for institutions undertaking public management functions under the agreements on self-government.

The Bank continues to support reforms in the management of public expenditure, with emphasis on improvements in the budget process, and the monitoring and execution of public expenditure programs. Public expenditure reviews are under way in the Baltic states, Romania, and the Russian Federation. Bank PSM assistance has also been provided to China and Indonesia through projects that seek to modernize accounting and auditing practices and to develop training programs for accountants and auditors. In Africa the Bank is helping to rebuild accounting and auditing capacities in government.

Bank aid for civil service reform has moved beyond its original focus on retrenchment and cost containment, and now involves such issues as performance improvement and effective management of resources. In Latin America and the Caribbean the Bank is supporting efforts to modernize the civil service in a number of countries; in South Asia, Bangladesh has requested Bank technical assistance for training public servants and improving civil service management; and in sub-Saharan Africa more than half the countries are receiving Bank aid to support their PSM reform efforts.

In recent years the Bank has been helping member countries to improve accountability in both the public and private sectors, and it has made progress in enhancing accountability and effectiveness in its own operations. A Bank task force on financial reporting and auditing recommended in 1993 that country efforts to establish sound financial management should include regular assessments of the country's financial accountability. For all regions, such assessments would review borrowing countries' accounting and auditing standards and examine their professional capacity and training arrangements. So far, assessments have been completed in Ghana and South Africa; they are in progress in other countries.

The Bank has employed a number of ways to help its members improve their legal frameworks for development. New laws or judicial reforms have been included as components in sector or economy-wide programs supported by adjustment loans; investment loans have contained legal system components; technical assistance projects have supported legal reforms; and grant assistance has been provided through the Bank's Institutional Development Fund (q.v.). Legal advice has been provided to many countries by the Bank's staff. In Eastern Europe and Central Asia countries moving from a command to a market economy have received Bank technical assistance in making new laws. Similar efforts are being made to assist the Lao People's Democratic Republic and Viet Nam. A large commercial law reform project has been prepared for China. In Latin America and the Caribbean the Bank is helping a number of countries to modernize their economic laws. Legal institutions relating to property rights have been strengthened in sub-Saharan Africa, and technical assistance projects for legal training and court infrastructure are under consideration.

The Bank believes that transparency and information assist governments to clarify their policies and programs, and that they are essential elements in efforts to improve governance. In Latin America and the Caribbean, the Bank has supported policies for improved financial management, more transparent budgetary systems, and revenue administration reforms, and it has financed programs in sub-Saharan Africa to simplify existing tax and tariff structures.

In the 1990s the Bank is most actively involved in governance issues in Africa and Latin America, but its future operations will probably expand in such regions as Eastern Europe and Central Asia, where the concept is relatively new. There, the Bank continues to stress openness in the ongoing PSM reform measures and presents seminars on economic management in market economies to encourage debate and greater understanding of its activities in support of good governance.

Governors, Board of. *See* Board of Governors.

Graduation of IBRD Borrowers. This is a process of slowly phasing out IBRD lending after a member country reaches a level of development, management capacity, and access to capital markets that enables it to continue its growth activities without borrowing from the IBRD. Graduation is normally achieved within five years after a country reaches the per capita gross national product (GNP) of $2,650 at 1980 prices. If the country's economic situation deteriorates during the phaseout period, the time for graduation may be extended. After a careful review of the country's economy, a flexible program is developed to limit IBRD lending and finally to end it. If requested, however, the IBRD will continue to provide support to member countries after its lending has ceased. This support can be in the form of technical assistance, continued access to the courses organized by the Economic Development Institute, or continued eligibility for operations of the International Finance Corporation (qq.v.).

Group of Five. The group originally comprised France, Germany, Japan, the United Kingdom, and the United States. After the addition of Canada and Italy it evolved into the Group of Seven (q.v.).

Group of Seven. This group consists of seven industrial countries—Canada, France, Germany, Italy, Japan, the United Kingdom, and the United

States. It was originally constituted as the Group of Five (q.v.), without the participation of Italy and Canada. Since 1974 the leaders of these countries meet each year at economic summits that play an important part in maintaining cooperation among the leading industrial nations. Their discussions can also affect the agendas for other international meetings, including the meetings of the Group of Ten, and the annual meetings (q.v.) of the Bank and the IMF.

Group of Seventy-Seven. Established following the United Nations Conference on Trade and Development in 1964, this group represents those developing countries that decided to form a group to promote and protect their common interests. Today the group has more than a hundred members.

Group of Ten. The Group of Ten consists of ten industrial countries— Belgium, Canada, France, Germany, Italy, Japan, Netherlands, Sweden, the United Kingdom, and the United States. It came into existence in 1962, when these countries agreed to participate in the IMF's General Arrangements to Borrow (q.v.). The group meets regularly, and continues to play an important part in international monetary negotiations.

Group of Twenty-Four. Officially established as the Group of Twenty-Four on International Monetary Affairs, this group came into existence in 1971, possibly as a counterbalance to the Group of Ten (q.v.). It consists of twenty-four finance ministers, or their equivalent. One-third of the Group's members are appointed by the African, one-third by the Asian, and one-third by the Latin American members of the Group of Seventy-Seven (q.v.). Although the Group is limited to twenty-four members, its meetings may be attended by any member of the Group of Seventy-Seven. In addition to its activities in connection with a reformed monetary system, the Group of Twenty-Four also participates in other international meetings, including those of the Development Committee (q.v.). It meets regularly, usually twice a year, when the Group of Ten meets.

Guarantees (World Bank). In fiscal year 1995 the Bank moved to mainstream its guarantee operations in order to catalyze the flow of private capital to infrastructure projects in developing countries. This was considered necessary because the financing of such large-scale, long-term projects is beyond the means of governments and multilateral agencies, and additional funding has to be obtained from private developers, operators, and financiers. The new guarantee initiative replaces the Bank's Expanded Cofinancing Operations (ECO) program by broadening country eligibility to any Bank borrower, by limiting fees, and by simplifying procedures.

Two new types of guarantees have been established under the initiative: partial risk guarantees and partial credit guarantees. The former are intended mainly for limited recourse project financing, in which lenders consider the project's revenues and assets to be more important than the sponsor's credit. Most "Build, Own, Operate" (BOO) projects are financed under these arrangements, and guarantees can cover risks associated with government contractual commitments to the project. Partial credit guarantees allocate risks in a different way. The Bank guarantees repayment, but only for a part of the period of financing, in order to improve the terms of borrowing through lengthening the maturity of the loan. Such guarantees usually apply to later repayments or they can be applied to a limited number of interest payments, or to a combination of both. Government counter guarantees are required when the Bank provides a guarantee. Although this requirement increases the time needed for processing, it strengthens the government's commitment to the project and indemnifies the Bank for any payments it may make under its guarantee. Bank guarantees carry fees. The standby fee, for the period of the guarantee when it is not callable, is twenty-five basis points; when the guarantee is callable, the fee is set between forty and one hundred basis points, depending on the risk.

H

Headroom. The IBRD's Articles of Agreement state that the Bank's total debt outstanding and disbursed, including guarantees, cannot exceed the total value of its subscribed capital, reserves, and surplus. The difference between the IBRD's statutory lending limit and actual total debt outstanding and disbursed is known as "headroom," and every three years it is subject to review. At the end of fiscal year 1995, the permissible increase of net disbursements (headroom) was $75.3 billion, or 38 percent of the IBRD's lending limit.

Health and the World Bank. After several years of informal activity in the health sector, the Bank adopted a formal health policy in 1974 that limited its operations in this sector to the financing of health components of projects in other sectors. In 1975 a Bank health sector policy paper suggested that poor health facilities were impeding development in many countries and that the improvement of health conditions should become a major development objective. Subsequently, the Bank increased its activities in the health sector, and between 1976 and 1978 it supported health components, amounting to $405 million, in seventy projects in forty-four countries. These financed the construction of facilities for family planning and nutrition, and provided for the training of health personnel. At the request of many of its members in the developing countries, the Bank began to prepare health sector studies. A formal agreement with the World Health Organization was signed in 1976, and health-related lending was coordinated with bilateral donor agencies.

In July 1979 the Bank's Executive Board reviewed Bank experience in financing health components in projects, and subsequently approved a proposal to provide direct financing to health projects. To support these new activities, the Bank established a Population, Health, and Nutrition Department. By 1982 the Bank had become the world's largest lender for health projects in the developing countries. Since then, the Bank has approved health, population and nutrition projects for more than $100 million in each fiscal year. From 1982 to 1986, lending for thirty-five projects in the health sector amounted to $1,010 million, and was mainly for the expansion of basic health services in rural areas. All these projects had a manpower development component, and most included efforts to improve family planning facilities.

In the 1990s, Bank and IDA lending for population, health, and nutrition has increased substantially, and in fiscal years 1990–94 rose to an annual average of $1,307 million. Projects approved in fiscal 1995 included support for basic health care services, training of health care workers, institutional development and reform, and efforts to prevent the transmission of the HIV virus and mitigate the AIDS epidemic (q.v.). The World Bank's growing involvement in the health sector has led several developing countries to adopt generally supported policies on family planning and nutrition. Bank activities also include health care financing, hospitals, pharmaceutical management, urban health services, and services for the poorest and least-served groups in rural areas. Health issues are assuming an increasingly important place in the Bank's assistance strategy in Africa. A recent Bank study, *Better Health in Africa* (1994), found that most African countries lag behind other developing countries in this sector, and proposed measures for health improvement by African governments and their external partners.

Housing and the World Bank. In the early 1970s emphasis in Bank assistance for housing shifted from support for total public housing provision to sites-and-services and slum upgrading projects. Policies changed because most urban residents in developing countries were unable to afford housing provided by the private sector, but the mass production of sufficient housing to meet their needs required massive subsidies that many governments were unable or unwilling to provide.

The Bank has found that provision of land tenure security and basic infrastructure services were sufficient incentives to poor households to invest their savings, labor, and management skills in housing. Through self-help and self-management of the building process, they could then acquire an affordable foothold in the housing sector without the need for subsidies. To ensure the successful implementation of such projects, it was necessary to introduce more affordable building standards and to provide core housing units instead of finished units. Although some of these projects have been relatively large, they were conceived as experimental demonstration projects intended to achieve three objectives: affordable but adequate housing for low-income families, cost recovery from beneficiaries, and the replicability of such projects by the private sector.

From 1972 to 1990, the Bank was involved in 116 sites-and-services and slum upgrading projects in fifty-five countries. Project costs averaged $26 million ($42 million if the cost of land was included). Such projects amounted to 30 percent of all urban projects, and represented 1.8 percent of total Bank lending during this period. The first objective, the provision of low-cost housing, was usually achieved, but the other two objectives, cost recovery from the beneficiaries and replicability, were not. The Bank found that there were substantial interest-rate subsidies in a number of the projects, while such features as the waiving of zoning and building regulations, access to government land at below-market prices, and availability of expertise could not always be replicated. It was possible to replicate some slum upgrading projects, such as the program carried out in Indonesian cities, although loans for such projects are smaller and more difficult to administer than housing finance loans. However, they will continue to be important in future Bank lending to this sector.

In the early 1980s Bank loans for housing gradually moved from sites-and-services to loans for housing finance institutions. This type of lending has been relatively successful. At the same time, the International Finance Corporation has helped to establish housing finance institutions in

Bolivia, Botswana, Colombia, Indonesia, Lebanon, and Senegal, as well as the Housing Development Corporation in India. From 1986 to 1991 Bank lending for housing and related residential infrastructure ranged from 3.5 to 7 percent of Bank lending, an average of more than $900 million annually. Recent loans in the housing sector, including a housing policy development loan to the Republic of Korea and an approved housing sector loan to Mexico, represent a new development in Bank policy which addresses broader sectoral issues and focuses on the performance of the sector as a whole. Emerging priorities for Bank lending in this sector include enhancement of housing finance, provision of infrastructure for residential development, efforts to increase the efficiency of the building industry, and support for regulatory and institutional reforms in the housing sector.

Human Resources Development and Operations Policy (HRO). The Bank's HRO vice presidency was established in 1993 to address all issues involving human resources development, poverty reduction, and operations policy. There are two sector departments within HRO, Education and Health, and Poverty and Social Policy. Each department has a team-based management structure. Work programs are organized by eight subject areas, the first four dealing with education and training, health, population and reproductive health, and nutrition. The remainder are concerned with a number of interrelated issues, including poverty and social safety nets, social security and labor supply, gender analysis and policy, and childhood development. A third department in HRO, the Operations Policy Department, oversees the operational complex as a whole. It is also responsible for portfolio management, operational directives, procurement, technical assistance, the Bank's relations with non-governmental organizations, activities relating to the Development Committee (qq.v.), Bank/United Nations relations, public sector management and governance (q.v.), and computer information services.

I

IDA. *See* International Development Association (IDA).

IDA Deputies. These are representatives of countries that donate funds to the International Development Association (q.v.). Each donor country appoints a deputy, who is usually a high-level official from the country's ministry of finance, ministry of foreign affairs, or its bilateral aid agency. Meetings of the IDA Deputies are held as necessary, usually every three years, to discuss the replenishment of IDA's funds and other issues. When the replenishment agreement has been negotiated, it is presented to IDA's Board of Governors for approval.

IFC. *See* International Finance Corporation (IFC).

IMF. *See* International Monetary Fund (IMF).

India and the World Bank. India became a member of the Bank in 1945. Over the years, it has received more assistance from the World Bank than any other country. In 1949, India obtained its first loans from the Bank, for railways, land reclamation, and a large project that included power generation, storage dams, and an extensive irrigation scheme. During the sucessful implementation of India's first five-year plan, 1951–56, the Bank made further loans for railways, irrigation, and electric power. Up to the middle of 1956 Bank lending to India grew rather slowly, averaging only about $20 million annually. India's second five-year plan, 1956–61, included a program of planned development for the country's heavy industries, which the Bank supported. Almost from the beginning, there was a foreign exchange crisis, and in 1958, at the government's request, the Bank organized an international meeting to discuss India's problems, attended by representatives from Canada, Germany, Japan, the United Kingdom, and the United States. Since then, this Aid to India Group, later known as the India Consortium (in 1995 it became the Indian Development Forum) has met regularly, chaired by the Bank. After the establishment of the Consortium, and the creation of the International Development Association (q.v.), the Bank's assistance to India increased, and a Bank resident mission was established in Delhi.

In 1960, Bank president Eugene Black proposed a mission, subsequently known as "the mission of the three wise men," to study India's economic situation. It consisted of Hermann Abs from Germany, Sir Alan Franks from the United Kingdom, and Allan Sproul from the United States. The mission reported favorably on India's situation, as did a 1961 Bank mission led by Michael L. Hoffman. Members of the Consortium pledged more than $1 billion annually in development assistance to India, with the Bank providing about 20 percent of this amount. In 1962 another Bank mission was critical of India's economic management, and its findings were endorsed by a 1965 mission, led by

Bernard Bell, which recommended a number of changes in the country's policies. The Indian government acted on these recommendations and devalued the rupee in June 1966. This move caused a political crisis, and it was suggested in India and elsewhere that the Bank and the IMF had put pressure on the government to devalue. Subsequently, India experienced debt-servicing difficulties. With the help of the Consortium, the Bank was able to organize the rescheduling of part of the country's debt.

From the late 1960s one of the Indian government's main objectives was to increase agricultural production, and in 1969 the Bank approved loans for projects to produce high-yielding food grain seeds. Other Bank loans and IDA credits went to new irrigation projects and the rehabilitation of existing facilities, to agricultural research and extension, and to rural development.

India's railway system is one of the largest in the world. Before 1962 the Bank lent more than $400 million for maintenance and repairs, and for the expansion of passenger and freight services. Since then, the International Development Association (q.v.) has also provided credits for the railways. In addition, the Bank and IDA assisted in the development of India's urban transport systems, and in expanding its port facilities. They also provided financing for increases in power resources and regional transmission networks. In the 1970s the Bank made a number of loans to improve India's telephone, telex, and telegraph services. The 1973 oil crisis put a strain on India's foreign exchange reserves, culminating in the crisis of 1975. The government was forced to request assistance from the IMF and the Bank. A growth strategy was agreed on that included measures to control the money supply, freeze wages, and provide incentives for private investment.

An examination of Bank and IDA projects completed in India between 1969 and 1985 concluded that overall performance was good. Visits by Bank staff from the Bank's permanent mission in Delhi, who knew India and worked on major projects with Indian experts, undoubtedly contributed to successful project implementation. The Bank's own evaluations of these projects show that time overruns occurred and that errors made during the preappraisal of projects may have caused additional costs and contributed to target failures. Some Bank-supported projects included successful pilot projects that usually involved agricultural credit and the upgrading of urban services and housing.

During much of the 1980s the Indian economy resumed growth, and the eradication of poverty, with help from Bank and IDA loans and credits, remained one of the government's main objectives. By the end of the decade, however, India's situation had begun to deteriorate. Events in the Middle East in 1991 precipitated an economic crisis, with India's foreign exchange reserves falling to such low levels that the country's credit rating was downgraded, necessitating urgent reform and stabilization measures. In fiscal year 1992 Bank Group loans and credits were approved to support the initial phase of India's program of macroeconomic stabilization and structural reform. Assistance was also provided for agriculture, education, electric power (with cofinancing by IFC), forestry, health services, housing, industry, irrigation, long-haul transport, maternal and child welfare, pollution control, public welfare, rehabilitation after the earthquake of September 1993, and water supply. In fiscal year 1995 the Bank made its largest ever loan to India, amounting to $700 million, in support of a financial sector development project to modernize the country's banking system.

Although the Bank's aid flows to India have been relatively small, measured by its population and as a share of its national income, they have made positive contributions to India's economy and society, accounting for about 8 percent of the country's total investment. Bank aid has increased agricultural production and has raised the level and stability of basic food supplies, so that bad harvests caused by adverse weather conditions have had less effect on India's economy. In recent years, some Bank-supported irrigation projects have contained measures to assist the poor, and a number of human resource projects, covering slum upgrading in urban areas, primary health care, family planning, and nutritional assistance, have been successfully implemented. India has many government controls superimposed on the working of market forces, but in recent years Bank assistance has supported greater liberalization, and the government is now introducing measures to relax controls and provide more support to India's private sector.

Information and Publications. Under Article 5 of its Articles of Agreement, the Bank is obliged to publish an annual report containing an audited statement of its accounts, and to circulate to its members "at intervals of three months or less" a summary statement of its financial position. It may also publish "such other reports as it deems desirable to carry out its purposes."

In the course of its operations, the Bank has access to much important economic and social data concerning its member countries. While the Bank makes every effort to keep constraints on information to a minimum, its effective functioning requires that some documents and material be kept confidential. These include the proceedings of the Executive Board, documents defining the Bank's country strategy, analyses of country creditworthiness, project supervision and completion reports, and information related to the Bank's activities in the financial markets. The Bank has no limit on the period of confidentiality, and Article 7 of its Articles states that "the archives of the Bank shall remain inviolable."

In 1993 the Bank undertook a major review of its disclosure policy, with the aim of increasing the amount of information available to the public. Under the revised policy approved by the executive directors, a number of Bank documents, previously treated as confidential, are now available to the public. In January 1994, a Public Information Center (q.v.) was opened at the Bank's headquarters in Washington, D.C., to supply information about these documents, and similar services are available through Bank offices in London, Paris, and Tokyo, and other Bank field offices.

Limited only by its own restraints concerning confidentiality, the Bank has published extensively on its work and on its research in order to broaden understanding of the development process, to provide policy advice to member countries, and to support education and indigenous research in those countries. Bank publications are listed in its annual *Index of Publications & Guide to Information Products and Services,* issued in printed form and on diskette. They are also included in the data file of the National Technical Information Service (NTIS) and are available in CD-ROM through DIALOG, OCLC, and SilverPlatter. Information about the Bank's publications is also included in a new Bank information service accessible through Internet.

Information Center (World Bank). *See* Public Information Center (World Bank).

Inspection Panel (World Bank). *See* World Bank Inspection Panel.

Institutional Development Fund (IDF). In June 1992, the Bank's executive directors approved the establishment of the IDF, and provided an initial fund of $25 million for its first year of operation. The IDF began operations in July 1992, providing grants of up to $500,000 per activity to cover the costs of institutional development and capacity-building. All Bank borrowers are eligible to apply for grants, and during the IDF's first year of operation fifty-seven grants were made to forty-six countries, for a total of $16.3 million. In 1994 ninety grants, amounting to $22.8 million, were made to fifty-four countries.

Inter-American Development Bank (IDB). The IDB's establishment was negotiated within the framework of the Organization of American States (OAS), and it began operations in December 1959. Its structure and charter are similar to those of the IBRD.

During the 1960s there was an implicit division of labor between the World Bank and the IDB, with the Bank making loans in Latin America mainly for power and transport, while the IDB's lending was directed toward agriculture, education, housing, industry, and water supply. Some joint financing arrangements between the two institutions were also negotiated. By the end of the decade, problems began to arise concerning this division of labor. The IDB, with increased resources, was making loans for power and transportation, while the Bank was increasing its lending in the social areas.

In June 1970 the Bank entered into an arrangement with the IDB and the Inter-American Committee on the Alliance for Progress (CIAP), to coordinate their procedures for country analysis. CIAP was to act as a policy review body for Latin American development programs that could rely on country economic reports by the World Bank. This annual review of operations in the common member countries was thorough and satisfactory to both banks.

Over the years the IDB has become the largest multilateral cofinancier of Bank-assisted projects. In fiscal year 1992, fourteen cofinancing operations were arranged with the IDB for a total of $2 billion, and during that year IDB provided 38 percent of all cofinancing funds from multilateral institutions. This growth in IDB's cofinancing with the the Bank is due to the recent introduction of sector lending into its lending program.

In the 1990s collaboration between the IDB and the World Bank continues, and staff from both institutions participate in a number of preparation, preappraisal, appraisal, and economic sector review missions. Senior staff from the IDB and the Bank's Latin America and the Caribbean region take part in monthly meetings on major issues concerning both institutions.

Interim Committee. The Interim Committee of the Board of Governors on the International Monetary System, generally known as the Interim Committee, was established by the International Monetary Fund in 1974. This Committee, together with the Development Committee, succeeded the IMF's Committee of Twenty (qq.v.). The Interim Committee is composed of governors of the Fund, ministers, or other high officials, and it advises the Board of Governors on management of the international monetary system, as well as on other matters. It is called an Interim Committee, because it was originally intended to replace this committee by a council, with similar members and functions, but possibly more power as an organ of the Fund. Because a special vote under the Fund's Articles of Agreement would be needed to create such a council, it seems unlikely at present that it will be established.

Internal Auditing Department (IAD). The Bank's Internal Auditing Department (IAD) performs an independent appraisal function that examines and evaluates Bank operations and activities. Its work program covers a variety of financial, accounting, administrative, and personnel activities. It also includes the lending and supervisory aspects of IBRD loans and IDA credits under disbursement. Some of these activities are reviewed annually, and others biennially or less frequently. In performing their assignments, IAD's director and staff have unrestricted access to all Bank records, documents, and personnel relevant to the activity under review. When required, the department coordinates its work with the Bank's external auditors, and makes its reports available to them. IAD reports to the senior vice president Finance, but its director also has direct access to the Bank's president and to the executive directors' Joint Audit Committee (q.v.). The JAC reviews IAD's work program, and receives reports on its activities.

International Centre for Settlement of Investment Disputes (ICSID). The Centre was established in October 1966, when the Convention on the Settlement of Investment Disputes between States and Nationals of Other States (q.v.) came into effect after ratification by twenty of the contracting states that had signed the Convention. According to Article 1 of the Convention, ICSID's purpose is to act as an impartial international tribunal to encourage foreign private investment by resolving disputes through conciliation and/or arbitration between a contracting state and a foreign investor.

Membership in ICSID is open to all member countries of the Bank. Its governing body is the administrative council that meets once a year, and consists of one representative from each contracting state. All members of the council have equal voting rights. The president of the Bank is the council's nonvoting chairman. The Centre is administered by its secretary-general, who is also head of its secretariat, which is located in the Bank's headquarters in Washington, D.C. ICSID's overhead expenses are borne by the Bank, but the expenses incurred during arbitration or conciliation proceedings are the responsibility of the parties involved.

The Centre's activities include the administration of its arbitration and conciliation functions, and arbitration, conciliation, and fact-finding proceedings under its Additional Facility. It also undertakes research and publication activities in connection with international investment law, with emphasis on ICSID arbitration. The Centre's publications include *ICSID Review: Foreign Investment Law Journal* (semiannual), and collections of *Investment Laws of the World* and *Investment Treaties.*

As of June 30, 1995, 119 countries had become members of ICSID, and 15 countries had signed but not ratified the Convention. During fiscal year 1995, two new requests for arbitration were received, and five cases were pending.

International Development Association (IDA). Because the Bank's Articles impose strict limitations on its lending, many of the poorer developing countries are not sufficiently creditworthy to borrow from the Bank and in any case cannot afford the rates of interest charged for Bank loans. In the 1950s these countries, in desperate need of help, put forward proposals in the United Nations for the establishment of a new UN institution to provide grants and low-interest loans. Although the IBRD's Articles could have been amended to make its lending more flexible, it was feared that such a step would make the Bank's bonds less attractive to investors and that it would be more difficult for the Bank to borrow. The richer countries opposed the establishment of a new UN agency, and proposed that any new institution should be established in collaboration with the World Bank. In October 1959 the Bank's Board of Governors requested the executive directors to prepare Articles of Agreement for an International Development Association. By the end of January 1960 IDA's Articles had been formulated, and were distributed to member governments. In September 1960 a sufficient number had approved the Articles and applied for membership in IDA, and the Association was formally established.

IDA's purposes, according to its Articles of Agreement, are "to promote economic development, increase productivity and thus raise standards of living in the less-developed areas of the world included within the Association's membership, in particular by providing finance to meet their important developmental requirements on terms which are more flexible ... than those of conventional loans." Countries eligible for assistance from IDA are those with an annual per capita gross national product (GNP) of $840 or less, but most of IDA's loans, called credits, go to countries with an annual per capita GNP of $675 or less. IDA credits have a period of thirty-five to forty years, with a grace period of ten years. Although no interest is charged, there is a small service fee to cover IDA's administrative costs. Apart from their different terms for repayment, IBRD loans and IDA credits have to satisfy similar criteria before they can be approved.

In theory, the Bank and IDA are separate institutions, but they share the same headquarters in Washington, D.C., and the Bank's president, governors, executive directors and staff all serve concurrently in IDA. Membership in the Association is open only to Bank members, but unlike the Bank or the International Finance Corporation (q.v.), IDA's members are divided into two categories: Part 1 countries, the high-income members that provide most of IDA's funds through government appropriations; and Part 2 countries, comprising the middle- and low-income members. IDA cannot raise funds in the capital markets, and its financial resources consist of members' subscriptions, loan repayments, and "replenishments" by its wealthier members. Subscriptions to IDA are in proportion to members' subscriptions to the capital stock of the IBRD. Part 1 countries pay their entire subscriptions in convertible currencies, and all these funds are immediately available for lending by IDA; Part 2 countries pay only 10 per cent of their subscriptions in convertible form and the remainder in their own currencies, which cannot be used by IDA without the country's consent. IDA's voting system is similar to the Bank's, with votes in proportion to members' subscriptions.

Schedule A of IDA's Articles lists its initial subscribers, with 14 high-income member countries contributing $763.07 million (the United States being the largest contributor), and fifty-one Part 2 countries $236.93 million. In July 1995 Eritrea and the Azerbaijan Republic became members of IDA, increasing its membership to 158, and action was pending on membership for Bosnia-Herzegovina, Brunei Darussalam, Ukraine, and the Federal Republic of Yugoslavia (Serbia/Montenegro).

Every three years, negotiations begin on the next replenishment of IDA. These usually take at least twelve to sixteen months to complete, and involve several meetings of the IDA Deputies (the representatives of the donor countries). Sometimes the slow process of obtaining agree-ment from Congress on the U.S. contribution to IDA has caused problems. On occasion, when delays have made it difficult to continue IDA's work, some of the other members have agreed to pay part of their contributions in advance.

IDA's first replenishment, for $750 million, was approved in less than two years; negotiations for the second, for $1,200 million, took nearly four years. In December 1969 Bank president Robert S. McNamara opened discussions with IDA's Part 1 members, and by July 1970 agreement was reached on a third replenishment of $2,400 million for the period from July 1971 to June 1974. Subsequently, in September 1973, twenty-four contributing countries agreed to increase IDA's resources for the fourth replenishment to $4,500 million for the period from July 1974 to June 1977. After more than a year of discussion on the fifth replenishment, the representatives of twenty-six donor countries reached agreement on $7,500 million for the period from 1978 to 1980. The sixth replenishment, for fiscal years 1981–83, had not become effective by the end of fiscal year 1981, as the U.S. was still seeking Congressional approval for its share. The replenishment, for $12,000 million, eventually came into effect in August 1981, but legislative delays in the U.S. and reduced appropriations resulted in a substantial reduction of IDA's operational program for fiscal 1982–84, and in a delayed start for negotiations on the seventh replenishment.

At a meeting in Washington in January 1984 the U.S. representative reiterated his country's decision to contribute no more than $750 million to IDA, and to limit the the U.S. share in IDA to 25 percent. As a result, IDA's seventh replenishment for 1984–87 was limited to $9,000 million. During this period the Bank transferred approximately $2,500 million to IDA. Negotiations for the eighth replenishment began in January 1986. The donors agreed on a basic replenishment of $11,500 million for 1988–90, with supplementary contributions from some donor countries. In February 1989 negotiations began on IDA's ninth replenishment, and agreement was reached on $15,500 million for 1991–93. The tenth replenishment, for 1994–96, was approved for approximately $18,000 million. With these funds, as well as an additional $4,000 million from repayments of earlier IDA credits, it will be possible for the Association to lend up to $22,000 million during the next three years. Replenishment meetings on IDA's eleventh replenishment began in 1995. Some donors were experiencing budgetary pressures, so there was uncertainty about the amount that would be available for the next repenishment. Further discussions will take place in 1996 on the lending projections for the IDA-11 period (1997–99), the overall size of the replenishment, and the burden-sharing among the donors.

IDA, like the Bank, has a formal agreement with the United Nations, and links with the regional development banks and other international organizations. About seventy countries are eligible to borrow from IDA; currently, a minimum of 45 percent of IDA lending has been allocated to sub-Saharan Africa, the remainder going mainly to poor countries in Asia, including Bangladesh, China, India, Nepal, and Pakistan.

In the 1960s most of IDA's credits were for infrastructure projects; in the 1970s they went mainly to projects directly benefiting the poor. During the 1980s IDA became more involved in projects supporting economic policy changes and institutional reforms. About 25 percent of all IDA lending is now for adjustment, but most of its credits still go to specific projects. Adjustment programs supported by IDA are often in conjunction with IMF stabilization programs, and since 1986 the two organizations have prepared joint policy framework papers.

IDA provides credits for rural development programs and projects intended to increase agricultural productivity and to raise living standards for the rural poor. It has also financed projects for education, health, family planning, and nutrition. It is the world's largest source of multilateral concessional loans and since its establishment has committed more than $71,000 million for more than two thousand projects. The Special Program of Assistance (q.v.), administered by IDA, assists low-income sub-Saharan African countries with external debt problems to implement their economic reform programs. IDA's Debt Reduction Facility helps the poorer developing countries to ease the burden of commercial debt. In addition, the Association works with other multilateral organizations and donor countries to coordinate assistance.

Recently, IDA has increased its lending in the social sectors, and governments, with IDA's assistance, have developed social safety nets that protect the poor from the initial consequences of adjustment. First introduced in 1985, social funds and social action programs have been established in a number of developing countries in Africa, Asia, and Latin America. These programs, originally designed to ease unemployment, to create jobs, and to promote training, now also assist the poor through immunization and nutrition programs. Since 1987, when the Bank began to emphasize its Women in Development initiative, more than half of all IDA operations have included components to help women, with support for education up to the secondary level, health and family planning activities, and measures to improve women's wage-earning capacity.

International Finance Corporation (IFC). Although the concept of an international finance corporation dates back to the late 1940s, IFC was not formally established until 1956, owing to lack of support from governments and the financial community. Both sides had doubts about an institution that would invest public funds in the private sector. Eugene R. Black, both as the U.S. executive director, and subsequently president of the Bank, expressed his interest in "a new international development corporation" to be established as a subsidiary of the Bank. Robert L. Garner, then vice president of the Bank and subsequently president of IFC, strongly supported its creation. President Truman's Advisory Board on International Development, chaired by Nelson Rockefeller, also recommended the establishment of the new corporation. Finally, an understanding was reached between the Bank and the United States government. It was agreed that the International Finance Corporation would be capitalized with $100 million, rather than the $400 million originally proposed, and that it would not be involved in equity financing. The Bank's executive directors then began work on Articles of Agreement for the proposed corporation, and IFC officially came into existence in July 1956, with Robert L. Garner (q.v.) as its president. After Garner's retirement in 1961, the president of the Bank subsequently served as the president of IFC, and IFC's executive vice president is responsible for the Corporation's overall management and day-to-day operations. Although IFC has a separate legal existence, its Board of Governors consists of the Bank's governors and their alternates who represent countries that are also members of IFC, and its Board of Directors is also composed of Bank executive directors that represent IFC member countries. The Corporation draws on the Bank for administrative and other services, but it has its own legal and operational staff, 1224 in number at the end of June 1995, including consultants, temporary staff, and staff in IFC's overseas missions, who are usually nationals of the host country. Owing to the Corporation's rapid expansion in the past ten years, it has outgrown the space it now leases from the IBRD. A decision was made in 1992 to purchase a site for a new building. Construction began in 1995, and IFC is expected to move into its new offices by 1997.

IFC's Articles state "The purpose of the Corporation is to further economic development by encouraging the growth of productive private enterprise in member countries, particularly in the less developed areas, thus supplementing the activities of the International Bank for Reconstruction and Development." In order to achieve this, IFC makes investments "without guarantee of repayment by the member government involved," seeks "to bring together investment opportunities, domestic and foreign capital, and experienced management," and helps "to create conditions conducive to the flow of private capital, domestic and foreign, into productive investment in member countries."

During its early days, the new Corporation encountered some difficulties, mainly caused by its Articles, which limited its investments to productive private enterprises in the territories of its members, and stated that its financing should not take the form of investments in capital stock. In 1961 IFC's Articles were amended to remove the ban on investments in capital stock, and its lending commitments began to increase. The transfer to IFC in 1962 of responsibility for development finance companies (DFCs) caused the Corporation to devote more attention to their organization and financing, but its major investments still supported manufacturing industries, mining, and public utilities. Through financing for Kenya Hotel Properties in 1966, IFC made its first investment in hotels and tourism. Before 1966 the Corporation's investments averaged less than $30 million annually, but this rate more or less doubled in the period 1966–68, and doubled again after Robert McNamara became president of the Bank.

IFC's organization in 1995 included six vice presidents: Operations (three); Personnel, Administration, and Business Development; General Counsel; and Finance and Planning. They form a management group that assists the executive vice president in decision-making and planning for the future. IFC's operational activities are organized in five regional investment departments, four specialist departments, a central capital markets department, and a corporate management services department. The three vice presidents for operations oversee IFC's regional and specialist departments. The regional departments cover sub-Saharan Africa; Asia; Central Asia, the Middle East, and North Africa; Europe; and Latin America and the Caribbean. They are responsible for strategies, business promotion, and investment programs, relations with the governments in these areas, and coordination with the IBRD. The four specialist departments (agribusiness; chemicals, petrochemicals, and fertilizers; infrastructure; and oil, gas, and mining) handle projects, maintain contacts with companies, and implement investment projects in all regions. The Central Capital Markets Department works with the regional departments on the design of capital market development and is responsible for a number of the Corporation's capital markets operations in developing countries. The Department also advises member governments, monitors emerging stock markets, maintains the *Emerging Markets Data Base,* and handles capital markets projects that are global or cross-regional in scope. IFC's Corporate Finance Services Department provides fee-based advisory services. It also advises state enterprises and governments on privatization and assists private companies in planning corporate and financial restructuring.

The International Finance Corporation has been described as a combination of a multilateral development bank and a private merchant bank. It is the largest source of direct financing for private sector projects in the developing countries, but it does not usually finance more than 25 percent of total project costs, is never the largest shareholder, and does not participate in company management. The Corporation's financing is in line with market rates, allowing for the cost of funds and profitable returns. Its minimum investment is usually $1 million. IFC makes direct investments, either in the form of loans or equity capital or a combination of both, undertakes standby and underwriting operations, and assists in the creation and support of local capital markets. Its advisory services include the Foreign Investment Advisory Service (q.v.), operated jointly with the Bank, which advises governments on methods of attracting foreign direct investment; and the Technical Advisory Service, which assists governments and business concerning projects. The Corporation also operates special facilities to assist small enterprises in sub-Saharan Africa, the Caribbean and Central America, and the South Pacific.

During the 1990s IFC has been playing an important part in the privatization efforts of the Russian Federation and other states of the former Soviet Union. In Central and Eastern Europe, the Corporation's activities include support for private sector projects, and advice to governments on the sale of state-owned enterprises. IFC has supported the private sector in Africa by promoting joint ventures with African entrepreneurs and by giving assistance to small- and medium-sized enterprises through its Africa Enterprise Fund and the Africa Project Development Facility, co-sponsored with the African Development Bank and the United Nations Development Programme (qq.v.).

In fiscal year 1994 IFC approved a total of $2,500 million in financing for more than two hundred projects in some sixty-five countries. Ninety-eight of these projects were in countries with per capita incomes of $830 or less. The Corporation continued its efforts to mobilize capital for private sector projects in developing countries; for each dollar in financing approved by IFC for its own account, other investors and lenders provided $5.43, some in the form of cofinancing. IFC's Board approved its participation in eight offerings of securities in 1994, with an aggregate value of $715 million.

Fiscal year 1995 was a record year for IFC, reflecting the strong demand for its financing and services in many member countries. Areas of particular activity included infrastructure (power, telecommunications, and transport), capital market development, and privatization. During the year, the Corporation's net worth rose to $3.6 billion. By the end of June 1995, one hundred and sixty-five countries were members of IFC.

International Monetary Fund (IMF). Together with the International Bank for Reconstruction and Development (IBRD), the International Monetary Fund was established at the United Nations Monetary and Financial Conference, held at Bretton Woods, New Hampshire, July 1–22, 1944. Officially, the Fund came into existence in December 1945, when its Articles of Agreement, or charter, had been signed by twenty-nine of the countries participating in the conference.

A number of factors contributed to the success of the conference and the establishment of the IMF. Many countries had suffered from the chaotic state of the international monetary system before the Second World War, and they were anxious to establish a more stable system for the postwar world. Although the conference lasted only three weeks, it had been preceded by years of discussion and planning. The main plans for postwar monetary stabilization were the work of two remarkable men: Harry Dexter White, special adviser to the Secretary of the United States Treasury, and John Maynard Keynes, afterward Lord Keynes, a distinguished British economist. At the Bretton Woods Conference (q.v.) White was chairman of Commission I, which dealt with the establishment of the Fund, and most of his proposals for the new institution were eventually adopted.

During its first decade, the IMF focused on the abolition of currency restrictions and the introduction of currency convertibility. It was then generally considered that lending would not be an important part of its functions, and that IMF resources would be used mainly on a short-term basis. Decisions by the Fund's Executive Board in 1952 had important effects on the institution's future development. The Fund was required, under its Articles of Agreement, to hold annual consultations with member countries maintaining exchange restrictions. These consultations were subsequently extended to cover balance of payments positions as well as exchange arrangements, so that eventually the Fund was able to exercise effective surveillance over members' policies. The principle of

Fund conditionality was also introduced when it was decided that a country could automatically use IMF resources to the extent of its reserve tranche, while use of its credit tranches would be conditional on the introduction of policies to correct balance of payments disequilibrium.

By the Fund's second decade, signs of strain were beginning to appear in the par value system established at Bretton Woods. There was concern about international liquidity, and the system lacked a satisfactory mechanism to control reserve assets. In 1962 the Fund arranged to increase its resources through the General Arrangements to Borrow (GAB), and in the following year the Compensatory Financing Facility (CFF) was established. A number of industrial countries, including Great Britain, had balance of payments problems after 1965, and many developing countries experienced severe deficits. In 1969 the first amendment to the IMF's Articles of Agreement came into effect, and a new facility based on the special drawing right (q.v.) was established. In August 1971 the United States suspended the convertibility of the dollar into gold. A new system of exchange rates was established by the Smithsonian Agreement of December 1971, and this remained in effect until February 1973, when the United States announced a 10 percent devaluation of the dollar. During these difficult years the Fund continued its efforts to exercise some control over international monetary relations, and at the same time work on monetary reform was continuing through the Committee of the Board of Governors on Reform of the International Monetary System, more generally known as the Committee of Twenty.

High inflation rates and rising oil prices in the 1970s caused widespread payments imbalances in many countries. The IMF introduced more facilities to assist its members, including two oil facilities in 1974 and 1975 and the Extended Fund Facility (EFF) in 1974, to support medium-term adjustment programs. The situation of the developing countries was especially difficult, and in 1976 the Fund established a Trust Fund, supported by the sale of some of its gold holdings, to provide loans on concessional terms to the poorer developing countries. Also in 1976, agreement was reached on reform of the international monetary system, which came into effect in April 1978, when a sufficient number of members had approved a second amendment to the IMF's Articles of Agreement. In the new system members could make their own exchange arrangements, but their policies were subject to Fund surveillance, gold was largely eliminated from the IMF's operations, and the institution was required to reduce its gold holdings by one third. In 1979, the Fund's Extended Facility was complemented by the Supplementary Financing

Facility (SFF), which provided additional access to IMF financing. Two years later, the new facility's resources were exhausted, and it was replaced by the enlarged access policy, offering similar access to the IMF's resources.

During the Bank/Fund annual meetings in 1982, Mexico announced that it could no longer service its debts, and this move initiated a debt crisis that persisted throughout the 1980s. Responding to Mexico's announcement the Fund, in cooperation with the Mexican government, prepared an adjustment program to be supported by SDR 3.6 billion of its own resources. However, the Fund's Managing Director insisted that Mexico's other creditors should agree on rescheduling existing loans, on adjusting interest rates, and on making new loans before the Fund actually committed its resources. Eventually, financing of $5 billion was arranged with more than five hundred commercial banks. The IMF adopted similar policies in its rescue operations for other countries. In March 1986 the Fund established the Structural Adjustment Facility to assist low-income countries with balance of payments problems. Conditionality under the new facility was tightened, with annual programs to be proposed in a three-year policy framework paper, that would be prepared by the borrower in collaboration with Bank and Fund staff.

To supplement the financing available under the Structural Adjustment Facility, the IMF established the Enhanced Structural Adjustment Facility in December 1987. It was funded partly by the Fund's special disbursement account and partly by contributions in the form of loans and grants from member countries, to be administered by a trust. Under the new facility monitoring was stricter and programs were subject to midyear reviews.

In the 1990s, after the collapse of the communist system, the countries in Central and Eastern Europe and the former Soviet Union applied for membership in the IMF and the World Bank. Both institutions provided financing and technical assistance to support these countries' transition to market economies. The Fund established a systemic transformation facility in April 1993 to provide balance of payments assistance to member countries during the period of transition, and Kyrgyzstan made the first drawing under the new facility in May 1993. Drawings from the Fund during financial year 1993/94 totaled SDR5.2 billion, the largest drawings being made by Russia, Argentina, South Africa, Poland, and India. More than forty developing countries were implementing Fund-supported adjustment programs in 1993/94, and its technical assistance to members continued to expand. By July 1994 the Fund had 179 members. *See also* World Bank-International Monetary Fund Relations.

Irrigation and the World Bank. Irrigation, the largest recipient of public agricultural investment in the developing world, accounted for about 7 percent of Bank lending between 1950 and 1993. During this period, the Bank lent approximately $31 billion for various forms of irrigation in 614 projects, which, with the contributions of borrowing governments, various cofinanciers, and farmers, made up a total investment of $52 billion.

The first Bank loan for irrigation was a component in a loan to Chile in 1948. In the 1950s, the Bank made only 6 loans for irrigation, and total annual lending averaged $37 million for projects that mostly involved dam construction and the main distribution canals in irrigation systems. There were forty-one Bank-supported irrigation projects in the 1960s, and they were expanded to include on-farm works, roads, agricultural credit and extension, marketing, processing, and research. This growth in world and Bank investment in irrigation occurred in response to food crises and high agricultural prices in the developing countries, with irrigation intended to promote increased grain production. Most Bank lending for irrigation (69 percent) went to Asia, with Bangladesh, India, and Pakistan the main recipients of Bank and IDA assistance. The remaining 31 percent supported projects in Africa, the Americas, and Europe. Most African projects were rather small, and Africa received only 12 percent of Bank lending for irrigation.

In the 1970s and 1980s the Bank made loans for more than five hundred irrigation projects, with average annual lending of between $1,120 and $1,273 million. New Bank policies were introduced in the early 1970s that supported integrated rural development, and from 1974 until the end of the 1980s only about half of the Bank's projects for irrigation had an irrigation content that was more than 50 percent of the total loan. In other cases, projects that were mostly for irrigation were sometimes called rural or area development projects. The benefits of such projects reached the poor, and the average irrigation project benefited more than seventy thousand farm families. Additional employment was also generated through increased farming intensity, so that millions in rural areas found work as a result of irrigation projects.

A typical Bank lending package for irrigation in the early 1990s is bigger, less geographically specific, more likely to be policy-based, and much more likely to cover the sector state-wide. The amount of Bank lending for irrigation in this period is slightly lower, averaging about $1,032 million annually. This reduction is probably due to increased food production, lower crop prices, and less concern about agricultural problems. Instead of developing new lands for irrigation, the Bank and its members are focusing on rehabilitating or modernizing existing systems. In India the National Water Management Project, initially limited to three states, has been developed from pilot projects that have demonstrated various ways of making a large project more productive. The Irrigation Operations Support Project in the Philippines is intended to improve the operating performance of the national irrigation systems and strengthen the institutional capacities of the National Irrigation Authority and private irrigation associations.

In order to improve the poor performance of some irrigation projects, the Bank is now emphasizing water resources management, closer coordination between agencies dealing with irrigation and agriculture, changes in water-use charges, and ways of increasing farmer participation. Various systems of irrigation have been financed, including spate irrigation in Yemen and Afghanistan, drip irrigation in Cyprus, and sprinkler irrigation systems in Romania, Morocco, and Tunisia. In some developing countries, remote centralized control technology has been successfully employed, and in others, such as the Persian Gulf states, where water is very scarce, drip irrigation systems and greenhouses have been used.

Technical advances in irrigation have solved some problems, but others remain. Of 256 irrigation projects supported by the Bank between 1974 and 1990, 128 projects included financing for research. Of these, 65 were for research on irrigation and drainage technologies (IDT). In 1991 the United Nations Development Programme (q.v.), and the International Commission on Irrigation and Drainage (ICID), established the International Program for Technology Research in Irrigation and Drainage (IPTRID), which promotes this type of research in developing countries, assists these countries in the identification of priority needs for research, and facilitates training and the exchange of information and experience. The Bank has contributed to this research effort through an inventory of its ongoing research in the irrigation and drainage subsector, and is actively engaged in the transfer of irrigation technology through seminars and training programs.

J

Japan and the World Bank. Japan became a member of the Bank in August 1952, soon after the Allied occupation ended. In October 1952, the Bank's first mission went to Japan, led by Robert L. Garner, the

Bank's vice president. The Bank decided to begin lending to Japan because it considered that this industrialized country would become an engine for growth among the less-developed Asian economies. In October 1953 the first loan agreement was signed to finance Japan's power sector. A good working relationship was established between the Bank and the government-owned Japan Development Bank (JDB), which handled more than two thirds of the $448 million that the Bank committed to Japan between October 1953 and June 1961.

In 1958, Japan requested a loan for the Nagoya-Kobe highway project. Although the Bank was prepared to finance part of the project, it suggested that some of the balance should be raised through an international bond issue. Eugene Black, then president of the Bank, personally encouraged the Japanese to reenter the New York market, and the issue, made in February 1959, was a success. From that time Japan's ability to borrow in the international capital markets determined the size of Bank commitments to individual Japanese projects.

Bank lending to Japan ended in 1966, when the IBRD made its last and largest loan to Japan for a $100 million highway project. This ended a thirteen-year lending program, during which the Bank had committed $862 million, mainly for infrastructure and heavy industry. In 1970 Japan made its first loan to the Bank, equivalent to $100 million, followed by other loans. Subsequently, through its Overseas Economic Cooperation Fund and the Export-Import Bank of Japan, Japan has provided the largest share of official cofinancing in support of the Bank's operations. In July 1990 a special fund for policy and human resource development (the PHRD fund) was established within the Bank, with financial support by Japan's Ministry of Finance. This fund, which supports the Bank's technical assistance and cofinancing activities, combines five previously existing funds administered by the Bank on behalf of Japan.

Joint Bank-Fund Library. Established to serve the staffs of the International Monetary Fund (q.v.) and the World Bank, the library is administered by the Fund, but its costs are shared by both institutions. The library's collections focus on economics, public policy, international and government finance, trade, development issues, and the world economic situation. It contains more than two hundred thousand volumes, including books, reports, and statistical publications; more than four thousand journals and newspapers; and research and working papers from a large number of institutions and organizations. The library has an on-line cataloging system, is a member of a national library network, and subscribes to a large number of commercial databases. The Joint Bank-Fund Library is not open to the public.

Joint Vienna Institute (JVI). Cosponsored by the World Bank, the International Monetary Fund (q.v.), the Bank for International Settlements (BIS), the European Bank for Reconstruction and Development (q.v.), and the Organisation for Economic Co-Operation and Development (OECD), the Institute, located in Vienna, Austria, began operations in October 1992. JVI conducts and hosts courses in market economics and financial analysis for officials from transitional economies. During its first year of operation, JVI arranged forty-four seminars, which were attended by more than a thousand officials and managers from Central and Eastern Europe and the republics of the former Soviet Union. In 1994 the Institute, which had been functioning under interim and informal arrangements, was established as an international organization with a board of directors composed of representatives of the sponsoring organizations. Four regional centers, in Kiev, Moscow, Prague, and Tashkent, were opened in 1995.

K

Keynes, John Maynard (1883–1946). John Maynard Keynes, later Lord Keynes, was a leading British economist, financier, and journalist, whose writings influenced economic thinking and policy throughout the Western world. His most important work, *The General Theory of Employment, Interest, and Money* (1935–36), rejected current theories on the causes of unemployment, presented an alternative explanation of its origins, and proposed remedies for unemployment and economic recession based on government supported policies of full employment.

During the Second World War Keynes worked for the British Treasury, and in the early 1940s he and Harry Dexter White (q.v.) of the U.S. Treasury prepared plans for new monetary and financial arrangements for the postwar world. After international negotiations, their plans were combined with plans put forward by other countries. These formed the basis of the discussions at the Bretton Woods Conference (q.v.) in July 1944, which led to the establishment of the International Bank for Reconstruction and Development and the International Monetary Fund (q.v.). During the Conference, Keynes chaired its Commission II, which was established to consider proposals for the Bank, and he took an active part in drafting the Bank's Articles of Agreement (q.v.).

L

Language of the Bank. The working language of the World Bank is English, and all Board discussions, publications, papers, reports, policy decisions, and documentation are conducted or issued in English. Over the years, some of the Bank's more important publications have been issued in French and Spanish also. Because of the expansion in the Bank's membership, its publications now appear in a number of other languages, including Arabic, Chinese, German, Japanese, Portuguese, and Russian.

Law (International) and the World Bank. The law of international organizations covers both their external and internal aspects, the former dealing with their relations with member- and non-member states, other international organizations, and private individuals, and the latter with their constitutional powers, their decisionmaking processes, and their administrative practices.

The agreements constituting the Bank and its affiliates have been described as "law-making treaties," which establish general rules for the future international conduct of nations, create new international institutions, and include declarations by member countries concerning their understanding of the law applying to certain sectors of international relations.

The charters of the Bank and its affiliated institutions involve lawmaking on a very broad basis. Article VII of the Bank's Articles establishes its position with regard to judicial process, and states that the Bank may be subject to suit in a competent court in a country in which it has an office, has appointed an agent to accept service or notice of process, or has issued or guaranteed securities. Suits may not be brought by member states, however, nor by persons acting for or deriving claims from member states. Article IX deals with the interpretation of the Articles of Agreement, and states that any questions about interpretation arising between a member of the Bank and the Bank itself, or between any members, should be decided by the Bank's executive directors, with the possibility of an appeal to the Board of Governors, the Board's decision being final.

The establishment of the World Bank Inspection Panel (q.v.) marks a new departure in the law of public international organizations. Previously, the review mechanisms of the decisions of international organizations were limited to staff appeals in personnel matters through an administrative tribunal, a staff appeals committee, or an ombudsman. The Bank established a staff appeals committee in 1977, an administrative tribunal in 1980, and the office of the staff ombudsman in 1981.

The principal legal instruments in the Bank's financing of projects are the loan agreement (IBRD) and the development credit agreement (IDA) with the borrower, and the project agreement with the agency executing the project. Drawn up by the Bank's Legal Department, these agreements contain the terms of the loan or credit, the repayment obligations, provisions for the use of the proceeds of the loan and for the procurement financed by it, and obligations with respect to the implementation of the project.

Although the Bank's Articles of Agreement place specific limits on the extent to which it can become involved with human rights of a civil or political nature, the Bank has played a significant part in supporting international laws relating to refugees, environmental protection, and involuntary resettlement. Bank loan or credit agreements contain specific covenants covering environment-related actions. The Bank has also taken part in a number of international negotiations involving environmental protection. In many member countries, it has been found that the national legal framework of resettlement operations is incomplete. Consequently, as part of a Bank-assisted project involving resettlement, new legislation must be introduced or existing laws modified.

In recent years, because of growing appreciation of the role of law in the development process, there has been increased emphasis on the borrowing country's legal and institutional framework. Problems frequently encountered in projects involving private sector development include the unenforceability of contracts or property rights, difficulties about land tenure, problems in restructuring or liquidating firms, difficulties with labor and tax laws, and insufficient or over regulation of investment and banking activities. Similar legal problems can arise in efforts to promote foreign direct investment. The Bank has responded to its members' requests for legal technical assistance, which may be provided through advice from Bank experts, in the form of free-standing loans, or as components in adjustment or investment loans.

Lending by the IBRD. The IBRD obtains most of its funds for lending through medium- and long-term borrowing in the capital markets of Europe, Japan, and the United States. It also borrows at market rates from central banks and other government institutions. Under the IBRD's

Articles of Agreement, the total amount of disbursed loans, participations in loans, and callable guarantees cannot exceed the total value of the Bank's subscribed capital, reserves, and surplus. This very conservative 1:1 ratio has restricted the Bank's ability to lend, but at the same time it has established its financial strength, has made Bank issues attractive to investors, has ensured the Bank's access to the financial markets, and has enabled it to make loans to its members at favorable rates.

All Bank loans are made to, or guaranteed by, its members, except loans to the International Finance Corporation. In fiscal year 1995 sixty-two member countries were eligible for IBRD funds only, and fourteen for a blend of IBRD and IDA funds. The Bank has never suffered a loss on any of its loans, although from time to time some of its borrowers have had difficulties in making their loan payments on time over long periods. Such loans are then placed by the Bank in nonaccrual status (q.v.). To guard against the risk incurred by such overdue payments, the IBRD maintains a provision for loan losses.

Originally, the IBRD lent only for projects offering high real rates of economic return to the borrowing country, but since 1980 it has also made adjustment loans to support programs of economic reform in its developing country members. Most IBRD loans have repayment obligations in various currencies based on a currency pooling system. In 1989 the pool was reconstituted, so that it is now approximately equivalent to 30 percent each of U.S. dollars, German marks, and Japanese yen; 10 percent is made up of other currencies. In fiscal year 1993 the IBRD introduced a $3 billion, two-year pilot project that offered eligible borrowers a choice of currencies as an alternative to the currency pool, and in 1995 the Bank's executive directors approved an expanded program that allows all Bank borrowers to choose the currency in which their loans are denominated. By the end of June 1995, $3 million in single currency loans had been approved, of which $1,507 million was under the expanded program.

The IBRD does not reschedule interest or repayments of principal on its loans, and it places in nonaccrual status (q.v.) any loan made to, or guaranteed by, a member if payments on the loan are overdue by more than six months. As soon as the overdue amounts are paid in full, the member's loans emerge from nonaccrual status, and its eligibility for new loans is restored. At the end of June 1995 Bosnia-Herzegovina, Iraq, Liberia, Sudan, the Syrian Arab Republic, and Zaïre were in nonaccrual status.

During fiscal years 1993–95 IBRD lending commitments amounted to $16,944.5 million (1993); $14,243.9 million (1994); and $16,852.6 million (1995). In fiscal 1995 the main recipients of IBRD loans were Mexico ($2,387 for six projects); China ($2,370 million for thirteen projects, including five "blend" projects); and Russia ($1,741 million for nine projects). Adjustment lending in fiscal 1995, which included $1,395 million in rehabilitation-import loans and $375 million in debt reduction loans, amounted to 24 percent of the Bank's lending commitments.

In recent years there has been only a slight increase in Bank loan commitments. Possible reasons for this may include lack of creditworthiness in some would-be borrowers; easier access to other forms of financing by some former Bank borrowers; stricter budgetary discipline in certain countries that reduces the amount of debt that governments are willing to assume; reductions in government subsidies, resulting in less demand for state-owned infrastructure projects; unwillingness by some countries to accept the Bank's conditionality and lending requirements for structural adjustment; and insufficient flexibility in Bank lending terms for members with access to other financing. Because borrowers have responded favorably to the Bank's introduction of single currency loans, it is possible that in future the Bank will introduce more flexible forms of lending that provide choices of rates and maturity as well as currency choices.

Libraries. The Bank has a number of libraries for staff use, including its Law Library, Sectoral Library, and smaller specialized collections. Together with the Fund, it maintains the Joint Bank-Fund Library (q.v.) to serve both institutions.

Living Standards Measurement Study (LSMS). In 1980 the Bank established this study to examine ways of improving the quality of household data collected by statistical offices in developing countries. Its objectives include the development of new methods to measure progress in raising living standards, the identification of the effects of government policies on households, and the improvement of communication among statisticians, analysts, and policy-makers. Publications by the LSMS include working papers that cover surveys of the LSMS data collection, reports on improved methodologies for employing this data, designs for surveys, questionnaires, data processing methods, and policy analyses.

Low-Income Countries. These are countries with a per capita gross national product (GNP) of $675 or less in 1992 U.S. dollar terms. *See also* Middle-Income Countries.

M

McCloy, John J. (1896–1989). The Bank's second president, John J. McCloy, was a lawyer who held office as Assistant Secretary of War during the Second World War. He had close ties with a number of New York banking firms and was well known and respected on Wall Street. Aware that Eugene Meyer, the Bank's first president, had experienced problems with the executive directors, McCloy did not accept President Truman's invitation to become president of the Bank until he had obtained assurances that he would have adequate authority. He assumed office as president in March 1947. Two months later the Bank made its first loan, for $250 million, to France's Crédit National. In June 1947 the Bank's first official mission, to Poland, was announced. Shortly afterwards, loans for reconstruction were made to the Netherlands, Denmark, and Luxembourg.

In McCloy's view, the major task of his presidency was to persuade American investors that Bank securities were good investments. Many difficulties had to be overcome, however, before the Bank could market its own bonds. McCloy, together with Robert Garner, the Bank's vice president, and Eugene Black, then U.S. executive director and subsequently the Bank's third president, made great efforts to secure support for the first issue of Bank bonds in the United States. They succeeded, and the issue, in July 1947, was successful and heavily oversubscribed. In May 1949 John J. McCloy resigned from the Bank to become U.S. High Commissioner in Germany.

McNamara, Robert Strange (1916–   ). Following three years as an assistant professor of business administration at Harvard University and a period of service during the Second World War, Robert S. McNamara joined the Ford Motor Company, becoming its president in 1961. He then served as Secretary of the U.S. Department of Defense until he took office as the fifth president of the Bank in 1968.

During his first days in the Bank, McNamara was surprised to find that there had been no recent loans to such countries as Egypt and Indonesia, nor to the majority of the poorest African countries. He called a meeting of senior Bank officers and asked why so many needy countries were not receiving assistance. McNamara then requested those present to make lists of all the projects and programs that they would like the Bank to undertake if there were no financing constraints. It was clear that acceptance of all these proposals would result in a doubling of the Bank's average rate of spending during the previous five years necessary, and McNamara proposed this scale of expansion at the Bank's annual meeting in September 1968. He had already begun to increase Bank borrowing and was able to announce that in the previous ninety days the Bank had borrowed more than in the whole of any previous year in its history. In anticipation of the increased workload, McNamara also began to expand the Bank staff. In 1968 the Bank's professional staff was about 760, and by 1982 it had grown to 2,689, out of a total staff of 5,278. As part of this expansion, McNamara intended to produce a staff that was fully representative of the Bank's membership, and during his years in office this policy was continued.

In his inaugural speech as Bank president, McNamara proposed not only a doubling of the Bank's lending but also a shift from the Bank's traditional financing of infrastructure projects to projects and programs designed to remove the main constraints on development, which McNamara considered to be increased population growth, malnutrition, and illiteracy. While visiting Indonesia in 1968, he decided to establish a Bank field office in Djakarta to advise on the restoration of the country's economy after the Soekarno regime. McNamara felt, however, that for the Bank to give advice to its members on development, it was necessary to improve staff knowledge and efficiency in this area. Consequently, the Bank's existing Economics Department was expanded, and it grew into the Development Policy Staff, led by Hollis Chenery, which worked with the Bank's country and technical staff to advise member countries.

From the beginning of his presidency, McNamara undertook intensive personal visits, especially to the developing countries. These visits took him to more than fifty countries. In Africa, where Bank assistance was most needed and where he made many of his visits, McNamara established friendly relations with a number of national leaders. In the course of these visits he also spent time in rural areas, and came to feel that poverty could only be reduced by direct action at the level of the small farmer.

In late 1971 the governors of the Bank began to consider the possibility of a second five-year term for McNamara. His achievements were recognized, but at the same time there was criticism of his poverty-oriented policy and of the increased size of the Bank. Among the industrial countries McNamara's policies were supported by the Scandinavians and the Dutch, but others saw him as a remote, primarily American figure.

Eventually, a consensus emerged that McNamara should be reappointed, but at first this consensus did not include the United States. McNamara's Vietnam years had left him with enemies in Congress, and there was opposition to his requests for increased foreign aid. American support for McNamara's second term has been described as "belated and grudging," but agreement was finally reached, and his reappointment was officially confirmed in 1972.

McNamara's second term began in April 1973. During the annual Bank/Fund meeting in Nairobi in September, the first to be held in Africa, he stressed the need for projects and programs that targeted those living in "absolute poverty." Agreement was reached on a replenishment of IDA's funds at a higher level than before, and this was regarded as an expression of confidence in McNamara and the Bank. Subsequently, OPEC raised oil prices, causing a crisis that affected both the industrialized and the developing countries. McNamara realized that the developing countries would need more external financing to maintain growth. Because of the difficulties faced by the industrialized countries, he believed that the new funds could come only from the capital-surplus oil producers. Early in 1974, he went to Iran for discussions about an OPEC fund for development. Although agreement was reached, McNamara found on his return that the U.S. was unwilling to cooperate, and the proposals came to nothing. The lack of American participation was a major setback for McNamara's efforts to obtain more funding for development. In addition, he had to face opposition from William Simon, U.S. Treasury Secretary from May 1974 to January 1977, who opposed any increase in the Bank's activities.

When President Carter assumed office in 1977, it was said that he intended to double U.S. foreign aid. In order to obtain Congressional approval, however, the new administration undertook an investigation of the salaries paid to the staffs of the Bank and the IMF, a frequent subject of complaint in Congress. Suspicions that the United States was trying to dominate or destroy the two institutions were strengthened by attempts in Congress to limit the use of IDA funds. McNamara insisted that under its Articles of Agreement the Bank could not accept "tied" funds. A compromise was reached, and it was agreed that the U.S. executive director would be instructed not to vote for such loans. The administration then tried to enforce its human rights policy by refusing to vote for loans to countries that it disliked. Again McNamara refused to change the Bank's policies because the Articles of Agreement stated that only economic considerations should determine Bank decision-making.

In spite of these problems the Bank continued to grow during McNamara's second term, and lending for agriculture, education, population, and rural development increased. McNamara's personal standing remained high, and his reappointment for a third term as Bank president was supported by the United States. In 1979 the United States again attempted to influence the Bank's policy by opposing two proposed loans to Vietnam. Vietnam invaded Cambodia during the negotiations for IDA's sixth replenishment, and McNamara was told that the replenishment bill would be defeated unless he assured Congress that there would be no further loans to Vietnam. A letter to this effect was sent to the chairman of the appropriate House committee. Subsequently, it was published, and the Bank's Executive Board unanimously protested McNamara's action and the bypassing of the Board.

These attempts to control Bank lending intensified efforts by the developing countries in the United Nations to change the Bank's weighted voting structure and so increase their influence in the Bank. The OPEC countries requested that a representative of the Palestine Liberation Organization should be an observer at the Bank/Fund annual meetings, but it was clear that a PLO presence would be viewed unfavorably in Congress and that the passage of appropriations for the Bank could be affected. McNamara obtained a vote from the Executive Board that postponed the issue for future consideration, but his action was criticized by many member countries. Such episodes, as well as the problems with Congress, undoubtedly made McNamara's last years in office difficult, and possibly influenced his decision not to complete his third term of office as Bank president. He retired in June 1981.

Mediation and the Bank. From 1950 to 1960, during the presidency of Eugene Black (q.v.), the Bank acted as mediator in three cases where its role was of wide international interest. The first case concerned Iran and the nationalization of the Anglo-Iranian Oil Company (AIOC). Established by predominantly British interests, the company had a large share of the world market for petroleum and petroleum products and had begun to develop oil interests outside Iran. In May 1951 the oil industry in Iran was nationalized, and AIOC appealed unsuccessfully to the International Court of Justice. The British government then requested the UN Security Council to call for a resumption of negotiations. In November 1951 Mohammed Mossadegh, then Iran's prime minister, visited

Washington, D.C., and a meeting was arranged with Robert L. Garner, the Bank's vice president. The Bank proposed some interim arrangements for the oilfields while negotiations were proceeding, but most of these proposals were rejected by Iran. Subsequently, the Bank sent a reconnaissance mission to Iran to report on the state of the oilfields. Its members included Torkild Rieder, formerly chairman of the Texas Oil Corporation. He and Garner were members of another Bank mission that met unsuccessfully with Mossadegh in Teheran. Rieder subsequently returned to Iran as oil adviser to the government, and the settlement finally reached in 1954 had some features in common with the earlier Bank proposals.

The second case of mediation involving the Bank was the dispute between India and Pakistan regarding the division of the Indus waters. In 1951 David E. Lilienthal, former chairman of the Tennessee Valley Authority, visited the Indus river valley and proposed that the system should be operated as a whole by an Indo-Pakistan agency or some supranational agency, possibly with financing from the Bank. Bank president Eugene Black visited India and Pakistan in February 1952, and it was agreed that engineers from the two countries would meet to prepare a plan for the division of the Indus waters. After discussions in Washington, each country agreed to present its own plan in October 1953. Faced with the prospect of a deadlock, Raymond A. Wheeler, the Bank's engineering adviser, prepared a proposal on behalf of the Bank. Negotiations dragged on for more than six months, and finally both sides agreed to proceed under terms of reference proposed by Black in August 1954. A Bank team headed by Sir William Iliff and accompanied by a group of engineers from India and Pakistan visited the Indus valley in 1955, and agreement was reached on transitional arrangements for use of the waters. No progress was made in formulating a comprehensive plan, however, and early in 1958 the Indus negotiations appeared to be at a standstill. Pakistan then put forward a new plan based on a Bank proposal that Pakistan should take the waters of the western rivers in the Indus system, and make no claim to the eastern rivers. In May 1959 Black and Iliff went to both countries with new heads of agreement for a treaty. After amendments and revisions they were accepted by both governments. More discussions followed and the Bank prepared a new draft for an Indus waters treaty, but disagreement on some issues continued. In the meantime the Bank had successfully negotiated the establishment of an Indus waters development fund, to be supported by friendly governments and the Bank. After further changes, both countries agreed to accept the Indus waters treaty in its new form. In September 1960, Iliff, for the

Bank, and the representatives of the donor governments signed the agreement for the Indus Development Fund, and the presidents of India and Pakistan signed the Indus Waters Treaty. The treaty negotiations, in which the Bank had been continuously involved, had lasted for nine years.

The Bank's third effort at international mediation began in January 1953, when the Egyptian minister of finance requested Bank president Black to consider Bank financing for the High Dam on the Nile. Black visited Egypt, and was impressed by the scheme, and by all the difficulties involved. In 1954 the Bank sent an aide-mémoire to the Egyptian government stating its position, and was then asked to undertake "a thorough and expeditious examination of the High Dam proposal." A Bank study, concluded in September 1955, was generally favorable, and a meeting was arranged with the Egyptian government, but after some discussion the talks were adjourned. In the meantime Black had had meetings with American and British representatives about possible participation in the project. They agreed, subject to certain conditions, but there was no firm commitment after the first part of the project. The Egyptian government then requested a definite commitment for financing the later stages of the project. Support from the United States and Britain began to weaken, and when the Egyptian premier declined their terms, they formally withdrew.

Although the negotiations were unsuccessful, Black and the Bank emerged with enhanced prestige and reputation. In July 1956 Nasser announced that the Egyptian government was taking over the property and operations of the Suez Canal Company, and in 1958 Black provided the Bank's good offices for the settlement of claims arising from the expropriation.

Membership of the Bank. According to the Bank's Articles of Agreement (q.v.), membership in the Bank is open to members of the International Monetary Fund (q.v.). A country applying for membership in the Fund is considered eligible if it controls its own foreign relations and is able and willing to fulfill the obligations of membership as described in the Fund's Articles of Agreement. The Bank's Articles also state that new members, as well as the conditions for their admission, have to be approved by the Bank's Board of Governors.

The first formal step toward becoming a member of the Bank is to submit a membership application, which has to be signed by the country's head of state or minister of foreign affairs and must include the name of a representative who can supply any required information. Most countries apply to the Fund and the Bank at the same time, so the two institutions usually coordinate the application process.

The Bank's executive directors (q.v.) are informed about applications for membership, and that they will be processed after the IMF has determined an appropriate quota for the prospective member. The quota is set after the Fund has examined detailed information about the prospective member's economy, population, trade, and other data. A member's quota in the Fund establishes its relationship with the institution and determines its subscription, its voting power, the amount that the member is entitled to borrow, and its share in the allocation of the Fund's special drawing rights (q.v.). The member's quota is expressed in special drawing rights (SDRs), and is equal to the subscription payable to the Fund. The amount of a member's quota in the Fund is used to determine the member's capital subscription to the Bank, and is calculated as a fixed ratio of the Fund's quota. For determining the new member's capital subscription to the Bank, the SDR is considered to have the same value as a 1944 U.S. dollar. Since 1945 the ratio has been changed at various times, owing to capital increases in the Bank and to quota increases in the Fund.

After the quota has been determined, the application for membership is sent to the Bank's Board of Governors for approval, together with a draft membership resolution and a report from the executive directors recommending adoption of the resolution. Voting on the resolution is by mail and it is adopted if approved by a majority of the governors. Certain additional requirements for completing the membership formalities include:

1. Enabling legislation adopted by the government of the prospective member, which authorizes the country to become a member of the Fund and Bank, and also provides for the necessary payments to both institutions.
2. A memorandum of law, signed by the appropriate legal representative of the prospective member country, which sets out the requirements for Bank membership and the obligations under the Bank's Articles.
3. The instrument of acceptance, in which the prospective member formally accepts the Bank's Articles.
4. The full powers, or authorization, for a representative of the prospective member to deposit the instrument of acceptance and to sign the original copy of the Bank's Articles.

The new member also has to appoint a governor and alternate governor, and is required to participate in the election of executive directors (q.v.).

Mexico and the World Bank. In 1949 the IBRD made its first loans to Mexico, totaling $34.1 million for 2 power projects. By the end of June 1971 the Bank had made ten loans, amounting to about $600 million, for the expansion of Mexico's power system. By then total Bank lending to Mexico amounted to $1.053 billion and also included support for projects in irrigation, livestock, and transportation.

In 1976 Mexico experienced severe balance of payments problems, and the government embarked on an adjustment program supported by the IMF. Because of increased oil production and extensive borrowing abroad, Mexico's economy rebounded between 1978 and 1981, and borrowing from the Bank increased for projects directed toward area and rural development, industry, and transportation.

By the end of 1981 the country's situation had again deteriorated, and in August 1982 the announcement that Mexico was unable to service its foreign debt marked the beginning of a worldwide debt crisis. A new Mexican administration adopted an adjustment program supported by an IMF extended arrangement and received additional financial resources and debt rescheduling from official and commercial bank sources. The adjustment effort could not be sustained, and in mid-1986 a new program was supported by a Fund stand-by arrangement. Moderate economic growth in 1987 was followed by a worsening in Mexico's balance of payments, and in 1989 the Fund approved a three-year extended arrangement, amounting to $3.6 billion. Negotiations with the Bank were concluded for several sectoral loans, and in June 1989 the Bank approved further loans amounting to almost $2 billion for reforms in the trade, financial, and fiscal sectors, of which $760 million was for debt and debt service reduction. The Bank also agreed to provide loans averaging $2 billion during the next three years, and in January 1990 it approved an additional $1.26 billion for debt and debt servicing operations. Mexico's recovery was limited by its large current account deficit and relatively modest growth, and in 1994 it was forced to devalue its currency, resulting in another major financial crisis. From January to June 1995, the Bank provided assistance to Mexico through a financial sector technical assistance project and supplementary financial assistance programs. Since then it has worked with the government on the restructuring of Mexico's banking sector.

Meyer, Eugene (1875–1959). Following a successful career as an investment banker in New York, Eugene Meyer held important posts in the U.S. government during the first and second world wars. Subsequently, he acquired the *Washington Post*. In June 1946 Meyer was asked by President Truman to become the Bank's first president. At the age of seventy-one, he was reluctant to accept, but felt that the Bank offered "the outstanding banking opportunity for world service in world history." Consequently, Meyer believed that it should be launched by an experienced financier according to sound banking practices. He accepted the office of president on the understanding that he would resign after the launching process had been completed.

Three major tasks awaited the new president: a competent staff for the new bank had to be appointed; the Bank had to show that it could sell its bonds in the markets; and a satisfactory working relationship had to be established between the Bank's president and the executive directors. He first addressed the task of creating the Bank's organization and staff. An outline of the Bank's organization was drawn up, and appointments were made to the offices of Secretary, General Counsel, Treasurer, and Director of Personnel. Meyer told the Executive Board that the staff should come from many countries, but he wanted an American vice president who would act for him in case of absence, and an American general counsel who would play an important part in establishing the Bank's organization. The Board agreed, and Meyer was able to fill these posts and some others, thus providing, in his words "a very good base . . . on which to build the Bank."

In August 1946, Meyer met a number of leading bankers in New York to reassure the financial community concerning the sound lending policies that would be adopted by the Bank. He then attempted to solve his problems with the executive directors. The Executive Board was in existence before the Bank had a president, and some of the directors, including Emilio Collado, the U.S. executive director, believed that the Bank's operations should be closely controlled by the directors. Meyer felt that he had responsibility as Bank president but lacked the necessary authority. In December 1946, after only six months in office, he submitted his resignation, saying that he felt that he had completed the Bank's initial organization.

Middle-Income Countries. These are countries with a per capita gross national product (GNP) of more than $675 but less than $8,356 in 1992 U.S. dollar terms. *See also* Low-Income Countries.

Multilateral Investment Guarantee Agency (MIGA). In 1985 the Bank's Board of Governors formally approved the Convention Establishing the

Multilateral Investment Guarantee Agency (q.v.), and it was opened for signature by member countries. The Convention came into effect on April 12, 1988, and MIGA was inaugurated on June 8, 1988, as an autonomous institution within the World Bank Group.

Membership in MIGA is open to all members of the Bank. By July 1995, 128 countries had become members, and 24 developing countries and countries in transition were in the process of fulfilling membership requirements. According to Chapter 1 of the Convention, MIGA's objective is "to encourage the flow of investments for productive purposes among member countries, and in particular to developing member countries, thus supplementing the activities of the International Bank for Reconstruction and Development, . . . the International Finance Corporation, and other international development finance institutions." To achieve this, MIGA issues "guarantees, including coinsurance and reinsurance, against non-commercial risks in respect of investments in a member country which flow from other member countries."

MIGA has an authorized capital of $1,082 million, subscribed by members whose subscriptions are in accordance with their allocation of shares in the Bank's capital stock. There is a council of governors, consisting of one governor and one alternate appointed by each member, and a board of directors. The president of the Bank is ex officio the president of MIGA, and the nonvoting chairman of its board of directors. The Bank's governors and directors also serve as governors and directors of MIGA.

The Agency promotes private investment in developing countries through insurance against:

1. Transfer risk resulting from host government restrictions on currency conversion and transfer.
2. Risk of expropriation or administrative actions or omissions of the host government that deprive the investor of ownership, control of, or substantial benefits from his investment.
3. Repudiation of contracts by the host government, where the investor does not have access to a competent forum, faces unreasonable delays, and is unable to enforce judicial decisions in his favor.
4. Armed conflict and civil unrest.

MIGA may act as sole underwriter or as coinsurer with other investment insurance agencies, and may also issue or buy reinsurance. The Agency's investment insurance is intended to be self-supporting.

In fiscal year 1995 MIGA issued fifty-four contracts, which facilitated total direct investment of about $2.5 billion and created an estimated

8,800 jobs in the developing countries. For the first time the Agency issued significant amounts of coverage ($142 million) for infrastructure projects.

N

National Environmental Assessment Plan (NEAP). This plan identifies a country's major environmental concerns and practices, and formulates plans and actions to address identified problems. A country borrowing from the Bank is responsible for preparing and implementing its NEAP, which forms a basis for the Bank's dialogue with a borrower on environmental issues. By the end of 1995 fifty seven active IDA borrowers had completed NEAPs or equivalent documents. NEAPs for 16 IBRD borrowers had been completed or were in advanced stages of preparation.

Negative Pledge Clauses. This clause is a standard feature of all IBRD loan agreements. It is intended to protect the Bank by prohibiting borrowing countries from establishing liens on public assets that would create a preference for other creditors on foreign exchange loans over the debt owed to the Bank. Most of the important assets of countries in transition are still publicly owned, so it is very difficult for state-owned enterprises to enter into financial relations with private creditors without either requesting a waiver of the negative pledge clause or granting equal security to the Bank. In fiscal year 1993 the Bank's Executive Board approved a policy by which countries in transition could be granted, in certain circumstances, a temporary waiver of the negative pledge clause. Since no waivers of the negative pledge clause had been granted, and substantial investments in several countries were being delayed, in fiscal year 1994 the Board approved a modification of its previous policy. Under this modification, the decision on the country's eligibility would be determined by the Bank's judgment that it was proceeding with privatization, moving toward a market economy, and that the waiver of the pledge would contribute to the achievement of its objectives. As a result, the Board approved negative pledge waivers for Kazakhstan, Russia, and Uzbekistan.

Nonaccrual Status. It is the policy of the IBRD to place in nonaccrual status all loans made to or guaranteed by a member of the IBRD if principal, interest, or other charges connected with such loans are overdue by more than six months, unless the IBRD's management determines that the overdue amount will be paid in the immediate future. If development credits by IDA to a member country are placed in nonaccrual status, all IBRD loans to that government are also placed in nonaccrual status. When a member's loans are placed in nonaccrual status, unpaid interest and other charges on outstanding loans are deducted from the IBRD's income for the current period, and only those payments actually received by the Bank are included in its income for that period. After a member country has paid in full all overdue accounts, its eligibility for new loans is restored, and all payments of overdue interest and other charges are considered part of the IBRD's income for the current year, even if they were incurred in previous years. The Congo and the former Yugoslav Republic of Macedonia paid off all their arrears during 1994, and their loans from the IBRD came out of nonaccrual status. At the end of fiscal year 1995 five member countries (Iraq, Liberia, Sudan, Syrian Arab Republic, and Zaïre), and two successor republics of the former Socialist Federal Republic of Yugoslavia (Bosnia-Herzegovina, and Serbia and Montenegro/the Federal Republic of Yugoslavia) were in nonaccrual status. Loans in nonaccrual accounted for 2.1 percent of the total IBRD portfolio at the end of fiscal year 1995.

Nongovernmental Organizations (NGOs) and the World Bank. The World Bank has defined NGOs as "private organizations that pursue activities to relieve suffering, promote the interests of the poor, protect the environment, provide basic social services, or undertake community development." In general, the term can be applied to all nonprofit organizations that are independent of government. Many NGOs are "value-based organizations" that depend to all or to some extent on charitable donations and voluntary service.

A useful source of information about NGOs is provided through databases maintained by the NGO unit in the Bank's Operations Policy Department. They contain material on more than eight thousand NGOs worldwide, a reference collection of more than seven hundred NGO directories and reports, and information concerning approximately eight hundred Bank-financed projects involving NGOs. These organizations are identified and selected in various ways for Bank-financed activities. In some cases, individual NGOs contact the project's task manager or borrowing government directly; in other cases, NGOs are selected on a sole-source basis or are invited to participate in a competitive bidding process. If NGOs are not directly funded by the Bank for their work on a particular project, other sources of financing include loan proceeds, consultancy trust funds, the Project Preparation Facility, the Institutional Development Fund, the Global Environment Facility (qq.v.), and supervision budgets. In addition, the Bank has a number of special programs through which relatively small amounts can be granted to NGOs for specific purposes. Under the Bank's existing policies, if procurement is involved, international competitive bidding (ICB) is the preferred method. Local competitive bidding (LCB) is permitted when projects are small and foreign bidders are not likely to be interested.

The World Bank usually deals with two main types of NGOs: operational NGOs, whose main purpose is the design and implementation of development projects, and advocacy NGOs, that support a particular cause and seek to influence Bank policies and practices. Operational NGOS fall into three main groups: community-based organizations (CBOs) that deal with a limited group in a small area, national organizations operating in individual developing countries, and international organizations, often with headquarters in a developed country, that are active in a number of countries.

Since the 1970s collaboration with NGOs has become increasingly important in Bank-financed operations. From 1973 to 1988, only 6 percent of such operations involved NGOs, but by 1993 more than 30 percent included some form of NGO involvement, and in 1994 the percentage rose to 40 percent. NGOs are most frequently involved in Bank operations concerned with agriculture, health, nutrition, population, and rural development. The Bank usually contracts with national or international NGOs to deliver services, design projects, or carry out research, while community-based organizations (CBOs) are more likely to receive contracts for project goods and services. CBOs also play an important part in Bank projects that promote participation, because they encourage a sense of ownership among the beneficiaries, and help to ensure long-term community support after project completion.

A Bank Operational Directive (O.D. 14.70), entitled *Involving NGOs in Bank-Supported Activities* (1989) contains guidelines for Bank staff working with NGOs. Although some NGOs are fundamentally opposed to the Bank and its policies, others have raised objections to Bank projects that are based on their experience and local contacts. The guidelines suggest that such concerns may be well founded. The objections should be carefully considered and efforts should be made to include NGOs in consultations about project design. To facilitate interaction early in the project cycle, the Bank periodically makes available to NGOs a list of prospective Bank-supported operations in which the staff consider that NGOs could be effectively involved.

The Bank has found that NGOs make useful contributions to the quality, sustainability, and effectiveness of Bank-supported projects. Often, they are able to provide effective institutional links with the poorest and most disadvantaged members of the community. On occasion they have facilitated direct consultation with persons affected by a Bank project, or have represented such groups in negotiations with the government or the Bank. NGOs have made useful contributions to the Bank's economic and sector work (ESW), especially in connection with poverty-related and environmental issues. The Bank is now conducting poverty assessments in all borrowing countries, and in some countries participatory poverty assessments (PPAs), involving the participation of poor people, have been completed. NGOs have taken part in preparing a number of PPAs, including those for Benin, Cameroon, Ghana, Guinea, Madagascar, and Rwanda. The Bank-NGO Committee continues to be useful in policy debate on such issues as participatory development and the social and environmental consequences of structural adjustment. In recent years special consultations have been convened outside the Committee to discuss problems of immediate concern. Some of these have involved energy, forestry, and water resource management. In 1993 the Bank organized a consultation with NGOs in Paris on the draft of *World Development Report 1993,* as well as one for African NGOs on "Better health in Africa."

Because many NGOs are small and flexible, they are able to develop new approaches and practices, and some of their successful innovations have been incorporated into Bank projects. OXFAM's "water harvesting" program in Burkina Faso has been a model for Bank operations in soil and water conservation throughout the Sahel. In 1988 CARE Canada established a private sector development project in Peru which involved the transfer of used equipment from companies in developed countries to small enterprises in developing countries. Staff from the Bank's Private Sector Development Department were impressed by the project's success, and worked with CARE and local NGOs to establish similar projects in Ghana and Zimbabwe. In other cases, NGOs working with the Bank on the Philippines Health Development Project and the Ghana Second Health and Population Project have played an important part in project design and implementation.

NGOs are usually hired by the Bank as consultants or implementing agencies, but sometimes they have contributed their own time, resources, and/or facilities to Bank projects. Large international NGOs or foundations have sometimes made financial grants in support of such projects. NGO involvement in project implementation is the most frequent form of Bank-NGO operational cooperation, which includes project management, service delivery, training, and community development. In recent years NGOs have also become involved in the monitoring and evaluation of Bank-financed projects. For example, in the Paraguay Caazapa Rural Development Project, local NGOs were contracted to monitor the status of indigenous communities throughout project implementation.

In 1995 41 percent of Bank-approved projects included NGOs. There was increased NGO involvement in the early stages of project preparation, and a number of workshops on the Bank's project cycle were organized for NGOs and government representatives to promote understanding and to encourage active participation. Collaboration between the Bank and NGOs has also presented opportunities to enhance the capacity of the NGO sector. The Bank has consulted with NGOs on strategies to support their institutional development, and has provided training, either as a project component or through programs arranged by the Bank's Economic Development Institute (q.v.). In some projects, the Bank has encouraged partnerships between international NGOs and local groups, and has promoted networking and information-sharing.

O

Official Development Assistance (ODA). This form of assistance is provided by official agencies to developing countries and multilateral agencies. Its objective is the economic development and welfare of developing countries. ODA is concessional in character, and includes a grant element of at least 25 percent.

Onchocerciasis Control Programme. Onchocerciasis, also known as river blindness, is a disease caused by parasitic worms which live and reproduce in the human body, and travel through the skin and other organs. When these worms reach the eyes, they cause blindness. This disease is spread by biting blackflies, which transmit the infant worms from infected to uninfected persons. By the 1970s the disease had affected up to 15 per cent of the population in eleven West African countries. This was the situation encountered by Bank president Robert S. McNamara during a visit to Upper Volta in 1972. After consulting experts, he found that the transmission of onchocerciasis could be interrupted by destroying blackfly larvae in the rivers. In theory, the disease could be brought under control within twenty years. McNamara proposed that the Food and Agriculture Organization of the United Nations, the United Nations Development Programme, and the World Health Organization (qq.v.) should join the World Bank in sponsoring a multidonor program to control the disease. By 1974 sufficient funds had been committed to launch the Onchocerciasis Control Programme, covering Benin, Burkina Faso, Côte d'Ivoire, Ghana, Mali, Niger, and Togo. The World Health Organization was designated as executing agency, and the Programme's headquarters were established in Ouagadougou, Burkina Faso. The Bank assumed responsibility for raising funds and for donor coordination, and it also acted as administrator of a fund supported by a number of donor nations and institutions.

The first phase of the eradication program (1974–79) received funding of $53.8 million; the second (1980–85) approximately $108 million. A funding agreement for a third phase was negotiated with the donors for the years 1986–91, and the eradication effort was extended to cover Guinea, Guinea-Bissau, western Mali, Senegal, and Sierra Leone. The estimated cost of this phase was about $133 million. The Bank's contribution to the costs of the first two phases was $18.5 million, and it contributed an additional $13 million, about 10 percent of the total cost, to the third phase. The Programme has been one of the Bank's most effective cofinancing operations, each dollar contributed by the Bank generating at least $9 from other donors.

By 1992 the Onchocerciasis Control Programme had doubled its operational coverage, had incorporated four more countries, and had gained support from 13 additional donors. The structure of the Programme remains the same, but the staff has been Africanized, so that now 97 percent are from the African countries participating in this Programme. The Bank has assumed additional responsibilities, including programs for the social and economic development of the areas in which onchocerciasis has been controlled. It also supports national capacity-building, so that the countries benefiting from this international program will be able to prevent any future recurrence of the disease.

Operations Evaluation (World Bank). After a Bank operation has been completed it is evaluated by the staff responsible for its implementation. A representative sample of completed operations is independently evaluated by the Bank's Operations Evaluation Department (q.v.). In the Bank's view, evaluation increases its internal and external accountability and transparency, offers a systematic, objective, and accessible record of its operations, and provides valuable lessons for its future activities based on its past experience.

The Bank has a number of evaluation mechanisms for its various activities. With regard to projects, evaluation procedures consist of regular reporting by borrowers, periodic field visits by Bank staff, regular reviews of progress by middle management, a semi-annual review by senior management, and an annual general discussion of problems in project implementation. Bank experience in the field is analyzed by the Central Projects staff. Since 1975 the Bank's economic and sector work has been evaluated by the staffs of Development Policy and Central Projects. Bank budgets are reviewed by the Programming and Budgeting Department. The Bank's organization is reviewed by the Organization Planning Department, and its accounting systems are reviewed by the Internal Audit Department. Recently, the Research Committee has begun to evaluate the Bank's research projects. The Economic Development Institute (EDI) has its courses evaluated by participants in its courses. Individual departments carry out periodic evaluations of their personnel, budget requirements, and projects.

Operations Evaluation Department (OED). The Bank first established a unit for evaluating the development effectiveness of its projects during the presidency of Robert S. McNamara in September 1970. The unit began by assessing the usefulness of individual projects and the effects of groups of related projects in individual countries. In April 1973 systematic project performance audits were added to the activities of the then Operations and Evaluation Division. During the following year, the Division was upgraded to department level, and in 1976 the post of Director General for Evaluation was established. In addition to the director, a chief evaluation officer and a number of senior evaluation officers direct the Department's operations. OED's functions include making periodical assessments of the Bank's operations evaluation system; carrying out performance audits of complete projects supported by the Bank; encouraging member countries to establish their own operations evaluation systems; assessing actions taken by the Bank in connection with OED's findings; and assisting in the dissemination of such findings within the Bank and the development community.

In order to assess the effectiveness of completed operations, the Department examines their technical, financial, economic, social, and environmental aspects. It also rates their performance and sustainability, using the criteria employed in identifying projects proposed for financing. Bank projects are examined from the perspectives of policy, effect, and efficiency. Regarding policy, the evaluators attempt to determine whether the project's objectives were consistent with the country and sectoral strategies agreed between the borrower and the Bank, and whether the project was designed according to the Bank's objectives of poverty reduction, environmental protection, human resource development, and private-sector development. Regarding effect, the evaluators review the results of the project in relation to its objectives. Regarding efficiency, the evaluators examine costs, implementation time, and the project's economic and financial objectives.

OED carries out a limited review of all completed Bank projects, and a detailed review of a number of selected projects. A brief project performance audit memorandum is prepared for about 50 percent of the projects evaluated. An in-depth analysis is performed for 10 to 20 percent of all Bank projects, while a third group of projects normally receives an intermediate level of evaluation, somewhere between the two procedures just described.

OED's evaluation begins with a review of the project completion report, which is prepared in the operational department responsible for the project. This report contains information about the project's costs, performance, economic returns, and institutional development; the efficiency of the Bank's work; and the extent to which the project was successfully implemented. OED's procedure for a detailed project performance audit report (PPAR) includes the preparation of a draft report based on its own audit memorandum and the project completion report. This is sent to the borrower, the Bank executive director for the country concerned, and the departments in the Bank responsible for the project. Comments on the draft are taken into account, and a final version of the PPAR is submitted to OED's director general, who releases it to the executive directors and the president. More detailed analyses of subjects or issues related to Bank operations are contained in OED's evaluation studies and operational policy reviews.

OED is linked administratively to the Bank's president (q.v.) and is also directly responsible to the executive directors (q.v.). Responsibility for assessing the efficiency of OED's work rests with the Executive Board's Joint Audit Committee (q.v.), which, among its other activities, reviews samples of OED's reports, and presents comments on its work to the executive directors.

Organization (IBRD). During the early years of its development, the Bank's organization, as described in its first Annual Report, consisted of the following offices and departments:

Office of the President
Office of the Secretary
Office of the Treasurer
Legal Department
Loan Department
Research Department (afterwards Economic Department)
Personnel Office
Office Services

Before 1952 staff members responsible for relations with member countries and for negotiating loans, and many of the technical and financial staff responsible for project evaluation, were in the Loan Department. Most economists, including those assessing the creditworthiness of member countries, studying commodities, or involved in general economic research, were in the Economic Department.

An interdepartmental committee, chaired by Sir William Iliff, was established in 1952 to examine the Bank's organization. It recommended the establishment of area departments, and the staffs of the Loan and Economic Departments were distributed among three area departments, a Technical Operations Department (which later became the Projects Department), and an Economic Staff. The new Technical Operations Department (TOD) was organized on a functional basis, with sub-units (later projects departments) for agriculture, industry, transportation, public utilities, etc. This framework, with its division of functions, remained basically unchanged for twenty years. It worked well as long as Bank lending remained relatively small. The rapid growth in the size and complexity of Bank operations that occurred after Robert S. McNamara became president in 1968 made changes necessary in the existing structure.

Following a comprehensive study of the Bank's organization in January 1972, five new regional offices were established at the Washington, D.C., headquarters (Eastern Africa; Western Africa; Europe, Middle East and North Africa; Asia; and Latin America and the Caribbean). Each office, headed by a regional vice president, was responsible for planning and supervising the Bank's development assistance programs in the countries assigned to it, and had under its direct control most of the experts (economists, financial analysts, and loan officers) needed in its new operations. Two country programs departments, with functions corresponding to the former area departments, and a projects department with its own sector specialists (for agriculture, education, public utilities, and transportation) were included in each office.

As part of the Bank's new structure, provision was made for a broad range of policy and operational support through the new Central Projects and Development Policy staffs, the former containing specialists responsible for projects in industry, population and nutrition, rural development, tourism, and urbanization; the latter dealing with global and country-wide policy issues, and having responsibility for the Bank's economic work, research program, and commodity analysis.

In May 1987 the Bank began to implement its first institution-wide internal reorganization since 1972. The Bank's functions were rearranged into four broad areas, each headed by a senior vice president, comprising Operations, Finance, Administration, and Policy, Planning, and Research (PPR). Financial intermediation and debt management were moved to the Operations complex, and the regions within this complex were reduced from six to four: Africa, Asia, Europe, the Middle East and North Africa (EMENA), and Latin America and the Caribbean (LAC). Each region, headed by a vice president, included a number of country departments, that combined the operational management functions formerly divided between the programs and the projects departments, as well as a technical department, consisting of several functional divisions. In addition to the four regional vice presidents, vice presidencies were established for cofinancing and financial intermediation services. Changes in the Finance complex were relatively limited, and related to the strengthening of key financial functions. Certain support activities, including Personnel, External Affairs, Information, Technology, and Facilities (ITF), and General Services, were moved to the Administration complex, and planning and budgeting to Policy, Planning, and Research (PPR).

In fiscal year 1992, following the appointment of Lewis T. Preston as the Bank's eighth president, some organizational changes were introduced. The Bank's senior vice presidencies were eliminated to create a flatter management structure; the Bank's presidency was strengthened through the creation of three managing director positions; a new department was created to manage operations in the republics of the former Soviet union; a vice presidency for sector and operations policy was created; the vice presidency for development economics was partially restructured; and the vice presidency for cofinancing and financial services was realigned. These changes were made to make the Bank's organization simpler, more flexible, more responsive to its clients, and more efficient.

Further organizational changes were made in 1993 to provide better support and leadership in the key areas of environmentally sustainable development, private sector development, and human resource development. The vice presidency for sector and operations policy was replaced by three new vice presidencies: Human Resource Development and Operations Policy; Finance and Private Sector Development; and Environmentally Sustainable Development. Within the regions, the sector operations divisions were strengthened, and the technical departments were reorganized to reflect the activities of the new thematic vice presidencies. In January 1994 the Personnel and Administration vice presidency was reorganized, and became the Management and Personnel Services vice presidency. A new department, Organization and Business Practices, was created. After James D. Wolfensohn assumed office as the Bank's ninth president in June 1995, the Bank began studies aiming at further institutional simplification and reduction in staff.

P

Pakistan and the World Bank. The Bank began lending to Pakistan in 1952. During the 1950s it made loans to modernize the country's railways, extend its port facilities, and construct a pipeline from the Sui natural gas field to Karachi. Although Pakistan's agricultural and industrial output increased during the 1960s, the country needed more assistance from abroad, and the Bank played a leading part in the establishment of an aid consortium for Pakistan in 1960. In the following year, Pakistan revised its development targets and asked the consortium for additional assistance. The request was approved, but the war between Pakistan and India in 1965 was a setback to international cooperation. Although the consortium continued, financial assistance to Pakistan was reduced, and the country was forced to modify its development plans.

Following a slowdown that persisted for much of the 1970s, Pakistan's economy began to recover after reforms were introduced in 1977. A program of structural adjustment was adopted in 1982, supported by a $60 million Bank loan and an IDA credit for $80 million. In 1988, following new economic and political difficulties, a medium-term adjustment program was agreed with the Bank and the IMF. The program was reasonably successful at first, but subsequently government changes and events in the Gulf delayed the implementation of policy reforms.

Early in 1991 the government attempted to resume the adjustment effort, and reforms were proposed in energy-related prices and railway tariffs, investment and import licensing, and the exchange control system. Measures to privatize a number of public enterprises were also announced.

The Bank has provided substantial assistance to Pakistan's agriculture, much of it in the form of loans to the Agricultural Development Bank of Pakistan to support its lending program. Other Bank loans and IDA credits have gone to agricultural extension and research, grain storage, development of edible oil crops, seed breeding and production, forestry, and dairying. The Bank has also supported Pakistan's irrigation program. For 9 years, it played an active part in the negotiations between India and Pakistan concerning the allocation of the Indus waters. The Indus Waters Development Fund, provided by donor nations to compensate Pakistan for the part of the waters diverted to India, and a later fund of $1.2 billion for the construction of the Tarbela Dam, have both been administered by the Bank. Assistance has also been provided in the management of Pakistan's water resources, with projects for salinity control and reclamation, drainage, and groundwater development. The country's On-Farm Water Management Projects, financed by IDA credits in 1982 and 1985, have increased farm production through more efficient use of water, and have encouraged farmers to participate in water users' associations.

The Bank participated in a major program for the development of Pakistan's power resources that provided more than 80 percent of the country's hydroelectric generation capacity. Bank loans and IDA credits have also gone to other investments in power generation, distribution and transmission, and have assisted in developing the country's coal, oil, and gas production. The Bank's assistance to Pakistan's industry has mainly consisted of loans and credits to the country's development finance institutions for financing new industrial ventures. The International Finance Corporation (q.v.) has also made investments in the country's industrial sector. Originally, much of Pakistan's industry was state-owned, but since the 1980s, as part of the reforms introduced through adjustment programs, the government has been withdrawing from the industrial sector. A plan was announced in 1991 that aimed at the almost total privatization of state-owned industries.

Education in Pakistan has been assisted by the Bank and IDA through support for primary education, literacy and basic skills, technical education and vocational training, and increased educational opportunities for girls and women. Help has also gone to programs for reducing poverty, expanding public health facilities, and improving urban services and housing.

In fiscal year 1995 the Bank made a $216 million loan for Pakistan's Financial Sector Deepening and Intermediation Project, to strengthen the regulatory framework for its banks, and to expand credit to private enterprises. Another Bank loan for $250 million was designed to increase the private sector's role in the power sector. IDA credits were approved in the same year for assistance to population activities, education, and the forest sector.

Participation and the Bank. In the 1960s and 1970s the Bank's experience with beneficiary involvement and community participation was associated with agricultural and rural development operations. This experience confirmed that stakeholder participation made an important contribution to successful project implementation, so that in recent years the Bank has endeavored to include participation by beneficiaries and others in all its projects. A number of learning initiatives have been established in various sections of the Bank to increase staff awareness of the importance of participation in Bank operations. The Operations Policy Department, in which the study of participation is a major activity, has coordinated a number of participatory development learning groups and has managed the Participation Fund (established in 1993) and its successor, the Fund for Innovative Approaches in Human and Social Development. The Bank has used the following methods to encourage participation in Bank-supported activities:

1. Information-sharing mechanisms (translations of informational material into local languages, presentations, and public meetings)
2. Consultative mechanisms (meetings, field visits, and interviews)
3. Joint assessment mechanisms (participatory evaluations)
4. Shared decision-making mechanisms (workshops, retreats, meetings to resolve conflicts)
5. Collaborative mechanisms (joint committees with stakeholder representatives)
6. Empowering mechanisms (capacity building of stakeholder organizations, self-management by stakeholders)

An example of successful participation by governments occurred during the appraisal stage of Ghana's first structural adjustment program. The government arranged a week-long series of workshops in which the program was open to discussion by members of the negotiating team, ministers and government officials, labor union and private sector representatives, local-level committees, and members of the Press. By the end of the week, consensus had been reached on most of the program, and feelings of suspicion about the Bank had been reduced considerably. Successful participation by local people also occurred in Morocco, where a Bank study on women in development used participatory techniques to consult with rural women.

In the Bank's experience, the costs of participation are largely incurred during the preparation and early supervisory stages of projects, the most costly elements being the salaries of Bank staff and consultants, and the additional staff weeks required for the design phase of participatory projects. The costs of such projects average 10 to 15 percent more than those without participation, but in most cases the extra time required during project preparation has been made up later during a smoother negotiating process.

Because the Bank's own institutional characteristics and procedures have tended, in the past, to limit the amount of participation in the operations that it supports, the following policies have been adopted to remove these constraints: a more flexible approach to project development, the use of more innovative funding mechanisms, the maintenance of a close field presence by the project's task manager, and the use of additional resources (from Japanese and other trust funds) to meet the additional costs of project preparation when participation is included.

In 1995 a Senior Managers' Oversight Committee was established to emphasize and oversee participation in Bank operations. One of the Committee's first tasks was to review the participation action plans prepared in each of the Bank's operational regions. Bankwide training courses in stakeholder participation were also held during the year. The Fund for Innovative Approaches in Human and Social Development (FIAHS), established in 1994, enabled the regions to hire a number of social scientists to provide direction in the area of participation.

Policy Framework Paper (PFP). The PFP process was initiated in July/ August 1986. Since then, policy framework papers for thirty-five countries have been discussed in the Bank's Committee of the Whole (q.v.) and reviewed by the IMF's Executive Board. Intended to ensure effective coordination and consistency in Bank/Fund policy advice and to support adjustment efforts in the developing countries, the PFP sets out the country's macro- and microeconomic objectives for the medium-term and identifies the policies and programs to achieve them. Because country commitment is essential to the successful design and implementation of adjustment, the borrower participates in joint Bank/Fund missions and in the drafting of PFPs in the field. IMF staff are responsible for macroeconomic projections and policy design, and Bank staff provide complementary support for sector and subsector policies. Recently, PFPs have also addressed social and environmental issues as part of the overall adjustment strategy.

Population and the World Bank. In September 1968, during his first address to the Board of Governors during the Bank/Fund annual meeting, Bank president Robert S. McNamara announced the Bank's intention to enter the population field "because the World Bank is concerned above all with economic development, and the rapid growth of population is one of the greatest barriers to the economic growth and social well-being of our member states."

The Bank's Population Projects Department was established in 1969, and Bank lending for population began in 1970 with a $2 million loan to Jamaica for a family planning program. In December 1975 a five-member external advisory panel, headed by Bernard Berelson, was appointed to examine Bank policies in the population sector and to advise on future policies. The Panel's report in 1976 recommended more Bank support for village-level projects, additional financing for population-related health activities, and more systematic treatment of population issues in Bank economic and sector work. In October 1979 the Bank established a new Population, Health, and Nutrition Department (PHND). Following the Bank's major institutional reorganization in 1987, activities connected with population and health were transferred to population and human resource divisions in the country departments within the Bank's new regions.

Two important Bank publications on population and women's health were issued in 1994, reflecting the Bank's intensified efforts relating to population and reproductive health. Population issues form an important part of the Bank's economic and sector work (ESW). A country's economic report provides a detailed analysis of a country's economy, often covering such issues as population and human resources development, while population sector work includes demographic analysis and examination of the potential effects of population growth on economic development. Research on population issues is undertaken at Bank headquarters in Washington, D.C. In recent years, it has focused on alternative family planning systems, the role of the private sector in contraceptive distribution, incentives to reduce family size, preparation of population projections, and population issues in Africa.

The Bank endeavors to influence population policy in member countries through its policy dialogue with government representatives, and through the participation of high-level officials and managers in Bank-sponsored seminars. An important participant in the policy dialogues is a Senior Population Adviser whose activities include leadership in general discussions of population policy, technical guidance for Bank staff, and support for cooperation between the Bank and other organizations in the population field.

Poverty Reduction and the World Bank. As recently expressed by Bank President Lewis T. Preston, the "overarching" objective of the World Bank has always been the reduction of poverty. Over the years, however, the Bank's policy emphasis and the methods it has employed to reduce poverty have changed in response to world conditions and the needs of its members.

During the 1960s the Bank focused on the promotion of economic growth as an essential element in its efforts to reduce poverty. Redistribution with growth and the satisfaction of basic needs were emphasized in the next decade, but at the same time the Bank was coming to realize that more investment in human resources was necessary to win the war against poverty. In the early 1980s the Bank's main objective was policy-based adjustment, but from 1985 onward there was more emphasis on the need to include poverty reduction measures in the adjustment program.

A special task force, composed of senior Bank staff, was established in 1987 to review the Bank's poverty work. It proposed an action program that combined growth policies and clearly defined poverty reduction efforts and was designed to eliminate poverty in the world by the year 2000. During 1988 and 1989 food security was included in poverty reduction initiatives, new efforts were made to protect the poor during periods of adjustment, and NGOs were more closely involved in Bank-supported operations. By 1990 each Bank region had developed a core program aimed at poverty reduction, and progress in the implementation of these programs was monitored.

The Bank's *World Development Report 1990*, which focused on sustainable poverty reduction, proposed a two-part strategy for reducing poverty, with emphasis on support for labor-absorbing economic growth and for increased investment in the development of human resources, especially among the poor. The *Report* also stressed the need to develop targeted transfers and social safety nets that minimized distortions and were fiscally feasible. The two main elements in the Bank's new approach were analysis and design. The first, analysis, attempts to assess the consistency of an individual country's policies, programs and institutions regarding poverty reduction; the second, design, contains proposals for the country's poverty reduction program and for the Bank's program to support and complement the country's efforts to reduce poverty. A policy dialogue is then initiated, based on the findings of the assessment, and on the country and sector work carried out in the Bank. The volume and composition of Bank lending would be linked to the country's own efforts to reduce poverty, often in conjunction with macroeconomic and sectoral efforts to achieve adjustment. Because Bank-supported adjustment programs can impose transitional burdens on the poor, measures would be included to protect the most vulnerable elements of the population. In its current poverty reduction policies the Bank emphasizes the development of institutional capacity in the country involved, so that efforts to reduce poverty can be sustained after project completion.

A recent Bank report, *Poverty Reduction and the World Bank: Progress in Fiscal 1994,* concluded that progress had been made in implementing the Bank's objectives and identified several problem areas still remaining. These included the integration of poverty reduction efforts into country-assistance strategies, the completion of poverty assessments by all borrowing countries, and the expansion of systems for monitoring poverty. The report found that during the year under review 25 percent of Bank investment loans and 43 percent of IDA investment loans were targeted to assist the poor. In fiscal year 1995, these increased to 32 percent for the Bank and 54 percent for IDA. Of the twenty-seven adjustment programs approved during fiscal year 1995, fourteen were poverty-focused. By June 1995 poverty assessments had been completed for thirty-three IDA-recipient countries out of sixty-nine countries that had recently received IDA credits.

President of the World Bank. The Bank's president is selected by the executive directors for an initial term of five years. Although the president is chairman of the Executive Board he has no vote except a deciding vote in case of an equal division. He may also participate in meetings of the Board of Governors, but does not vote at such meetings. The president of the Bank is chief of its operating staff and conducts, under the direction of the executive directors, the ordinary business of the Bank. Subject to the general control of the executive directors, the president is responsible for the organization, appointment, and dismissal of the Bank's officers and staff. According to the Bank's Articles of Agreement "the president, officers, and staff . . . in the discharge of their duties, owe their duty entirely to the Bank, shall respect the international character of this duty, and shall refrain from all attempts to influence any of them in the discharge of their duties." The president is also enjoined "subject to the paramount importance of securing the highest standards of efficiency and of technical competence [to] pay due regard to the importance of recruiting personnel on as wide a geographical basis as possible." The president of the IBRD is also ex officio president of the other members of the World Bank Group. Since its establishment the Bank has had nine presidents: Eugene Meyer (1946–47), John J. McCloy (1947–49), Eugene R. Black (1949–62), George D. Woods (1963–68), Robert S. McNamara (1968–81), A. W. Clausen (1981–86), Barber B. Conable ((1986–91), Lewis T. Preston (1991–95), and James D. Wolfensohn (1995–   ). The president of the Bank has always been an American, and the managing director of the Fund a European.

Preston, Lewis Thompson (1926–95). Formerly board chairman and president of New York's Morgan Guaranty Trust Company and its parent company J.P. Morgan & Co., Lewis T. Preston became the eighth president of the World Bank Group in September 1991. During his presidency, all fifteen of the former Soviet republics joined the Bank, Bank programs were initiatd in the new South Africa, banking relations with Vietnam were resumed, and peace efforts in the Middle East were encouraged through Bank support for economic development in the West Bank and Gaza.

Lewis T. Preston worked to make the Bank more efficient, more flexible, more cost-effective, and more sharply focused on the changing needs of its members. Some important institutional changes were introduced during his presidency which were intended to make the Bank leaner through removal of some layers of its bureaucracy. He supported the establishment of an independent Inspection Panel, introduced new cost-accounting practices, and called for more information about Bank business to be made available to the public. Preston declared poverty alleviation to be the Bank's "overarching objective" and promoted increased Bank lending to benefit health, education (with emphasis on girls' education), and the environment. Owing to ill-health, he decided to retire in 1995. Lewis T. Preston died after a brief illness in May 1995, shortly before his successor, James D. Wolfensohn, was to assume office.

Private Sector Assessment (PSA). To strengthen its work on private sector development (q.v.), the Bank introduced private sector assessments in fiscal year 1992 as part of its program of economic and sector work (ESW). PSAs examine the structure of the private sector in a particular country, identify the constraints to its development, and propose economically efficient ways to remove these constraints. They also suggest ways in which the private sector can provide infrastructure or other services currently provided by the government. Because they involve formal cooperation with the International Finance Corporation (q.v.), the assessments differ from other Bank work. By the end of 1995 private sector assessments for thirty-four countries had been completed or were in progress. In some countries, including Côte d'Ivoire, Egypt, Hungary, the Philippines, and Sri Lanka, the findings of such assessments have been discussed with governments and with a variety of private sector participants to encourage future self-sustaining dialogue.

Private Sector Development (PSD) and the World Bank Group. During the 1960s and 1970s the development strategies of many low-income countries emphasized import-substituting industrialization with economic growth led by the state. State-owned enterprises dominated the industrial sectors of these countries, and state-owned banks financed them with resources derived from taxes on trade and agriculture. Initially, this model of development was successful, but experience in many countries showed that these non-market approaches had been less effective than anticipated, and that efforts to expand the public sector had actually limited economic growth. As a result, by the 1980s many countries had begun to adopt a more 'market friendly' approach toward development, because it was realized that competitive markets and increased entrepreneurial activity could play an important part in fostering economic growth.

In 1988, the World Bank Group established a task force to assess the role of the private sector and to propose ways in which the Bank could assist its members to strengthen the development contribution of this sector. An action program was approved in 1989 that included the creation of business environments to support the private sector, the restructuring of public sectors to improve efficiency and encourage concentration on services complementary to private activity, and the fostering of private enterprise through resource transfers and support for entrepreneurial efforts. The International Finance Corporation (q.v.) also established a central coordinating unit to make the Bank Group's work for private sector development more effective. IFC also agreed to provide or mobilize the necessary resources for projects or joint ventures that could be financed on market terms, that would meet IFC ownership guidelines, and that could be funded without government guarantees. Both the Bank and IFC agreed to expand their capacity to advise on privatization strategies, and to increase research efforts in this area. During its September 1990 meeting the Development Committee (q.v.) welcomed the progress made under the program, and called for high priority for PSD in Bank Group operations, for additional resources for IFC, and for increased collaboration between the Bank and IFC in their efforts to promote the private sector.

The Bank reorganized and strengthened the existing Private Sector Development Committee in 1991, restructured and expanded selected divisions within the Bank to support PSD development, and began the preparation of private sector assessments (q.v.). The first twenty assessments were scheduled for completion by the end of 1993. As part of its effort to support the private sector, the Bank used its adjustment operations to assist member countries to create more supportive business environments for this sector. By 1992 more than 50 percent of Bank adjustment lending included components for dismantling barriers to market entry, and investment opportunities open to private agents had been substantially increased. The Bank also supported government efforts to increase the role of the private sector in the production, delivery, and financing of public goods and services, and from 1990 onwards at least 50 percent of all the Bank's social services projects have included private sector development components. The involvement of the private sector in infrastructure development and maintenance has been promoted in such countries as Argentina, Colombia, Poland, Rwanda, and Tanzania, while Bank-supported projects in water supply and sanitation have included the private sector in Madagascar and Mexico. To increase capacity and improve operation, the private sector has also been involved in power projects in Chad, Pakistan, Turkey, and Uruguay.

In 1995 the Bank's financial intermediation loans of nearly $2 billion supported $4 billion in private investment. During the same year, the International Finance Corporation (q.v.) provided $2.9 billion that supported about $18 billion of investment, and the Multilateral Investment Guarantee Agency (q.v.) guaranteed about $600 million, supporting about $2.5 billion in private sector investment. The World Bank Group continued its support for local financial institutions and markets, and assistance was increased to small businesses in low-income developing countries with little or no access to financing.

Privatization and the World Bank Group. The privatization of state-owned enterprises (SOEs) is supported by the World Bank Group as part of its effort to achieve economic development and poverty reduction. Privatization is considered complementary to the development of the private sector in member countries. The Bank has found that privatization, when correctly conceived and implemented, has increased efficiency, promoted investment, and freed public resources for infrastructure and social programs.

During the 1960s and 1970s, many developing countries considered that economic development could be most rapidly achieved through industrialization with government support. Although state-owned enterprises dominated the industrial sectors of these countries, many of them were inefficient. The spread of their losses through the economy affected saving, investment, and economic growth. In the late 1970s many developing countries attempted to improve the poor performance of these enterprises. Some of their programs had positive results, but they were difficult to implement and even more difficult to sustain. As a result, support for divestiture and privatization began to increase.

Bank lending for divestiture began in 1981. Between fiscal year 1981 and the first half of fiscal 1992, 182 Bank operations supported privatization in sixty-seven countries. Half of these countries were in sub-Saharan Africa. About 70 percent of all Bank structural adjustment loans (SALs) and 40 percent of sectoral adjustment loans (SECALs) supported privatization. More than sixty Bank operations during this period financed technical assistance for privatization, mainly in sub-Saharan Africa and the Caribbean.

Privatization accelerated in 1994, with emphasis on small-scale privatization. This has now been more or less completed in the Czech Republic, Hungary, and Poland, and substantial progress has been achieved in Albania, the Baltic States, the Kyrgyz Republic, Romania, and Russia. In 1995 more than twenty of the Bank's private sector development loans approved during the year included privatization as a key component. Direct technical assistance was also provided to member governments organizing and implementing privatization schemes.

Procurement. Because the World Bank cannot provide all the external financial resources needed by its member countries, borrowers are encouraged to obtain additional funds in the form of cofinancing from other sources. The funds provided by the Bank and cofinanciers make it possible for borrowing countries to procure the goods, works, and services for their development projects and programs. When Bank funds are involved, the Bank regulates the procurement process, requiring suppliers and borrowers to observe the requirements and procedures laid down in Bank guidelines. If the funds come from cofinancing, different procedures may apply, because sometimes they are "tied," i.e., they may only be available for specific purchases or for purchases from the country providing the financing, or they may be subject to other restrictions.

When the Bank makes a loan to a member country, that country is responsible for implementing the project, and for making procurement arrangements. The Bank is involved in the procurement process to ensure that the loans it has made are used for the purpose laid down in the loan agreement, that goods and services are obtained economically and efficiently, and that all eligible bidders are able to compete for the contracts to supply them. The Bank's objectives in procurement are achieved through the use of international competitive bidding (ICB) available to qualified contractors in all Bank member countries. After the project appraisal process has been completed, the borrower prepares a general procurement notice that describes the goods and services to be acquired through the ICB process and invites prospective bidders to express their interest. The notice appears in the Bank's *International Business Opportunities Service (IBOS)* and in the United Nation's *Development Business*. It is also published in one of the leading newspapers in the borrower's country, circulated to local or trade representatives of possible supplying countries, and also sent to bidders who responded to the general procurement notice. Bids are evaluated on a cash price basis, exclusive of any financing terms offered, and they must be opened publicly. Contracts are awarded to the lowest evaluated responsive bid, not necessarily to the lowest price offered. Contractors are paid in the currency of their bid proposal and are fully protected against foreign exchange risk.

Since the Bank usually finances only part of the cost of a project, the borrowing country may use different procurement procedures for the part of the project that it finances, provided that these procedures do not have adverse effects on the project's timetable, quality, or financial and economic viability. In cases where the cofinancier has procurement procedures that are incompatible with the Bank's guidelines, a parallel financing arrangement may be used, in which the Bank and the co-lender finance different goods and services or different parts of a project under separate loan agreements. A large hydroelectric project is a good example of a project where parallel cofinancing is used. Another form of financing, also used when procurement procedures vary, is a joint financing arrangement in which the cost of all goods and services to be procured is shared between the Bank and the cofinancier in agreed proportions. In such cases orders for all goods and service must be placed in accordance with the Bank's approved procedures, and bidding must be open to all parties eligible under the Bank's guidelines.

Official aid agencies are one of the main sources of cofinancing, because of the procurement opportunities they offer to national suppliers. Other sources of cofinancing include export credit agencies and private institutions, especially commercial banks. Export agencies normally provide financing only for the purchase of goods from their own countries, to a maximum amount of 85 percent or less of the cost of items to be procured. The borrower has to arrange financing for the remaining 15 percent, or the Bank can enter into a joint financing arrangement with the agency. Another method of financing with export credit agencies is to parcel the procurement into a number of separate packages for which simultaneous bidding is invited from all eligible suppliers. The Bank and the borrower then determine which packages can best be financed by the Bank.

Program of Targeted Interventions (PTI). These targeted programs are intended to reach the poor in disadvantaged rural and urban regions, the disabled, unskilled workers, recent migrants, those lacking land, and certain ethnic groups. A project is included in the PTI if it has a specific mechanism for targeting the poor and if the proportion of the poor among the project's beneficiaries is higher than the proportion of the poor in the country's total population. During fiscal year 1994 approximately $4.4 billion, (about 21 percent of World Bank lending) came under the PTI, and included projects designed to raise agricultural productivity, improve the quality of basic health care, increase access to primary and non-formal education, raise living standards, support safety net measures, and address environmental concerns. Lending for PTI projects in fiscal year 1995 was 32 percent of the Bank's total investment lending, and 54 percent of IDA's lending.

Project Cycle. The various phases of the Bank's traditional project cycle have been described in two articles by Warren Baum, that first appeared in *Finance & Development* in June 1970 and Dec. 1978. They formed the basis for *The Project Cycle,* which was first published in 1979. A revised edition was issued in 1982, and the seventh printing appeared in June 1994.

As described by Baum, the project cycle comprises six phases: identification, preparation, appraisal, negotiation, implementation and supervision, and evaluation. During the first phase projects that appear suitable for Bank support are identified. Both the Bank and the borrower are involved in the identification process. Over the years, the Bank has assisted its borrowers to develop their project identification capacities, and the Bank's own methods for identifying projects have been improved. Once identified, projects are incorporated into a multi-year lending program for each country that is used for budgeting future Bank operations, and for ensuring that there will be sufficient resources to complete the project.

An identified project then moves into the second phase of the cycle, preparation. During this phase, which normally lasts one to two years, a project brief is prepared that describes objectives, identifies the main issues, and establishes a timetable for future processing. Although the borrower is formally responsible for project preparation, the Bank often provides technical and financial assistance. Such assistance can take various forms, including special loans or advances from the Bank's Project Preparation Facility. The preparation phase of the project cycle has to cover all the technical, institutional, economic, and financial conditions required to achieve successful project implementation. It also includes the identification and comparison of possible alternative methods for achieving the project's objectives.

In the third phase of the project cycle, appraisal, all aspects of the project are reviewed. The Bank is solely responsible for the appraisal stage, which is usually conducted by Bank staff, sometimes in cooperation with consultants, who spend three or four weeks in the member country. Their work covers the technical, institutional, economic, and financial aspects of the project. Technical appraisal is concerned with questions of scale, layout, location of facilities, types of equipment and processes, and provision of services. Institutional appraisal, on the other hand, deals with such questions as the organization of the project, the adequacy of management, the effectiveness of local capacity, and possible policy or institutional changes outside the project that may be necessary to achieve implementation. During economic appraisal, the investment program for the sector, the state of public and private institutions in the sector, and government policies are closely examined. Financial appraisal covers all aspects of the project's cost. Bank loans normally meet all the project's foreign exchange costs, while the borrower or the government concerned is expected to meet some or all of the local costs. Frequently, other agencies or banks are involved in cofinancing Bank-supported projects, so at this stage it is important to ensure that sufficient funds are available for project completion. Financial appraisal is also concerned with recovering investment and operating costs from the project's beneficiaries. Finally, the Bank appraisal team prepares a report that is carefully reviewed, and redrafted if necessary, before submission to Bank management.

During negotiation, the fourth stage of the project cycle, the Bank and the borrower discuss the measures required to assure successful project implementation, and agree on a timetable for progress reports to be submitted by the borrower. When the Bank and the borrower are agreed on all points, the loan documents are prepared. These, together with the Bank's final appraisal report, and the president's report, are presented to the executive directors. If they approve the project, the loan is signed.

Implementation and supervision form the next phase in the project cycle. Implementation is the responsibility of the borrower, with agreed assistance from the Bank taking such forms as organizational studies, staff training, and managers or consultants to supervise project implementation. The supervision of the project, in some ways the most important part of the project cycle, is the responsibility of the Bank. Supervision of a project takes many forms. The progress reports submitted by the borrower are reviewed by the Bank, and problems encountered during implementation are dealt with by correspondence or by the field missions sent to each project. An important element in project supervision involves the procurement of goods and services financed under the loan. The borrower is responsible for preparing the specifications and evaluating bids, while the Bank has to make sure that the work is done properly and that its guidelines for procurement have been observed. Only then can funds be disbursed for the project. As a final step in the supervision process, a completion report on each project is submitted at the end of the disbursement period.

In 1970 the Bank established an evaluation system as the final stage in the project cycle, and all Bank-assisted projects were made subject to an ex post audit. This audit is the reponsibility of the Bank's Operations Evaluation Department (q.v.), which is entirely separate from the operating staff. The project completion report is reviewed by OED, which then prepares a separate audit report. Both reports are then submitted to the executive directors. The borrower is asked to comment on these reports and to prepare a project completion report. The Bank encourages borrowers to establish their own evaluation systems. Because it is impossible to make final judgments on the success or failure of some projects whose effects extend beyond the end of the disbursement period, OED prepares project evaluation reports at least five years later for a small number of selected projects.

In response to the changing needs of its members, the Bank has recently developed a new action plan to increase the development impact of its projects. This plan focuses on the needs of the borrower and the beneficiary rather than on the requirements of the development agency, provides for participation and capacity building, introduces more effective risk management, and reduces the amount of time and resources expended before initiating action on the project. The Bank's new plan for the project cycle comprises four phases: listening, piloting, demonstrating, and mainstreaming. In the first or listening phase the borrower, potential beneficiaries, and Bank staff are involved in discussions that shape project goals and strategies. The second phase, piloting, explores alternatives identified during the listening phase, and assesses risks through pilot projects. Because these projects are small, they can be funded without elaborate internal review, and alternative sequencing of investments can be tested without incurring major costs or risks. Training of project leaders and the design of participatory techniques are regarded as essential elements of the piloting phase. During the third phase of the new project cycle, demonstrating, the project's concepts are fine-tuned and adapted in accordance with the results achieved during the piloting phase. The final stage, mainstreaming, includes the large-scale adoption of the methods, techniques, and programs tested during the pilot and demonstration phases of the project. It is believed that this new approach to project design, which emphasizes collaboration and lasting commitment to the project's goals, will be more effective in achieving successful project implementation.

Project Preparation Facility (PPF). This Bank facility, established in 1975, is intended to assist borrowers in completing project preparation, and to support those responsible for the preparation or implementation of a project. When the facility was established, it was thought that typical costs would be in the range of $50,000 to $150,000, but in 1978 the limit was raised to $1 million, and in 1986 to $1.5 million. It was then possible to advance up to $1.5 million for each project, either to fill in gaps in project preparation (up to a limit of $750,000) or to assist in institutional strengthening (up to a similar limit). In 1991 the Bank's executive directors approved amendments to the facility that removed the distinction between these two types of PPF assistance, and permitted the Bank's operational regions to authorize one or more advances up to the previous limit of $1.5 million per project. By the end of 1993, 138 PPF advances had been approved, mainly to countries in sub-Saharan Africa on IDA terms. During fiscal year 1994 a new ceiling of $2 million per advance was established except in connection with loans exceeding $200 million; for these a new limit was set at $3 million. Unlike advances under the Bank's Special Project Preparation Facility (q.v.), PPFs are either refinanced through Bank loans, or are repaid by the borrower. By sector, the facility has been used most in the agricultural sector, followed by technical assistance and transportation.

Public Information Center (World Bank). On January 3, 1994, the Bank expanded access to its operational information by opening a Public Information Center (PIC) at its headquarters in Washington, D.C. The Center is part of the Bank's more open information policy, which was approved by its Executive Directors on August 26, 1993. PIC field offices were subsequently opened in the Bank's London, Paris, and Tokyo offices. Each office has a public reading room with a workstation connected to the Internet. For those without access to the Internet, a catalog of available Bank documents is distributed by mail and is updated monthly by fax. Academics, investors, nongovernmental organizations, and any other groups or individuals may use the Center, which offers access to documents relating to all projects approved by the Bank's Board as of January 3, 1994. For documents relating to projects approved before that date, the Bank country department in charge of the project should be contacted. Bank resident missions play an important part in the PIC network, ensuring that relevant documents concerning projects are available to affected people and local organizations in borrowing countries.

Those seeking information must request specific documents, as the Center is unable to handle general requests for information. The following documents are now available to the public:

1. Project information documents (PIDs) for Bank (IBRD, IDA, and IFC) projects, and for Global Environment Facility (GEF) projects
2. Environmental assessments to review the possible environmental impact of individual projects

3. Environmental assessments and executive summaries for projects funded by IFC (in Category A: projects that are expected to have major environmental effects)
4. Environmental data sheets (updated quarterly for each Bank-funded project)
5. National environmental action plans (available with government consent for publication)
6. Staff appraisal reports (available after projects have been approved by the Board)
7. Summaries of evaluation reports (prepared by the Bank's Operations Evaluation Department)
8. Country economic and sector work reports
9. Sectoral Policy papers

A catalog of available documents is accessible through the Internet system, and a World Bank information service is also available. By the end of 1994 the PIC offices had received nearly seventeen thousand requests for information. *See also* Documents and Information; Information and Publications.

R

Research in the IBRD. In the Bank's first *Annual Report,* published in September 1946, its Research Department is listed among the first offices and departments established in the Bank. The Bank's research program was formally established in 1971, and by 1980 more than one hundred research projects had been completed.

Research projects are usually initiated within the Bank and often involve collaboration between Bank staff and the outside research community, especially institutions in the developing countries, as it is the Bank's policy to support the development of indigenous research capacity. Except for such collaborative undertakings, the Bank does not provide funding for research to outside individuals or institutions. The results of completed Bank research projects appear as articles in professional journals, as books published under the Bank's auspices or by independent publishers, or as papers in one of the many series issued by the Bank. Details of publications issued by, or on behalf of, the Bank are included in its annual *Index of Publications,* and information on current research projects is provided through an annual publication, *World Bank Research Program: Abstracts of Current Studies.*

Early in 1980 an external advisory panel, chaired by Sir Arthur Lewis, submitted a report on the Bank's economic and social research. It recommended closer collaboration with research institutions in developing countries, closer links between the Bank's operational activities and its research program, and expansion of the Bank's research effort, especially in the application and dissemination of its results. By the end of the year a news bulletin on Bank research had been launched, and a series of workshops were held in which research staff communicated the results of their work on topics of current interest. In 1982 five Chinese researchers worked with Bank staff to design a program of joint research that included the construction and use of a macroeconomic model.

Research accounts for about 3.5 percent of the Bank's administrative budget. In 1990 it amounted to about $21 million, including $6.1 million for the research support budget. Staff apply for funds from this budget by submitting proposals to the Research Committee. The research program is reviewed annually by the executive directors, and priorities for research are established by the Bank's Research and Publications Policy Council.

During recent years Bank research has concentrated on the Bank's main operational activities including adjustment, the decentralization and reduction of govenment activities, environmental protection, human resource development, natural resource management, poverty reduction, the private sector, the promotion of foreign capital investment, public sector management, the reform of centrally planned economies, and taxation. Bank research staff also provide comprehensive statistical information to assist operational staff in the development of programs and projects for developing countries. In addition, they are assisting the countries of the former Soviet Union in their transition to market economies with advice on policy reform and other issues such as agriculture, banking and finance, labor markets, privatization, and social safety nets.

Resident Representatives (World Bank). Early in its institutional development, the Bank realized that its effectiveness was increased through direct personal contacts with governments and officials in member countries, and it was decided to assign staff as resident representatives. A request for a Bank resident mission, or a Bank field office, is made by the member country concerned. The final decision, however, rests with the Bank, which considers current and potential lending to that country, as well as available Bank staff. Cost effectiveness is always of concern, as the expenses of maintaining staff are much higher in the field than at Bank headquarters. Because, from the beginning, India and Pakistan have received a large share of Bank and IDA financing, resident missions were established in both countries in the early 1960s. In 1965 resident missions were established for Eastern Africa (in Nairobi, Kenya) and for Western Africa (in Abidjan, Côte d'Ivoire), mainly to help governments in these areas identify and prepare projects for Bank financing.

Although staff on such assignments constitute a very small part of the total Bank staff, they make useful contributions to the Bank's work by explaining institutional policies and procedures, monitoring programs and projects, and providing technical assistance. They also keep headquarters informed of current developments in the country's economy, politics, and administration. Representatives are responsible for facilitating the implementation of Bank programs and projects, coordinating the activities of visiting Bank missions, and maintaining good relations with officials in the appropriate ministries and agencies. They assist member countries in project preparation and also keep headquarters informed about individual views and needs, so that if necessary more appropriate analysis and advice can be developed in Washington. Since the establishment of the Bank's Public Information Center (PIC) in January 1994, Bank resident missions have been playing an important part in the PIC network, by ensuring that relevant documents are available to those affected by a Bank project and to local organizations in borrowing countries.

Bank representatives normally serve in a posting for three years, which may be extended by an additional year. Many of these postings are to one-person offices in individual countries. Bank offices vary in size, some being very much larger. A number of the larger offices have taken on some of the economic and sector work previously performed in Washington, including country economic reporting and project identification, preparation, and supervision.

The number of Bank staff on external assignment has grown over the years, together with the number of resident missions. In 1971 the Bank had eleven resident missions, of which eight were in individual countries. An office in Paris now functions as the headquarters for Bank missions. In June 1995 there were seven regional missions, fifty-nine resident missions (the majority in developing countries) and a number of smaller Bank field offices. This expansion reflects the increasing volume and complexity of Bank lending, as well as the Bank's concern for the administrative problems encountered in many newly independent states, including those in the former Soviet Union.

Resources (IBRD). See Financial Resources (IBRD).

Rights Accumulation Program. Originally introduced by the International Monetary Fund (q.v.), this program allows member countries in arrears to the Fund to establish a record of performance in connection with policy implementation and payments. A similar program was adopted by the Bank in 1991. A country in arrears is permitted to establish a record on adjustment measures during a pre-clearance performance period that may last several years. In this period the Bank may develop and process loans, but does not sign them nor disburse any funds. When the period is over and the country has cleared its arrears to the Bank, the borrower receives disbursements on loans approved during the period, as well as on loans that were suspended while the country was in arrears.

River Blindness. See Onchocerciasis.

Rotberg, Eugene Harvey. Mr. Rotberg, formerly associate director of the division of trading and markets, U.S. Securities and Exchange Commission, was invited by Robert S. McNamara to join the Bank's staff as Treasurer. He held this office for nearly 20 years. During his first months Rotberg was asked to increase Bank borrowing to support the expanded program of lending envisaged by McNamara, and was very successful. When he began, Bank borrowing was around $100 million a year, and by 1987 it had increased to more than $11 billion.

In spite of the great expansion in Bank borrowing, Rotberg's skill as a financial manager was such that the Bank's credit-worthiness was always maintained. He introduced a very sophisticated cash management system to manage the Bank's liquidity, and he was an innovative borrower in the international capital markets. The Bank began using currency swaps in July 1981, and this considerably reduced the cost of its medium- and long-term borrowings. In July 1982 the Bank decided to change the way it priced its loans to the developing countries. Instead of offering long-term, fixed-rate loans, the Bank introduced variable rate loans, with a rate that was reset every six months, based on the cost of funds to the Bank. In spite of some opposition from the Bank's Executive Board regarding short-term borrowing by a long-term lending agency, Rotberg introduced new borrowing vehicles for the Bank, including floating-rate-note issues, short-term discount notes, and short-term borrowings from central banks, all expertly handled. Without his financial skills, it is possible that the Bank would not have become the world's largest international development agency.

Rural Development and the World Bank. A new strategy for the Bank, which emphasized rural development (RD), was announced by its president Robert S. McNamara (q.v.) during the Bank/Fund annual meetings in Nairobi in September 1973. Intended to provide additional resources for poverty reduction in the rural areas of developing countries, the RD strategy was broadly based and included the following elements: policies to promote productivity in the poor, support for land and tenancy reform, better access to credit and public services, and expansion of agricultural research and extension facilities. Its aim was to increase production by small farmers so that by 1985 their output would grow by 5 percent annually. The new strategy was to be implemented mainly through projects, although the importance of complementary economic and sector work (ESW) was emphasized in the identification of target groups in rural areas.

It was proposed that Bank lending for rural development in 1974–79 would be doubled by earmarking 50 percent of its greatly expanded agricultural lending for RD projects. These were defined as projects in the agricultural sector in which 50 percent or more of the direct benefits were intended to go to targeted poverty groups. As a result, some Bank projects in agricultural subsectors, such as tree crops, livestock, and agricultural credit, were classified as rural development projects, as were other projects that were mainly for infrastructure (roads and canals). During this period 446 agricultural projects were approved, and of these, 251 were classified as RD projects, with $6.5 billion in Bank lending. From 1980 to 1986, 497 agricultural projects were approved, with 247 of these classified as RD projects, supported by $12.6 billion in Bank lending.

Although the RD strategy was not directly intended to assist the poorest of the rural poor (the landless and the laborers), many Bank RD projects indirectly benefited this group by increasing their employment opportunities and by providing access to increased rural facilities and services. To implement the new strategy, various types of activity were proposed in a Bank rural development sector policy paper issued in 1975. These activities included area development projects, coordinated national programs, minimum package programs, and sector and special programs.

RD project results were uneven, but in most cases those with irrigation components were successful. Area development projects, which comprised 40 percent of all RD projects, performed somewhat worse than RD projects as a whole, especially in Eastern and Southern Africa. The poor performance of some projects was attributed in Bank documents to deficiencies in project design. In other cases, evidence from audited projects suggests that there may have been over-optimism, and sometimes even error, concerning the level of available agricultural technology in the country involved.

Because Bank operational managers and staff were geared toward rapid expansion of lending in the 1970s, bigger and more complex projects were approved. In some cases, the socioeconomic and political complexity of multicomponent area development projects may have been underestimated, while in others the capacity for project execution may have been overestimated, especially in sub-Saharan Africa and Latin America. Integrated rural development projects (multicomponent projects involving 2 or more agencies) performed so badly that questions were raised about the utility of that particular approach.

The Bank's RD strategy has influenced its lending program and operational policies. It has benefited millions of rural people in poor countries through improvements in rural infrastructure and services, increased food production, and assistance to subsistence farmers. Not all the strategy's ambitious objectives were achieved, and it has been suggested that the Bank proceeded too rapidly from a generalized global strategy for RD to approval for individual projects without full consideration of all the issues involved in very different regions and countries. Although there has been reduced emphasis on Bank lending for RD projects in recent years, it is probable that this reflects changes in the Bank's approach to the problems of the developing countries, rather than a lessening of its support for rural development.

Russia (Federation) and the World Bank. After the formal dissolution of the U.S.S.R. in December 1991, the government of the Russian Federation formally applied for membership in the IMF and the World Bank Group in January 1992, claiming successor status to the U.S.S.R. The other republics of the former Soviet Union also applied for membership. Since then, the Bank has been engaged in one of the largest operations in its history, establishing working relations with all the states, setting up new resident missions and offices, and preparing new projects. The Bank's initial lending instrument for the Russian Federation was the rehabilitation loan, in which quick-disbursing funds finance imports for the maintenance of critical components in production and infrastructure. Subsequently, a major Bank-supported oil sector project, cofinanced by the European Bank for Reconstruction and Development (q.v.), has provided about $1 billion for the rehabilitation of oil-producing operations in Siberia. The Bank has also financed programs for highway rehabilitation.

Inflation has been reduced in the Russian Federation since early 1994, and the Bank has supported policies for further structural reform, liberalization of the incentive regime, and increased allocation of credit. Progress in privatization has continued, with the Russian program privatizing more enterprises than anywhere else in the world. Through a pilot project in the Nizhny Novgorod region, supported by the International Finance Corporation (q.v.), members of collective farms could elect to divide their farms and then bid on parcels of land to work individually or in partnership with other owners. Housing privatization began in 1992, and to date more than one million units in Moscow and other cities have been privatized. A second oil rehabilitation project in Russia includes a component for preventing future negative environmental effects and remedial policies to correct past damage. Poverty assessment work has also begun.

In fiscal year 1995 a permanent working group was established, comprising government officials, and Bank resident mission staff, to coordinate Bank project work and ensure that projects were implemented without delay. The Bank made its first environmental loan to Russia (a $110 million environmental management project), intended to strengthen environmental policy, to improve hazardous waste and water quality management, and to promote pollution abatement projects. During 1995 the Bank responded to an environmental emergency, when help was urgently requested to contain an oil pipeline spill in Russia's Komi Republic. In addition to financing containment infrastructures, the $140 million project was made up of $99 million in IBRD funds, cofinancing by the European Bank for Reconstruction and Development (q.v.) and the pipeline operator, and consultant services supported by Canada and the United States. *See also* Soviet Union.

S

Sardar Sarovar (Narmada River) Project. In 1985, after several years of negotiation, the World Bank approved credits and loans, totaling $450 million, to the government of India and the states of Gujarat, Madhya Pradesh, and Maharashtra for the construction of the Sardar Sarovar dam and canal on the Narmada River. This project was one of the largest water resource projects ever undertaken. It was intended to bring drinking water to the drought-prone regions of Gujarat and to irrigate large areas in all three states. The Indian government and the Bank considered that this project would benefit many people and increase India's agricultural productivity.

Although the construction of a dam on the Narmada had been considered for some years, the governments of the three states involved had been unable to agree on the division of benefits and costs. Finally, the dispute was referred to the Narmada Water Disputes Tribunal in 1969. After ten years of deliberation, the tribunal reached a decision about the distribution of benefits. It also laid down conditions regarding the resettlement and rehabilitation of those displaced by the project. Certain environmental conditions were imposed by the Indian government, and the Bank's loan agreements for the project also contained requirements relating to resettlement and the environment.

In 1980 the Bank had adopted a general resettlement policy which stipulated that there must be rehabilitation as well as resettlement in projects causing involuntary displacement. A Bank policy statement was issued in 1982 relating specifically to tribal peoples. It provided that their customary usage of land should be respected and that they should be displaced only when the borrowing country could implement measures to protect their integrity and well-being. Normally, in connection with projects involving resettlement, the Bank requires the borrower to provide information about the resettlement involved and to submit a plan for resettlement with the main project plan. Both plans can then be examined by the Bank's appraisal team, with recommendations being made for or against approval.

Because Bank staff working on resettlement issues were concerned, a request was sent to India in 1983 for full information about the resettlement plan for the Sardar Sarovar projects. Thayer Scudder, an expert on resettlement from the California Institute of Technology, was hired by the Bank as a consultant. He made two visits to India and found that the information available about the magnitude and implications of displacement was inadequate and that there had been little effort to carry out a full investigation. Scudder also noted that India's record of reservoir-related relocation was unsatisfactory, and that the three states involved did not have adequate institutional frameworks to achieve resettlement. Because the Indian government and the Bank had been very eager to approve the Sardar Sarovar projects, India's regulations and the usual Bank procedures concerning resettlement and environmental protection seem to have been more or less ignored.

Work on the project began and continued in spite of opposition from those displaced by it and a number of environmental groups. In June 1991 the Bank responded to growing criticism, both in and outside India. An American, Bradford Morse, former Administrator of the United Nations Development Programme, and Thomas R. Berger, a Canadian lawyer, well known for his work on aboriginal, environmental and human rights issues, were asked to undertake an independent review of the Sardar Sarovar Project.

Morse and Berger presented their findings in June 1992. They suggested that the Bank and India had failed to carry out adequate assessments of the project's impact, that there was inadequate understanding of the resettlement involved, and that the situation had been made worse by lack of consultation with those directly affected by the project. Because of India's unsatisfactory record regarding resettlement and rehabilitation, they considered that the Bank should have insisted from the beginning on specific plans for resettling those displaced by the project. Morse and Berger also pointed out that the Indian Ministry of Environment and Forests had never given the project environmental clearance. Although the Bank had requested an environmental workplan by the end of 1985 (subsequently extended to 1989) it had not been completed before the authors presented their review. As a result, the project's possible ecological and health effects had never been sufficiently considered during its appraisal stage. In conclusion, Morse and Berger recommended that the Bank should step back from the projects and consider them afresh.

In October 1992 the Bank's Executive Board met to discuss the review's recommendations and management's proposals for future action. It was agreed to continue Bank support for the project on the basis of a detailed plan worked out with the Indian government and the states involved, provided that a number of key benchmarks were met in the following six months. The Bank also agreed to review the lessons learned from Sardar Sarovar, and to establish a task force to review all projects with a resettlement component in the Bank's active portfolio. Subsequently, in March 1993, India requested the Bank to cancel the remaining undisbursed part of its loan for the Sardar Sarovar project, since the government had decided to complete the work without the Bank's assistance. In spite of continuing opposition and threatened withdrawal by one of the states involved, work on the project still continues in 1995. However, owing to rapidly mounting costs that far exceed the original estimates, it may not be possible for India to complete the project as originally designed.

Social Action Programs and Social Funds. These are multisectoral operations mobilizing several sources of financing to support special programs and targeted projects or project components designed to alleviate poverty and the social costs of adjustment. Financing is provided in such areas as public works, retraining, severance assistance, and for schemes involving nutrition, basic education, and health. Subprojects in social action programs are usually appraised by the Bank, but social funds, which are often parastatal quasi-financial institutions, support small subprojects, and sometimes bypass existing bureaucratic procedures.

Social Dimensions of Adjustment Initiative (SDA). In response to fears concerning the adverse effects of structural adjustment programs on the poor, the SDA initiative was launched in 1987 by the World Bank in association with the African Development Bank and the United Nations Development Programme (qq.v.). Its objective is to provide assistance to African governments in designing and implementing programs that will help the poor during periods of adjustment. Subsequently, a number of other donors agreed to take part in the initiative and funding has been provided for a $10 million regional project for sub-Saharan Africa. More than thirty countries have applied to participate in this project, which, among its other activities, encourages research carried out in African countries, as well as joint ventures between African and non-African research institutions. SDA participants also support efforts to improve data collection, emphasizing the design of household and community surveys, and the analysis of the data obtained from them. The working paper series *Social Dimensions of Adjustment in Sub-Saharan Africa,* published by the SDA project, includes three subseries: *Surveys and Statistics,* focusing on data collection; *Policy Analysis,* covering analytical studies based on existing and newly collected data; and *Program Design and Implementation,* dealing with the conceptual framework and policy designs for the SDA project.

Initially, the SDA initiative was received enthusiastically. Following criticism, however, it was terminated at the international level in 1992, although SDA projects at the country level still continue. The Bank has established a successor initiative, the Poverty and Social Policy Program for Africa (PSPPA), which is also being supported by a number of donors.

Social Safety Net. This form of assistance is intended to help those among the poor who are unlikely to benefit from economic growth or human resources development. It includes income transfers and other assistance for those unable to work and for those temporarily affected by natural disasters or economic recessions. The Bank has supported a relatively small but steadily growing number of safety net interventions for the most vulnerable countries, either as freestanding operations or as components of projects. Their numbers have increased since the 1980s, especially in sub-Saharan Africa, Latin America, and the Caribbean, through efforts to protect the poor from the effects of stabilization policies. In the 1990s the Bank is assisting countries in Central and Eastern Europe, as well as in the former Soviet Union, to establish social safety nets during their transition to market economies.

Soviet Union and the World Bank. The Soviet Union attended the Bretton Woods Conference (q.v.) and participated in the discussions leading up to the establishment of the IBRD and the IMF. Although it signed the Articles of Agreement, and attended the first meeting of the Boards of Governors in 1946, the U.S.S.R. did not ratify the Articles, and did not become a member of the two institutions. Possibly, the Soviets mistrusted the new system because their requests for a large recovery loan and reparations from the defeated countries had been denied; they might have thought that the new institutions would be dominated by the United States; or they might feared that participation in the IMF would involve sharing information about the Soviet economy and gold reserves that the government did not wish to divulge. In any event, Stalin and his successors attempted to establish two world systems by creating the Council for Mutual Economic Assistance, the International Bank for Economic Cooperation, and the International Investment Bank, which were critical of the Bank and the Fund.

Beginning in 1985, the government of the U.S.S.R. introduced economic reforms. In July 1990 the leaders of the Group of Seven (q.v.), after consulting the Soviet authorities, requested the World Bank, the International Monetary Fund, the Organisation for Economic Co-Operation and Development, and the European Bank for Reconstruction and Development to make a detailed study of the Soviet economy. This study was intended to show how a market-oriented economy could be established in the Soviet Union, and how Western economic assistance could effectively support the proposed reforms. In July 1991 the Soviet Union applied for membership in the International Monetary Fund. In the following October it entered into a special association with the Fund, through which immediate technical assistance was provided while the application was being considered. After the dissolution of the U.S.S.R.

in December 1991, the government of the Russian Federation formally applied for membership in the IMF and the World Bank in January 1992, claiming successor status to the Soviet Union. *See also* Russia (Federation).

Special Assistance Program (SAP). Initiated in February 1983 for a 2-year period, this program was designed to increase assistance to countries attempting to cope with the exceptionally difficult economic situation caused by the global recession. Its major elements consisted of increased lending for high-priority operations supporting structural adjustment, policy changes, production for export, fuller use of existing capacity, and the maintenance of essential infrastructure; accelerated disbursements under existing and new commitments to ensure implementation of high-priority projects; expanded advisory services on the design and implementation of appropriate policies; and efforts to persuade other donors to take similar action. The SAP program related mainly to countries receiving loans from the IBRD.

Progress in the implementation of the program was reviewed in 1984 and again in 1985, and it was concluded that the SAP had been very successful in achieving its objectives. The program had facilitated the completion of some 260 priority projects, amounting to about $50 million. The adjustment process was rendered less painful because the program's fast-disbursing assistance permitted imports of the raw materials and spare parts needed to maintain production. The Bank's efforts to lessen the economic difficulties of its developing country members benefited the policy dialogue between the Bank and these countries, and it also affected the actions of other multilateral agencies. The Asian Development Bank, and the Inter-American Development Bank (qq.v.) followed the Bank's lead, and the African Development Bank (q.v.) took similar action. As a result of the program, disbursements to forty-four recipient countries totaled $4.5 billion, almost double the amount estimated when the program was launched.

Special Drawing Right (SDR). The first international reserve asset to be created by international law, the SDR came into existence in 1969, under the authority of the first amendment to the IMF's Articles of Agreement, as a supplement to existing reserves. It is used by countries participating in the SDR facility for settling accounts among national monetary authorities, and also employed as a unit of account in certain international and regional organizations, as well as in some private arrangements. The SDR's value is calculated daily, and is based on a weighted average of the currencies of the G-5 countries (France, Germany, Japan, the United Kingdom, and the United States).

Special Facility for Africa (SFA). In February 1985 an agreement was reached between fourteen donor countries and the Bank to mobilize additional resources of more than $1.1 billion, to be committed over a three-year period for the operations of the SFA. The facility was designed to provide quickly disbursing assistance to IDA-eligible countries in sub-Saharan Africa that had undertaken, or were committed to undertake, medium-term programs of policy reform. The International Development Association (q.v.) was designated in May 1985 as SFA's administrator.

Two types of resources were made available to the facility: funds in the form of direct contributions (60 percent), and funds in the form of special financing (40 percent). The Bank's contribution amounted to $150 million. Eligible countries received "African Facility Credits" to support structural and sectoral adjustment, and rehabilitation and emergency reconstruction. Credits, made on current IDA terms (fifty-year maturity, including a ten-year grace period) would have an annual .75 percent service charge and a yearly .50 percent commitment charge. All operations would be approved and administered by Bank staff, and be subject to approval by IDA's Executive Directors.

The Facility began operations in July 1985. By the end of 1986, assistance, totaling $782 million, had been approved for fifteen countries. In 1987 twelve operations were financed with facility credits of $421 million, and 20 countries received assistance.

Special Program of Assistance (SPA). At a meeting in Paris in December 1987, representatives of the industrialized countries agreed to establish a three-year program (1988–90) for low-income, debt-distressed countries in sub-Saharan Africa. A framework for adjustment assistance was established through increased flows from IDA, concessional debt relief, additional cofinancing of adjustment operations, and support provided by the IMF's Enhanced Structural Adjustment Facility. Eligibility for the SPA is determined on the basis of poverty (countries ineligible for IBRD loans); indebtedness (countries with project debt-service ratios of 30 percent or more); and efforts to adjust (countries implementing reform programs endorsed by the Bank and the IMF).

During the program's first phase, evaluation missions from several donor agencies and the Bank visited six SPA countries and concluded that this assistance had substantially improved their economic performance. By March 1990 twenty-three countries were taking part in the program, and the donors agreed to extend it for three more years (1991–93). SPA-2 was officially initiated in October 1990, when eighteen donors pledged $7.4 billion in cofinancing and coordinated financing. At the SPA meeting in April 1992, the donors were asked to increase their commitments to offset the effects of drought in Eastern and Southern Africa and to meet the needs of new SPA countries (raising the number of eligible countries to twenty-six). Under the Bank's leadership, the donors agreed in October 1992 to support the next phase of SPA, and a joint program was prepared. SPA-3, launched in October 1993, will cover the years 1994–96. The number of participating countries is now twenty-nine, and the estimated requirement for donor commitments in the third phase is $12 billion.

Special Project Preparation Facility (SPPF). As opposed to the Project Preparation Facility (q.v.), the SPPF is one of the Bank's few technical assistance grant instruments. Established in 1985, the facility is intended to assist IDA-eligible countries in sub-Saharan Africa to finance their project preparation activities, including the preparation of proposals for project financing by other donors if this cannot be financed from other sources. Reimbursement of SPPFs is required only if a Bank-financed project is approved within five years from the date of approval for the SPPF.

Sri Lanka and the World Bank. The Bank's involvement in Sri Lanka began in 1954 with a loan for power production. At that time the United National Party (UNP) was in power. In 1956 the Sri Lanka Freedom Party (SLFP) won a majority in the elections and remained in power until 1965. When the UNP was in power (1951–55, 1965–70 and 1977 onward) there was more reliance on market-oriented policies and private enterprise, while under the SLFP (1956–65 and 1970–77) the economy was controlled by the state. The Bank made fewer loans to Sri Lanka during the years of state control and lent more extensively during the market-oriented periods. When the UNP was returned to power in 1965, it was faced with an acute foreign exchange crisis and asked for the Bank's help in organizing an aid group to obtain foreign assistance. The UNP then introduced reforms that were in line with the Bank's recommendations, and from 1968 to 1970 Sri Lanka received a number of loans from the Bank. In 1970 the SLFP returned to power, and Bank lending was halted, owing to doubts about the new government's economic policies. However, the Bank continued to maintain a presence in Sri Lanka, and this, combined with the country's increased financial needs after the first oil shock, led to a resumption of Bank lending in 1973.

When the UNP was returned to power in 1977 Bank loans and IDA credits to Sri Lanka increased. On a per capita basis, the country became one of the main recipients of IDA funds. In the period up to June 1985, the Bank made eleven loans to Sri Lanka, amounting to $211 million, IDA provided thirty-nine credits, totaling $783 million, and IFC made eight investments. Most Bank loans to Sri Lanka have supported directly productive projects. From 1978 to 1985, 56 percent of Bank loans went to agriculture, almost 12 percent to industrial development, and the remainder to infrastructure. Earlier Bank loans to Sri Lanka's agricultural sector were mainly for irrigation, but during the second half of the 1970s Bank lending to this sector became more diversified, and it included financing for tree crops (mainly rubber and tea), rural development, agricultural support services, dairying, and forestry.

Large amounts of Bank aid continued to go to the Mahaweli development program, which comprised the development of about 365,000 acres of land in Sri Lanka's dry zone, and to the construction of fifteen reservoirs, and eleven power stations. The Bank provided $183.1 million in loans and credits to support this program.

Over the years, much of IDA's assistance to Sri Lanka has supported water supply and sanitation projects, and it has also promoted industrial development. The Bank has been Sri Lanka's main source of foreign financing for electric power development. In 1981 a joint United Nations Development Programme/World Bank energy assessment mission prepared a comprehensive energy policy framework for Sri Lanka. Many of the mission's recommendations have been accepted by the government, and steps have been taken to implement them.

A number of challenges confronted Sri Lanka in the 1980s and early 1990s. The government had to restore peace in the north and east, and maintain economic stability. Today, it is continuing its efforts to implement the growth-oriented structural reforms recommended by the Bank and the International Monetary Fund.

Staff of the Bank. Unlike the United Nations, the Bank and its affiliates are not subject to nationality quotas regarding staff recruitment. According to Article 5 of the Bank's Articles of Agreement. "the president, officers, and staff of the Bank, in the discharge of their offices, owe their duty to the Bank and to no other authority. Each member of the Bank shall respect the international character of this duty, and shall refrain from all attempts to influence any of them in the discharge of their duties." The president of the Bank is required, when appointing the officers and staff, to "pay due regard to the importance of recruiting personnel on as wide a geographical basis as possible," subject only "to the paramount importance of securing the highest standards of efficiency and of technical competence."

When the Boards of Governors of the Bank and the Fund held their inaugural meeting in Savannah, Georgia, in March 1946, the staff of the Bank numbered seventy-two. The staff grew slowly during the 1950s, rising from 430 in 1951 to 646 in 1960. The numbers of professional staff increased from 159 to 283. During the 1960s, the staff increased much more rapidly, especially after Robert S. McNamara became President of the Bank in 1968. By June 30, 1982, the Bank's staff amounted to 5,278, of whom 2,689 were higher-level staff representing 104 nationalities. At the end of June 1994 Bank regular and fixed-term staff numbered 6,185, of whom 4,145 were higher-level staff from 123 countries. In addition to its regular staff, the Bank employs a number of outside experts and consultants, on contract for varying periods. Approximately 1,166 higher-level, long-term consultants (those with contracts for six months or more) were working for the Bank in 1994.

In August 1995 it was announced that reductions in Bank budgets for the next two fiscal years would be accompanied by staff reductions. Regular and fixed-term staff then numbered 6,059. Through downsizing and changes in skills requirements, some 590 staff were expected to be declared redundant by the end of fiscal year 1996. To assist redundant staff, a job search center has been established to provide individual consultations and arrange workshops and seminars on visa issues, financial planning, and employment opportunities.

Stern, Ernest. Ernest Stern retired in February 1995 as a Managing Director of the World Bank Group after a Bank career of twenty-three years. Previously, he had been senior vice president, Finance, senior vice president, Operations, vice president, South Asia, and director, Development Policy. Stern came to the United States from Amsterdam in 1947, and worked for thirteen years in the U.S. Agency for International Development (USAID) before joining the Bank. He was actively involved in the Bank's structural adjustment lending program and in initiatives to aid the least developed countries. As senior vice president, Finance, Stern chaired the negotiations for the International Development Association's ninth replenishment, which was agreed on December 14, 1989.

Structural Adjustment Loan (SAL). In his address to the Board of Governors during the 1979 annual meeting, Bank president Robert S. McNamara (q.v.) indicated that he was ready to recommend consideration of requests for "structural adjustment" assistance. Increases in petroleum prices, continuing inflation, and a prolonged period of slow growth in the industrialized countries were causing acute problems for many of the developing countries. It was feared that the petroleum importing developing countries would have large current account deficits, and that their growth rates would be significantly lower.

A structural adjustment loan was regarded as an effort to supplement, with longer-term financing, the relatively short-term finance available from the commercial banks and the resources provided by the International Monetary Fund (q.v.). It was expected that countries in difficulties would be able to reduce their current account deficits over the medium-term and to support adjustment programs that included "specific policy, industrial, and other changes designed to strengthen their balance of payments, while maintaining their growth and developmental momentum." Although these programs were intended to be flexible, borrowing countries would have to meet certain prerequisites for loans, conditions would be established, and there would be a limit on Bank and IDA lending for adjustment.

From a modest beginning in 1980, structural and sectoral adjustment lending by the Bank increased fairly steadily until 1989, when it amounted to $6.5 billion. During 1990 and 1991 it averaged a little less than $5 billion a year, and in 1993 amounted to slightly more than $4 billion. Originally, it was expected that structural adjustment lending to a country would continue for three to five years and be supported by a number of loans. It was also thought that this form of lending, with longer-term objectives, would have more enduring effects than the crisis-oriented operations of previous Bank program lending.

A study performed in the Bank's Operations Evaluation Department (q.v.) in 1992 analyzed the outcome of ninety-nine structural and sectoral adjustment loans in forty-two countries in the period from 1980 to September 1991. Of the countries reviewed, twenty-eight had Bank-sponsored adjustment programs in their industrial sectors, and of these thirteen had very successful or successful results. In the agricultural sector, twelve completed operations in eleven countries were examined.

Half of these received IBRD loans, and the other half received IDA credits or other concessional funds, with agricultural sector adjustment loans (ASALs) varying in size from $5 million to $303 million. Satisfactory performance was achieved in half the cases examined. The study also compared the performance of thirty adjusting countries that had received adjustment loans before 1985 with the performance of sixty-three countries that had not, concluding that the performance of countries that had received support for adjustment was moderately better than that of the countries without support. There was, however, great variation in the success of implementation, the policy changes under adjustment being successful in some countries but slower and less successful in others. Progress was slowest in sub-Saharan Africa, but the study showed that by the end of fiscal year 1989 nearly thirty of these countries were implementing programs of structural adjustment with encouraging signs of success.

T

Task Force on Concessional Flows. Established by the Development Committee (q.v.) in May 1982, the task force contained official representatives from donor and recipient countries. The donor countries included Canada, Finland, Germany, Japan, Kuwait, the Netherlands, and Saudi Arabia, with Belgium and Italy sharing representatives. Among the recipient countries were China, Costa Rica, the Dominican Republic, India, Indonesia, Senegal, and Tanzania. John P. Lewis was appointed the first chairman, and the Bank's International Relations Department acted as the secretariat of the task force. Its terms of reference included the study of the problems affecting the volume, quality, and effective use of concessional flows and evaluation of the effects of such flows on developing countries and on the world economy.

Task Force on Portfolio Management. Shortly after his election as president of the Bank, Lewis T. Preston asked Willi A. Wapenhans, a senior manager in the Bank, to head a task force on portfolio management. He was concerned about criticism of the Bank's policies, that had originated both inside and outside the Bank. The task force was asked to examine the quality of the World Bank portfolio, and to make recommendations for policies to reduce the decline in the number of successful projects that had occurred during the previous decade.

Following a detailed analysis of Bank materials and operations, that included three international workshops with borrowers, cofinancers, and contractors, the task force issued its report, *Effective Implementation: Key to Development Impact,* generally known as the Wapenhans report, in September 1992. It found that more than 75 percent of Bank-assisted projects had good performance during the project-completion stage and that the actual rate of return for 120 projects completed in fiscal 1991 was 16 percent, 6 percent more than the 10 percent minimum required by the Bank. However, the task force also found that in recent years there had been a decline in the quality of the Bank's portfolio. The number of problem projects had risen from 11 percent in fiscal 1981 to 18 percent in fiscal 1992, while the number of projects considered satisfactory by the Bank's Operations Evaluation Department (OED) had fallen from 85 percent in fiscal 1981 to 63 percent in fiscal 1992. Although the task force felt that conditions in the world economy accounted to some extent for the increase in problem projects, it suggested that some types of Bank practice might have contributed to difficulties in portfolio management or were ineffective in dealing with them. In particular the members of the Task Force found that the Bank's "pervasive preoccupation" with new lending was at the expense of effective implementation of existing Bank-assisted programs and projects. The report concluded with recommendations for changes in Bank practice that would improve portfolio management, increase attention to project management, and achieve a better balance between the implementation of new projects and the preparation of new ones.

The Bank's executive directors endorsed the general conclusions of the report, and met several times to discuss its findings and recommendations. In July 1993 they approved a detailed action plan prepared by the Bank's management, which responded to many of the criticisms put forward by the task force, and proposed far-reaching changes in Bank policies and procedures.

Task Force on the Multilateral Development Banks. During fiscal year 1995, the Development Committee created a special task force to assess the effects of economic change on the aims, operations, and management of five multilateral development banks, and to determine whether changes could strengthen their impact on the development process. The banks involved included the African Development Bank, the Asian Development Bank, the European Bank for Reconstruction and Development, the Inter-American Development Bank (q.v.), and the World Bank. The task force is expected to present its report at the end of 1995 or early in 1996.

Technical Assistance and the World Bank. Bank-supported technical assistance falls into three main categories: assistance directly connected with Bank lending operations, assistance funded by outside sources but administered by the Bank, and assistance directly funded through the Bank's administrative budget. Bank assistance in the first category can either be a project component intended to support the project's effective implementation, or it can be "freestanding," not tied to a particular project but in itself directly devoted to technical assistance. Examples of projects in the second category of Bank technical assistance include those funded by the United Nations Development Programme (q.v.) and administered by the Bank as executing agency. The third category, Bank technical assistance that is supported through its administrative budget, provides direct assistance through the Bank's Economic Development Institute (q.v.). Assistance can also be provided indirectly as part of the Bank's economic and sector work, or it can be given to borrowers to supervise or to implement projects more efficiently.

In recent years member countries have sometimes requested the Bank's assistance to improve or to reform their legal systems. Technical assistance for this purpose has been provided through adjustment loans, components in investment loans, and freestanding technical assistance and capacity-building loans. Bank staff have also undertaken legal studies and given advice on general legal matters.

During 1992 the Bank's technical assistance operations were reviewed by a special task force which recommended some improvements in the management of Bank technical assistance, and the strengthening of aid coordination, especially with the United Nations Development Programme (UNDP). The task force also proposed the creation of a technical assistance grant facility, the Institutional Development Fund (q.v.). Because many previously centralized economies are adapting their institutions during their changeover to open markets, the Bank is providing technical assistance for institution building in these countries.

Bank-financed loans (freestanding and components) for technical assistance in 1993 amounted to $2.2 billion. Ten countries, led by Brazil, China, Indonesia, and Mexico, accounted for more than half of all Bank assistance for this purpose. In 1994 Bank-financed technical assistance amounted to $2.6 billion, of which $2.2 billion supported project components. The remainder went to nineteen freestanding projects. Fifty-two percent of technical assistance components were for capacity building, and the remainder for implementation support (41 percent) and policy support (7 percent). Latin America and the Caribbean accounted for most of this technical assistance, followed by East Asia and the Pacific, and Europe and Central Asia. Indonesia was the largest single user of Bank technical assistance in 1994, followed by Mexico and Russia.

Telecommunication and the World Bank Group. The Bank has assisted in the development of telecommunication since the mid-1960s. At first Bank lending supported investment to modernize and expand physical plants, but in the 1970s efforts were also made to strengthen the organization and management of telecommunication enterprises. From the mid-1980s the Bank has continued to expand its support for telecommunication, emphasizing sectoral reforms and, where appropriate, the privatization of state enterprises.

From 1965 to 1995, the Bank lent about $5 billion for more than one hundred stand-alone telecommunication investment projects in fifty-four developing countries. Approximately 20 percent of all nonsector Bank lending in recent years has included support for telecommunication. The International Finance Corporation (q.v.) has also made major investments in this sector and has raised significant amounts of financing for privatized telecommunication companies in such countries as Chile and Argentina, and also for new private businesses.

Third Window. During its meeting in January 1975, the Development Committee urged the Bank to examine the possibility of establishing a "Third Window," which would provide development assistance to eligible countries on terms between those of the IBRD and the International Development Association (q.v.). A resolution establishing the Intermediate Financing Facility, more generally known as the "Third Window," was adopted by the executive directors in July 1975. It became effective in December 1975 after pledges of $100 million in contributions to the interest subsidy fund for the Third Window had been received. As of June 30, 1976, contributions of $124.9 million had been received, sufficient to subsidize $600 million in loans.

Tourism and the World Bank Group. For a number of developing countries, the money brought in by tourists amounts to 15 percent or more of foreign exchange receipts, playing an important part in the country's development. Because of the importance of tourism to these countries, the Bank established a tourism projects office in 1969 to assist member countries in identifying, preparing, and implementing projects to encourage tourism. Bank loans were made either to finance integrated programs of infrastructure in areas where the main activity was tourism or to support the construction of hotels and other tourist facilities in areas where basic infrastructure already existed. In 1969 and 1970, Bank missions went to sixteen member countries to explore tourism development. The Bank also acted as executing agency for a UNDP-financed project to design a tourism master plan for Bali, and Morocco received a Bank loan to assist in building tourist hotels. Before 1969, much of the Bank Group's direct assistance to the tourism sector had come from the International Finance Corporation (q.v.), through investments in Central and South America, and participation in projects in Africa and Asia. In 1971 the Bank assisted in the financing of a $24 million complex in Yugoslavia, and carried out additional UNDP-financed studies on tourism possibilities in Afghanistan, the Dominican Republic, and Fiji. The Bank also supported an international study on the financial aspects of tourism. In fiscal year 1972 the Bank financed infrastructure for tourism in Mexico, an IDA credit was approved for hotel construction in Nepal, and joint Bank/IDA financing was approved for a project to promote tourism in Tunisia.

By 1973 tourism had become a significant source of foreign exchange earnings in Asia, and the Bank Group supported projects in Nepal and Indonesia to increase hotel capacity. In fiscal year 1974 an IDA credit of $16 million was approved to develop an area in southern Bali as a tourist resort, the Bank made two loans to Korea, totaling about $30 million, for tourism development, and Tunisia received financing to establish three hotel training centers. From 1975 to 1977, a Bank loan to the Dominican Republic was approved for resort sites and international airport facilities; a loan went to Crédit de la Côte d'Ivoire for on-lending to finance the construction of twelve hundred hotel rooms; IDA credits were approved for infrastructure supporting tourism in The Gambia and Jordan; and Bank loans went to Mexico, Morocco, Senegal, and Turkey for tourism development.

After the Bank introduced structural adjustment lending in 1979, assistance to hotels and tourism has come mainly from the International Finance Corporation. In 1995, for example, IFC's investment portfolio shows that assistance has been provided in the following areas: Sub-Saharan Africa (Cape Verde, Gambia, Ghana, Kenya, Mali, Mauritius, Mozambique, Nigeria, Seychelles, Tanzania, Uganda, Zaïre, Zambia, and

Zimbabwe); Asia (Indonesia, Nepal, Philippines, Sri Lanka, Thailand, and Vietnam); Central Asia, Middle East, and North Africa (Egypt, Pakistan, and Tunisia); Europe (Cyprus, Poland, Turkey, and Yugoslavia); and Latin America and the Caribbean (Belize, Brazil, Costa Rica, Dominican Republic, Mexico, and St. Lucia).

Training and the World Bank. The Bank offers training through its Economic Development Institute (q.v.), which was established in 1955 to provide courses for officials concerned with development programs and projects in the developing countries. Originally conducted in English only, courses were subsequently offered in French and Spanish at EDI's headquarters in Washington, D.C. Today, they are held in many other languages worldwide. In the 1970s the Institute began to hold more of its courses outside the United States, and it increased its efforts to develop training capacity in the developing countries. By 1987 more than 85 percent of EDI's activities were taking place overseas. The Institute's courses now cover a wide range of subjects, including many of current interest, and include more training in basic skills, much of it through training-of-trainers programs in cooperation with institutions in member countries. EDI is now organizing courses for countries in transition from centrally planned economies. It also works with the Joint Vienna Institute (q.v.), as well as with institutions in the countries themselves, to provide additional training.

Transport and the World Bank Group. The share of transport in total Bank Group lending has varied over the years, from 18 percent in the period before 1960 to about 40 percent in the early 1960s, subsequently declining to about 30 percent in later years. Until 1960 lending for railways accounted for more than half of all Bank transport loans, amounting to more than twice the amount lent for highways. Because of the lag in investment caused by World War II and postwar shortages, much of this lending was for equipment. Between 1960 and 1971 the situation changed, because many of the Bank's new members were dependent on highways. During this period, highway lending totaled $2.4 billion, as opposed to $1.4 billion for railways. Many loans were made for the construction of relatively high standard paved roads. Most railway projects were for rolling stock, equipment, and materials, or for track maintenance and rehabilitation. Bank-supported port projects were mainly for increased berthing capacity, and loans for pipelines supported the construction of nearly 1,200 km of new lines. There was some indirect involvement in vehicle manufacture and assembly through Bank and IDA industrial import credits, and the International Finance Corporation (q.v.) made loans and equity investments in firms manufacturing vehicles in Brazil and Yugoslavia.

Over the years the Bank has acted as executing agency for many transportation-oriented preinvestment studies financed by the United Nations Development Programme (q.v.). Both the Bank and IDA have provided technical assistance to the sector in their lending operations, and most loans or credits for transport have included studies or technical assistance to help the borrower or to prepare future projects. In the period 1971–81 the Bank Group's program included lending for some four hundred transport projects. It also supported transportation components in projects designed for urban development, tourism, agriculture, and industry.

Current Bank operations in the transport sector are focusing on changes in pricing, regulatory and investment policy reforms, the achievement of appropriate financial targets, the strengthening of management, and private sector participation. Highway projects are emphasizing the construction of feeder roads, highway maintenance, and the development of local contracting capacity. Loans to the railway sector are directed toward breaking or preventing the present cycle of railway decline, and stress rehabilitation, institutional reform, rate revision, and withdrawal from overextended systems. There is more emphasis on assistance to coastal and inland shipping for borrowers with long coastlines, navigable rivers, and large lakes. Port projects now include modifications to existing infrastructure and new designs for handling the large oil tankers and container ships coming into service. Bank lending for urban transport now involves efforts to deal with congestion and pollution problems, and supports projects for mass transit, urban roads, traffic control systems, and terminal facilities. Research is playing an important part in the Bank's attempts to deal with all the new problems in transport, and plans have been made for closer cooperation between developed and developing countries in an expanded program of transport research.

Tropical Forestry Action Plan (TFAP). Cosponsored by the Food and Agriculture Organization of the United Nations (FAO), the United Nations Development Programme (qq.v.), the World Resources Institute, and the Bank, this five-year, $8 billion plan came into effect in 1986. The plan was intended to increase forest productivity, to improve forestry's contribution to food security, and to promote equitable distribution of the socioeconomic benefits of forestry activities. In 1991 work began on a major restructuring of the plan because studies by NGOs and an independent panel appointed by FAO had revealed a number of shortcomings in its implementation.

U

United Nations, Relations with. The IBRD became a member of the United Nations system on November 15, 1947. The formal agreement between the Bank and the UN confirmed the Bank's status as a specialized agency of the United Nations and also established it as an independent international organization. In its early years, the Bank's relations with the United Nations were not very close. Article 102 of the UN Charter requires all treaties and international agreements entered into by its members to be registered with and published by the UN secretariat. In 1948 the Bank offered to file and record its agreements with member countries, but not to register them. Finally, in 1952, it was agreed that the Bank would register loan and guarantee agreements between the Bank and member states of the United Nations, and would submit agreements with non-UN member states for filing and recording. As a result, these agreements are published in the United Nations Treaty Series. In the Bank's view, this arrangement indicates that they are open agreements, and that they are treaties in the broadest sense of the term.

Dag Hammarskjöld, who became Secretary-General of the United Nations in 1953, made efforts to establish friendly relations with Bank President Eugene Black (q.v.). In 1956 Black agreed to allow the Bank's engineering adviser and a Bank consultant to assist the United Nations in the task of clearing the Suez Canal of the ships and bridges sunk in it during the Middle East war. Also at the UN's request, the Bank acted as its agent for the funds contributed by various governments toward the cost of clearing the Canal.

Following the establishment of the UN Special Fund, and its successor, the United Nations Development Programme (q.v.), collaboration between the Bank and the United Nations became closer. George Woods, who became president of the Bank in 1963, attended the first meeting of the United Nations Conference on Trade and Development (UNCTAD), and pledged Bank support for its activities. Subsequently, the Bank entered into cooperative arrangements with other UN agencies, including the Food and Agriculture Organization of the United Nations, the United Nations Educational, Scientific, and Cultural Organization, and the World Health Organization (qq.v.).

The Bank has an office in the United Nation's headquarters in New York, and its special representative to the United Nations is responsible for maintaining close relations with the UN. The president of the Bank also participates in certain UN functions, addresses meetings of the UN Administrative Coordinating Committee, speaks at sessions of the Economic and Social Council and the United Nations Conference on Trade and Development, and, when invited, addresses other UN meetings and conferences.

United Nations Children's Fund (UNICEF). Established in 1946 as the United Nations International Children's Emergency Fund, UNICEF was intended to meet the emergency needs of children in post-war Europe and China. In 1950 its mandate was changed to include the needs of children in developing countries, and in 1953 it was extended to cover the needs of children everywhere. The Bank is working with UNICEF in activities concerning children's health and education.

United Nations Conference on Environment and Development (UNCED). This conference, the largest ever held by the United Nations, met in Rio de Janeiro, Brazil, in June 1992. Also known as the Earth Summit, the conference was attended by 120 heads of state and their delegations, representing 177 nations, as well as nongovernmental organizations, religious groups, educators, business executives and specialists in development. The conference ended with the Rio Declaration on Environment and Development, the Agenda 21 Action Programme, and a statement of principles concerning forests. Two legally binding conventions, one on climate change and one on biodiversity, were signed by the participating governments. A number of issues were raised during the conference, including financing for Agenda 21, the next replenishment for the International Development Association (q.v.), and funds for the Global Environment Facility (q.v.).

United Nations Development Programme (UNDP). The UNDP, with its headquarters in New York, is the main source of technical assistance provided through the United Nations. It was established in January 1966 following a merger between the United Nations Expanded Programme of Technical Assistance (established 1949), and the UN Special Fund (established 1959). UNDP works closely with the specialized agencies of the United Nations, including the World Bank, to act as executing agencies for its projects. During the 1990s there has been a steady decline in the amount of funding provided by UNDP for Bank-executed projects. The decline is due to a decrease in donor support and to UNDP's preference for national execution of its projects.

United Nations Educational, Scientific and Cultural Organization (UNESCO). Established in 1946, UNESCO's main activity is in the area of education, with emphasis on the spread of literacy, adult education, universal primary education, education for people with disabilities, and education for women and girls. It also promotes international intellectual cooperation, provides operational assistance through advisory missions, and supports research. The Bank cooperates with UNESCO in the educational field. In 1990, together with UNDP and UNICEF, the Bank cosponsored the World Conference on Education for All, which was held in Thailand.

United Nations Environment Programme (UNEP). Established in December 1972, UNEP's headquarters are in Nairobi, Kenya. It promotes international cooperation in the area of environment and sustainable development, provides policy advice on environmental programs within the UN system, and reviews national and international environmental policies in the developing countries. Together with the World Bank and the United Nations Development Programme (q.v.), UNEP sponsors the Global Environment Facility (q.v.).

United Nations Monetary and Financial Conference, Bretton Woods, New Hampshire, 1944. *See* Bretton Woods Conference.

United States and the World Bank. Much of the initial work on the proposed Bank for Reconstruction and Development was done within the U.S. Treasury by Harry Dexter White, then special adviser to Henry Morgenthau, Secretary of the Treasury. In 1941, White had already begun working on plans for a postwar stabilization fund and international bank, which were first described in a memorandum entitled *Suggested Program for Inter-Allied Monetary and Bank Action.* The Bank was originally conceived as an institution that would work with private financial agencies in supplying long-term capital for reconstruction and development. It was also intended to provide additional funding when such agencies were unable to meet all needs for capital for productive purposes. In the 1940s it was thought that the Bank's most important function would be to guarantee loans so that investors would have "a reasonable assurance of safety in placing their funds abroad." Direct lending by the Bank was envisaged as a secondary function only.

The Bank's Articles of Agreement that emerged from the Bretton Woods Conference (q.v.) contained many of the ideas embodied in White's original plan. Legislation to authorize U.S. participation in the Bank and the Fund was presented to Congress in February 1945, and received overwhelming approval, the votes being 345–18 in the House, and 61–16 in the Senate. By submitting the Bretton Woods Agreements Act to Congress as a bill rather than as a treaty, the U.S. administration set a precedent that gave the House and the Senate new opportunities to influence U.S. international economic policy.

In order to finance its operations, it was necessary for the Bank to sell its bonds in U. S. markets. There were initial problems, however, because the Bank did not fit into existing state banking laws, and many American investors felt that foreign bonds were risky investments. To gain investor support, the Bank's second president, John J. McCloy, his chosen vice president Robert L. Garner, and Eugene Black, the U.S. executive director, made speeches at American bankers' conventions and lobbied for legislative changes at a number of state legislatures. Their efforts were very important for the Bank's financial future, because in its early years the U.S. dollar subscription to the Bank was the only fully usable subscription, eighty-five percent of its bonds were denominated in U.S. dollars, and most were sold in the U.S. market. By the mid-1950s investor confidence in the Bank had been established, and Bank issues had achieved a triple A rating.

Because many developing countries were unable to borrow from the Bank, they began to press in the United Nations for the creation of a new agency that would provide technical and financial assistance on concessional terms and operate under the UN rule of one country, one vote. The U.S. strongly opposed such proposals, but finally the administration decided to support the establishment of the International Finance Corporation (q.v.), as an affiliate of the Bank. In 1955 Congress formally approved U.S. membership in IFC. This did not end the pressure from the developing countries for a UN fund for economic development, and in 1959 the Secretary of the U.S. Treasury proposed that the Bank's executive directors should prepare draft articles of agreement for an International Development Association (q.v.). The draft was accepted by the United States, and IDA was established in September 1960, with the U.S. assuming a 42 percent share of the initial contribution to IDA and taking an active part in the mobilization of support from other countries.

In the 1960s the United States encouraged the Bank to expand its lending to the developing countries. It increased its own long-term economic assistance efforts out of concern that the developing countries would succumb to communism and offers of support from the Soviet Union. The United States took the lead in the first replenishment negotiations for IDA, but the negotiations for the second IDA replenishment were slower and much more difficult because of the changed economic situation in the U.S. and its domestic policy concerns. The United States then began to press for a reduction in its share of IDA's replenishments, an objective that continued to be emphasized in subsequent negotiations.

U.S. relations with the Bank during the 1970s were affected by the relative decline of the United States in the world economy, the effect of the war in Vietnam on foreign aid, and more active congressional involvement in foreign economic policy. Although the Bank usually fared better in Congress than the other multilateral aid agencies, the administration's requests for appropriations were closely examined. The Bank was frequently criticized, not only by Congress, but also by church groups, nongovernmental organizations, and the Press.

In 1971 the United States cast its first negative vote on a Bank loan. This loan to Guyana was opposed by the United States as part of its policy against the expropriation of U.S. property. Previously, Congress had shown little interest in the allocation of Bank loans, but it then began to oppose loans to certain countries, India being a frequent target. Congress opposed Bank loans for the production of commodities in developing countries that could compete with those produced in the United States; it also established a practice of attaching directives to its approval for Bank funding bills. In 1974 the funding bill for IDA's fourth replenishment was defeated in the House. Although the vote was subsequently overturned, it demonstrated the vulnerability of Bank requests for funding. During the Bank/Fund annual meetings in 1976, William Simon, Secretary of the U.S. Treasury, expressed U.S. opposition to McNamara's call for increased Bank lending and a general capital increase.

When the Carter administration came into office, it had already made commitments to expand U.S. foreign aid and to eliminate the arrears in payments to the multilateral development banks (MDBs). Although its attempts to gain support for increased IDA funding and for a general capital increase for the Bank were unsuccessful, the administration was able to persuade Congress to appropriate funds in one package for the last payment of IDA-4 and for the first of IDA-5. This action put the United States on the same payment schedule as other donors, and it also raised the IDA appropriation, for the first time, to more than $1 billion. To appease critics in Congress, the administration tackled the issue of Bank salaries. In 1978 it made a proposal to the Bank/Fund Joint Committee on Compensation that eventually provided the basis for salary reductions and a guide for future salary increases. In the same year, Representative Bill Young proposed an amendment to a Bank appropriation bill that would prevent U.S. funds from being used for loans to certain socialist countries, including Vietnam. This amendment was subsequently defeated, but if it had become law, the Bank would have been forced to refuse the U.S. contribution, because its Articles do not permit the acceptance of earmarked funds. To break this deadlock, the administration promised that the U.S. executive director would vote against all loans to the countries in question.

The Reagan administration, which came into office in January 1981, was critical of the Bank and other multilateral agencies, and it favored reduced U.S. support for them. In a statement to Congress, the new administration announced that it would undertake a reassessment of previous policies and establish new policy guidelines and a budgetary framework for U.S. participation in the multilateral development banks. The assessment, which was performed by the U.S. Treasury, was fairly favorable, and some banks, including the World Bank, were praised for their overall performance. In 1983, during the negotiations for IDA's seventh replenishment, the United States insisted on holding its pledge to less than the amount contributed to IDA-6. The Bank had asked for a larger replenishment to accommodate the entry of China, but the administration insisted that both China and India should rely more on commercial borrowing. Subsequently, in 1985 the administration refused to participate in the new special facility for Africa, administered by IDA.

Before the negotiations for the next IDA replenishment began, James Baker had replaced Donald Regan as Secretary of the U.S. Treasury. Faced with the deepening financial crisis in the developing countries, the Reagan administration adopted a more favorable attitude toward the Bank. At the Bank/Fund annual meetings in September 1985, James Baker proposed a plan for the debt crisis that called for new lending and a greater role for the Bank. During the 1987 IDA negotiations, the United States agreed to a replenishment that brought IDA lending back to its 1981–83 levels, but it also insisted on a number of policy changes. These included increases in IDA credits for policy-based lending, a larger share for sub-Saharan Africa, a reduction in the maturity of IDA credits, and a limit of 30 percent of annual IDA funding for China and India combined. In March 1989, Secretary of the Treasury Nicholas Brady proposed another plan for the debt crisis that encouraged the multilateral institutions to support voluntary write-offs of commercial bank debt.

As part of the U.S. efforts to resolve the debt crisis, the Treasury and the Federal Reserve Board participated in Bank, Fund, and commercial bank negotiations with debtor countries. Some critics said that the United States "directed" the Bank's lending. During the negotiations for IDA's ninth replenishment, the U.S. agreed to maintain lending levels in real terms, but insisted on a ceiling for its own contributions that reduced its share to 21.6 percent. The United States also proposed that the Bank should adopt some of its policy positions, including continued emphasis on Africa, closer collaboration between IDA and the IMF, poverty alleviation policies by countries as a criterion for IDA assistance, and new measures for environmental protection.

In 1990–91, while negotiations were proceeding for a capital increase for IFC, the United States attempted to increase the Bank's role in the development of the private sector. As a condition for its support, it recommended a number of changes in the Bank. While these proposals were being considered, the administration withheld support for the IFC capital increase. In May 1991 the Foreign Operations Subcommittee of the House Appropriations Committee supported funding for the U.S. share of the IFC capital increase and expressed disagreement with the administration's proposals. Some weeks later, the U.S. executive director announced that the United States would support the IFC capital increase, and called for discussion of papers prepared by the Treasury on possible changes in the Bank and IFC. The Bank's Board expressed strong opposition to many of these proposals, and the U.S. executive director, on instructions from the Treasury, said that the United States would withdraw its support for the IFC capital increase. A week later, however, the U.S. reversed its position, and agreed to the increase.

In the 1990s, the United States continues to be actively involved in the World Bank. U.S. influence is based on the role that it played in founding the Bank and in drawing up its Articles of Agreement. It also remains the Bank's largest shareholder. The president of the Bank has always been an American. Because of the Bank's location in Washington D.C., the United States has paid close attention to its activities, especially as Congress plays an important part in funding for the Bank and IDA. Although its relative importance in some of these respects has declined, the United States remains the dominant member of the Bank and, for the most part, U.S. and World Bank views and policies have evolved in similar directions.

Urban Policy and the World Bank. The Bank's active involvement in the urban sector began in 1972, when its Urban Projects Department was established. In the same year, the Bank made its first urban development loans, totaling $26 million, to Senegal and Turkey. Initially, Bank assistance in this sector went to slum upgrading and to sites and services projects, which provided shelter, water supply, sanitation, and urban transport for the growing numbers of poor migrants to the cities. The Bank supported a number of pilot projects, with the idea that public subsidies would eventually be replaced by the mobilization of private savings, and that public agencies would be able to recover their investment costs. Such projects were intended to alleviate urban poverty while relieving the public sector of the financial burden for such services. The principal agents for these projects were usually central government housing or public works ministries. Most of these projects were successful in meeting their investment targets, but problems occurred after project completion when arrangements for continuing operation and management did not work well. Because of these problems, the Bank made changes in the design of its projects, new components being added to improve the performance of municipal governments and to increase local property tax yields. Examples of these new designs can be found in the Calcutta urban development projects, the Nairobi site and service project, the sixth Indonesian urban development project, the Brazil medium-size cities project, and a series of urban and municpal development projects in the Philippines.

In the 1980s responsibility for Bank lending to the urban sector was transferred from the Urban Projects Department to six regional projects divisions in the Bank's regional projects departments. A new Urban Development Department was established in 1983 that became responsible for sector policy, operations review, evaluation, and research. There was more emphasis on local government administration and housing finance. On a national scale, the Bank became involved in urban service delivery through municipal infrastructure fund projects. From 1980 to 1982 the Bank approved twenty-five projects of this type, which focused on ways of allocating capital financing among local governments and attempted to introduce systematic economic and financial criteria into what were often seen as arbitrary systems of funding distribution. Examples of these projects are found in Jordan and Morocco. Other Bank projects attempted to change the terms on which governments provide funds for local capital works. These projects supported a shift from grants to loans. In some cases, municipalities were required to present financial action plans as one of the conditions for eligibility. Intergovernmental fiscal relations were addressed in several sector studies, including those dealing with problems in Brazil, Kenya, and Pakistan. Other changes in Bank urban policies included reform of local finance, with Bank aid going to improve local tax administration and municipal capital expenditures; the strengthening of technical capacity for infrastructure maintenance and solid waste collection and disposal; the reform of housing finance; and the application of corporate management concepts to city management. In 1988 Bank lending to the urban sector rose to $1,700 million, the peak year to date.

In the 1990s the Bank is receiving a growing number of requests from member countries for assistance with urban problems. The Bank made four large loans involving the urban sector in 1991. The largest project with an urban component was the Iran earthquake recovery project, in which the Bank's loan to the urban sector was $250 million. While the Bank is still actively involved in efforts to relieve urban poverty and to solve urban environmental problems, the main emphasis of its lending in the 1990s is shifting from direct investment in shelter and infrastructure to policy reform at the national as well as the city level; institutional development; and infrastructure investments that support the country's overall development and are not limited to the urban sector. Such operations include the reform of central-local financial relations, measures to improve urban productivity, and more emphasis on private sector and participatory involvement in urban projects.

V

Vehicle Currency. This is a currency in which the Bank borrows and at the same time enters into a currency swap (q.v.) in order to convert its liability in the "vehicle currency" into a liability denominated in another currency, the "target currency."

Venezuela and the World Bank. Venezuela became a member of the Bank in 1946, and received its first loan in 1961. From 1961 to 1974 the Bank disbursed $342 million for thirteen loans to Venezuela. After oil prices rose in the 1970s, Venezuela did not need further loans from the Bank. It repaid all its outstanding Bank loans and invested some of its profits from oil in Bank bonds. During the 1980s oil prices fell, Venezuela's income was reduced, and the country's situation was made worse by poor economic policies. In 1986 the executive directors renewed Venezuela's eligibility to borrow from the Bank, and discussions began on measures to solve the country's economic and sectoral problems. Following the election of President Pérez in 1989, the Bank and the IMF worked closely with the new government to provide support for programs of economic reform and structural change. Five adjustment loans and four sectoral loans totaling $1,700 million were provided by the Bank, and a $5,000 million Extended Fund Facility by the IMF.

The main elements of the reform program included trade reform (supported by the Bank's $353 million trade policy loan); control of public spending (supported by the Bank's $402 million structural adjustment loan); financial system reform (supported by the Bank's $300 million financial sector adjustment loan); social policy (supported by the Bank's $100 million social development project loan); and agricultural reform (supported by the Bank's $300 million agricultural investment loan). In December 1990 a program of debt and debt service reduction was completed, with assistance from the Bank through an interest support loan ($300 million). The Pérez government also wished to reduce the number of state-owned enterprises and by the end of 1991 seven had been privatized, including the national telephone company and the country's international airline. These privatization and restructuring measures were supported by a Bank public enterprise reform loan. Other reforms, including a basic education program, an endemic disease control project, and a hospital modernization project, also received Bank support. Projects approved for Bank assistance to Venezuela in fiscal years 1994–95 included agriculture, highway rehabilitation, improvements in port facilities, natural resource management, and urban transport.

The International Finance Corporation (q.v.) is playing an important part in developing Venezuela's private sector as it adjusts to the opening of the economy. IFC has increased its role in syndicating and underwriting to encourage the inflow of foreign capital. It is also assisting small- and medium-sized enterprises to establish new credit and agency lines to financial institutions. Between 1988 and 1991, IFC's investments in Venezuela increased from $10 million to $179 million, and included chemicals, cement, banking, and iron and steel. IFC also invested in several new projects, and assisted in company expansions and restructurings.

Voting. Unlike most international organizations, in which voting power is based on the principle of "one person, one vote," the Bank and the International Monetary Fund (q.v.), have adopted a weighted system of voting. According to the Bank's Articles, membership in the Bank is open to all members of the International Monetary Fund. A country applying for membership in the Fund is required to supply data on its economy, which are compared with data from other member countries whose economies are similar in size. A quota is then assigned, equivalent to the country's subscription to the Fund, and this determines its voting power in the Fund and its access to the IMF's financial resources.

Each member country of the Bank is allotted 250 votes plus one additional vote for each share it holds in the Bank's capital stock. The quota assigned by the Fund is used to determine the number of shares in the Bank held by each member country. As a result, the industrialized countries have larger shareholdings than Third World countries. This variable allocation of shares recognizes the differences among members' holdings, and is designed to protect the interests of the countries that contribute more to the Bank's resources.

The Board of Governors (q.v.) is the Bank's senior organ, and each governor is entitled to cast the votes of the country that has appointed him or her. The Governor cannot cast fewer votes than his country's allocation, and must either cast all his votes or abstain from voting. The Board's decisions are usually based on a simple majority of the votes cast, but there are certain decisions, such as those involving amendments to the Bank's Articles of Agreement, that require special majorities of up to 85 percent of the total voting power. *See* World Bank Inspection Panel.

W

Wapenhans, Willi A. In February 1992, Willi A. Wapenhans, an experienced senior manager in the Bank, was asked by Bank president Lewis T. Preston (q.v.) to lead a task force on portfolio management (q.v.), which would examine the quality of the Bank's portfolio and recommend ways to reduce the decline in the proportion of successful projects that had occurred in the previous decade. After a detailed analysis of Bank materials and operations, the task force issued its report, generally known as the Wapenhans Report, in October 1992.

Water Resources Development and the Bank. Since the 1950s the Bank has been active in water resources development, and investments in this area have played an important part in its efforts to reduce poverty and improve living conditions. Irrigation systems have increased food production, improved nutrition, and increased rural incomes; investments in water supply and sanitation have raised health and living standards; and hydropower projects have provided important sources of energy for rural, agricultural and industrial development. By the end of 1991 the Bank had lent more than $19 billion for irrigation and drainage, $12 billion for water supply and sanitation, and about $9 billion for hydropower projects, representing more than 15 percent of total Bank lending.

In the Middle East, North Africa, Central Asia, and sub-Saharan Africa, many of the Bank's member countries have limited renewable water resources and fast growing populations. Other countries, such as northern China, western and southern India, western South America, and parts of Mexico and Pakistan, have fewer problems at the national level but severe water shortages in certain areas. In some parts of Eastern Europe, water pollution is a serious problem, and in much of Africa frequent droughts have exacerbated the problems caused by limited water supplies. As part of a new approach to water resource management, the Bank is giving priority to projects in member countries where water is scarce, or where there are serious difficulties in water allocation, service efficiency, or environmental degradation. Water resource management is now included in Bank country policy dialogues and assistance strategies.

The Bank's operational policies and guidelines provide the basis for its investments in water resources and are designed to make operations efficient, equitable, transparent, and environmentally sound. In the past, however, as indicated in operational reviews, evaluations by the Bank's Operations Evaluation Department (q.v.), and other studies, the Bank has not always been guided by its own rules. Some earlier mistakes in water resource management have included failure to address such issues comprehensively, insufficient attention to financial covenants and cost recovery, lack of consideration of environmental assessments and pollution control, inadequate investments in sewage treatment and drainage systems, neglect of operations and maintenance, delayed and poor-quality construction, lack of concern for project sustainability, and inadequate programs to address erosion problems. In its review of 234 Bank-supported water projects in the years 1974–88, the Bank's Operations Evaluation Department (q.v.) found that 88 percent of investments in water supply and sanitation, and 80 percent of those in irrigation, were satisfactory. This compares with an 81 percent average for all types of Bank projects reviewed by OED.

In many developing countries, the development and management of water resources are under the control of the central government, but deteriorating irrigation systems and inadequate water supply services have exposed serious institutional deficiencies in many government agencies. Current Bank assistance to water resource management now includes support for institution building and management training, consideration of such issues as pricing and decentralization, emphasis on participation by users and communities in water resource management, and involvement of the private sector through management contracts and increased private ownership. For example, a rural water supply and sanitation project in Pakistan has been designed to ensure that rural communities will, as far as possible, operate and maintain the services themselves; Bangladesh is allowing the private sector to sell and maintain low-lift pumps and shallow tubewells; and the Bank is assisting a number of countries, including Colombia, Indonesia, Mexico, and Tunisia, to strengthen water user associations and transfer irrigation management to them. The Bank has also provided support for the privatization of water supply systems in cities in Chile, Côte d'Ivoire, Guinea, and Indonesia, and in rural areas in Bangladesh, Bolivia, Colombia, Kenya, and Paraguay.

Since the 1980s, the Bank has been working closely with the United Nations Development Programme, the Food and Agriculture Organization, the World Health Organization (qq.v), and other United Nations agencies to implement the aims of the Water Decade (1981–90) to ensure "safe water and sanitation for all." This aim has not yet been achieved, in spite of investments of about $10 billion in developing countries. For the Bank this failure has meant a change in direction that emphasizes the systemwide effects of water resource management. In the past, the Bank was prevented from adopting a comprehensive approach to this sector by the institutional structure in most countries, where specialized agencies deal with irrigation and drainage, water supply and sanitation, and hydropower generation. In the 1990s the Bank has developed a new approach, integrated water resources planning (IWRP), to deal with the many problems involved in the optimal allocation of water resources.

White, Harry Dexter (1892–1948). Together with John Maynard Keynes (q.v.), Harry Dexter White played a leading part in the establishment of the International Bank for Reconstruction and Development and the International Monetary Fund (q.v.). He joined the staff of the U.S. Treasury in 1934, became director of the Division of Monetary Research in 1938, was appointed special assistant to the Secretary of the Treasury in 1941, and became Assistant Secretary of the Treasury in 1945. White began work on a plan for a postwar monetary and financial system in 1941. A first version, entitled *Preliminary Draft Proposal for a United Nations Stabilization Fund and Bank for Reconstruction and Development of the United and Associated Nations,* was issued in March 1942. His proposals, and Keynes's plan for a Clearing Union, were combined with other plans and debated internationally during the next two years. Subsequently, they formed the basis for the discussions at the Bretton Woods Conference (q.v.), and the establishment of the Bank and the Fund. In 1946, White resigned his office at the Treasury to become U.S. executive director (q.v.) of the IMF. He resigned from the Fund in 1947, and died in the following year.

Wildland Management and the Bank. The need to maintain natural land and water areas in a state more or less unchanged by human activity forms part of the World Bank's concern with the environment, since the conversion of wildlands to more intensive land and water uses is sometimes part of a development objective, and as such can be an element in a Bank-supported project. Although wildlands are rapidly diminishing in many of the Bank's member countries, those that survive can make important long-term contributions to economic development, especially if they are maintained in their natural state. Consequently, the Bank is attempting to achieve a balance between preserving the environmental benefits of some of the remaining wildlands while converting others to more intensive uses.

Beginning in the 1970s, the World Bank has assisted in the financing or implementation of at least forty projects with wildland management components. Many of these components have involved the establishment or strengthening of wildland management areas (WMAs) in forest reserves, national parks, and wildlife sanctuaries, or have included the management of wildlife and the people that utilize it. In some cases, the location of Bank-supported projects has been changed to preserve important wildlife areas. Although wildland management components in Bank projects are relatively inexpensive, normally accounting for less than 3 percent of total project costs, they have achieved significant benefits and have also contributed to the preservation of biological diversity, which the Bank has undertaken to support.

Lessons derived by the Bank from its experience with wildland management include the systematic and routine incorporation of wildland management components as early as possible into Bank-supported projects, the provision of effective measures to ensure project implementation and continuation, and the promotion of government commitment and local support for the project.

Wolfensohn, James David (1933–   ). Described by the *New York Times* as a "Renaissance banker," James D. Wolfensohn, an international investment banker, became the ninth president of the World Bank on June 1, 1995. Born in Australia, he is a naturalized U.S. citizen, and holds degrees from the University of Sydney and the Harvard Graduate School of Business. In 1956 he was a member of the Australian Olympic fencing team. From 1981 until he became Bank president, Mr. Wolfensohn was president and chief executive officer of his own investment bank, James D. Wolfensohn Incorporated. Previously, he had extensive experience with other investment banks, including Salomon Brothers in New York, Schroders Limited of London, and Darling & Co. in Australia. Among his other responsibilities, Wolfensohn serves as chairman of the Institute for Advanced Study at Princeton University, is on the Board of the Population Council, and is a member of the Council on Foreign Relations. In 1990 he became chairman of the Board of Trustees of the Kennedy Center for the Performing Arts in Washington, D.C., and for many years was associated with the Metropolitan Opera and Carnegie Hall in New York.

During his first months in office, Mr. Wolfensohn visited a number of developing countries, especially in Africa. He has also endeavored to introduce reforms that will make the Bank more effective as a development agency. In a speech to the Bank's senior managers on March 12, 1996, he appealed for their support in changing the internal culture of the institution and in moving from "cynicism, distrust, and distance to risk-taking and involvement."

Women in Development (WID) Initiative. In January 1977 the Bank appointed its first WID adviser, and in the following April, during a speech at the Massachusetts Institute of Technology, Bank President Robert S. McNamara stressed the importance of raising women's socioeconomic and political status. The following year, the WID adviser began producing a series of papers, entitled *Notes on Women in Development*. In 1979 the Bank published *Recognizing the 'Invisible' Woman in Development: The World Bank's Experience*. This work included an overview of the economic and social barriers to women's participation in development, examples of Bank projects designed to remove these barriers, and a listing of gender-related factors to be considered in project preparation. Robert McNamara's final address to the Bank's Board of Governors in 1980 emphasized "the immensely beneficial impact on reducing poverty that results from educating girls." Although the Bank's shift toward macroeconomic policies in the 1980s meant that poverty alleviation and gender issues became less immediate concerns, the new Bank President, A. W. Clausen, shared his predecessor's interest in WID issues. His address to the Board of Governors in 1983 reported increased attention to women in development, and the Bank's *Annual Report* for 1984 contained four pages on WID.

During the second half of the 1980s, the Bank began to devote more attention and resources to gender-related issues. In September 1985 a senior economist was appointed to succeed the first WID adviser. Barber B. Conable assumed office as Bank President in June 1986, and during his address to the Bank's Board of Governors in September 1986, he announced that the environment, population, and WID would be included among the Bank's areas of special emphasis. Conable also mentioned the Bank's program in his address to the Safe Motherhood Conference in Nairobi in February 1987, promising that "the World Bank would do its part." Later that year, the Women in Development division, with a professional staff of seven, was established in the Bank's Population and Human Resources Department. Some innovative strategies were introduced, including efforts to integrate women into project design in such areas as microenterprises, natural resources management, water and sanitation, and finance. Three stand-alone projects for women were approved: in Mexico in 1989, in Gambia in 1990, and in Côte d'Ivoire in 1991. WID coordinator positions were created in the Bank's regions in 1990, and each country department in each of the regions was asked to appoint a WID resource person, who would "ensure the systematic integration of WID concerns in the department's lending and ESW programs."

Under a mandate that required women's country assessment reports to be prepared in each of the Bank's regions, additional efforts were made to gain more knowledge of women's roles, constraints, and contributions to development. Approximately fifty of these assessments have been made and discussed with the governments concerned. The Bank has also examined WID issues in country economic memoranda, poverty assessments, and economic and sector work. A number of special studies have focused on regional issues involving women in development, especially in the areas of employment and human capital formation. In addition, Bank policy and research work has examined women's issues in education, agriculture, forestry, health, and credit facilities for the poor.

After a Bank reorganization in 1993, the Women in Development division became a team, located in the Education and Social Policy Department (ESP) of the Human Resources Development and Operations Policy vice presidency. The team, renamed Gender Analysis and Policy (GAP), made systematic reviews of initial executive project summaries. At this early stage, the team was able to identify opportunities for enhancing the role of women or any possible negative impact on women when it could still influence the project design.

In 1994 an overall portfolio evaluation was carried out that covered the distribution, funding, and performance of 615 projects with gender-related components for the period from 1967 to 1993. Africa had the largest number of these projects (41 percent), followed by South Asia, and Latin America and the Caribbean (15 percent each). Human resource projects, including education, health, population, and nutrition were the most numerous (46 percent), followed by agriculture (39 percent), and urban projects (18 percent). More than two-thirds of the projects examined were funded by the International Development Association (q.v.).

Over the years, the Bank has supported the following strategies to improve women's status and productivity: expanding educational opportunities for women and girls; improving women's access to health and family planning programs; increasing women's participation in the labor force; expanding women's role in agriculture and in the management of natural resources; and providing financial services to women. The Bank has also assisted efforts by member countries to remove the legal and regulatory barriers that prevent women from participating fully in the development process.

Woods, George David (1901–82). In January 1963 George D. Woods became the fourth president of the World Bank and held office until April 1968. Formerly chairman of the First Boston Corporation, Woods had considerable experience in industrial financing, and was well-known and respected in U.S investment banking circles. In his first address to the Bank's Board of Governors, Woods proposed an expansion of the Bank Group's assistance to industry. During Woods's presidency, Bank and IFC commitments to industry and to development finance companies for support to industry grew considerably. He also favored the use of IDA credits to finance equipment and raw materials for industrial production.

Woods endeavored to widen the range of the Bank's activities, stressing the need for more assistance to agriculture and education. Bank Group lending to the agricultural sector increased during his presidency, and a close relationship was initiated between the Bank and the Food and Agriculture Organization of the United Nations (q.v.), which focused on the identification and preparation of agricultural projects. Bank loans for education increased, and similar arrangements about educational projects were worked out with UNESCO. Efforts were also made to coordinate aid more effectively through the establishment of consultative groups and other coordinating mechanisms.

The Bank expanded the scope of its economic studies during Woods's term of office. Technical assistance to member countries was increased also. In the 1960s, when the problem of external debt became one of the Bank's major concerns, Woods proposed a second IDA replenishment of $1 billion, which was much larger than the amount agreed on for IDA's first replenishment. Only $400 million was eventually agreed on, and this after considerable delay.

World Bank. Officially, the "World Bank" comprises the International Bank for Reconstruction and Development (IBRD) and the International Development Association (IDA), but the term is often used in referring to the IBRD alone.

World Bank and International Monetary Fund Relations. Although the Bank and the Fund were both created in 1944 at the Bretton Woods Conference (q.v.), from the beginning they were considered to be completely separate organizations, each with its own Articles of Agreement (q.v.) and its own governing bodies and staff. Until recently, their purposes were very different. The Bank was intended to support reconstruction efforts after the Second World War, and to assist in "the development of productive facilities and resources in less developed countries." The Fund, on the other hand, was conceived as an institution to promote international monetary cooperation, encourage exchange rate stability and orderly exchange rate arrangements, establish a multilateral system of payments, and assist its members to reduce disequilibrium in their balances of payments. Its resources include a pool of currencies that, subject to certain safeguards and limitations, can be drawn on by member countries.

The Bank and the Fund have their headquarters in the same part of Washington, D.C., and cooperation between them has always been close at all levels. According to the Bank's Articles of Agreement, a country has to be a member of the Fund before it can become a member of the Bank. Guidelines for collaboration between the Bank and the Fund have been in place since 1966, and they are updated periodically. Since the beginning of the 1980s Bank and Fund staff have participated in many joint and parallel missions. In March 1989, after agreement had been reached on additional administrative and procedural steps for enhanced collaboration, new guidelines were issued to the staff of both institutions that included increased sharing of information, cross-attendance by staff at selected Executive Board meetings, and temporary staff exchanges. The 1989 guidelines also stress the importance of early agreement among working-level Bank and Fund staffs when conditionality or advice on major development issues is involved, and emphasize the need for full cooperation between parallel missions in the field.

The Bank is a much larger organization than the Fund, and over the years it has grown into the World Bank Group, comprising the International Bank for Reconstruction and Development, the International Development Association, the International Finance Corporation, the International Centre for Settlement of Investment Disputes, and the Multilateral Investment Guarantee Agency. The Bank Group has a staff of more than seven thousand, and maintains a number of offices throughout the world, mainly in the developing countries. To support its many development activities, the Group employs economists and experts in a wide range of fields, including agriculture, communications, education, engineering, health care, population, rural development, transportation, and water supply. The Fund, on the other hand, is still a relatively small institution with a staff of about two thousand that includes economists specializing in finance and macroeconomics. Most Fund staff are based at its headquarters in Washington, D.C., although the Fund also has small offices in Geneva, Paris, and at the UN headquarters in New York.

Both institutions have resources subscribed by their members, but the Bank obtains most of its funds through market operations, while the Fund relies on the resources provided by members and borrows only from official sources. The Bank uses its resources to invest in development projects and in structurual and sectoral projects in member countries;

Fund members make use of its resources according to their quotas in the institution and their balance of payments needs. The International Development Association (q.v.), which lends on concessional terms to the poorer countries, obtains its resources from "replenishments" provided by its wealthier members. The Bank now lends only to its developing country members and to countries in transition, but the Fund's resources are available to all its members, and most have made use of them in time of need.

During the 1950s and 1960s, the Bank and the Fund participated in very different operations, the Bank's support going mainly to long-term development projects for irrigation, electric power, transportation, and roads. The Fund, on the other hand, provided medium-term financing to correct balance of payments disequilibrium in member countries and also worked to establish orderly exchange arrangements. In the 1980s, however, in response to the debt crisis and the adjustment needs of their members, the work of the Bank and the Fund began to move into areas of common concern. In addition to its long-term project lending, the Bank introduced structural and sector adjustment loans, while the Fund began lending for longer-term adjustment through its extended fund facility, its structural adjustment and enhanced structural adjustment facilities, and its enlarged access policy. As a result, cooperation between the two institutions has increased, but they have maintained their identities as independent institutions and have continued to support the confidential relationships each has established with individual member countries. Both institutions have succeeded in avoiding "cross conditionality," in which the conditionality established by one institution for providing finance is not regarded as a condition for receiving a loan from the other. By the second half of the 1980s, members' overdue obligations to both institutions had become a serious problem. As a result, the Bank and the Fund worked closely with each other, the member, and the regional development banks to restore normal relations. *See also* International Monetary Fund.

World Bank Annual Report. The *World Bank Annual Report,* which covers the period from July 1 to June 30 each year, is prepared by the executive directors of the International Bank for Reconstruction and Development (IBRD), and the International Development Association (IDA), in accordance with their respective by-laws. The *Annual Report,* together with administrative budgets and audited financial statements of the IBRD and IDA, is presented by the president of the World Bank (which comprises the two institutions) to the Board of Governors. The other members of the World Bank Group, including the International Finance Corporation (IFC), the Multilateral Investment Guarantee Agency (MIGA), and the International Centre for Settlement of Investment Disputes (ICSID), issue their annual reports separately.

World Bank Economic Review. Published three times a year, this journal publishes the results of Bank-sponsored research, emphasizing its operational, rather than theoretical, aspects. The research described in the *Review* is mainly the work of Bank staff and consultants.

World Bank Group. The Group consists of the International Bank for Reconstruction and Development (IBRD), and its affiliated institutions, the International Centre for Settlement of Investment Disputes (ICSID), the International Development Association (IDA), the International Finance Corporation (IFC), and the Multilateral Investment Guarantee Agency (MIGA).

World Bank Inspection Panel. The decision to create an independent inspection panel within the World Bank was taken in response to two concerns, the first being Bank president Preston's concern that the management of the Bank's investment portfolio could be improved. The second concern, expressed by many outside the Bank, was that the Bank "was less accountable for its performance and less transparent in its decision-making than it should be."

In February 1992 Willi A. Wapenhans, an experienced senior manager in the Bank, was asked to lead a task force to examine the Bank's management of its loan portfolio. Its report, generally known as the Wapenhans report, was submitted to the Executive Board in November 1992. The report suggested that Bank projects had become too complex, and that the Bank's staff had failed to ensure borrower commitment to project implementation and ownership. A number of changes in current Bank policies and practices were proposed. In response to the report, an action plan prepared by Bank management was submitted to the Executive Board. The plan called for more efficient and client-oriented policies, concluding that "the interests of the Bank would be best served by the establishment of an independent inspection panel."

The Panel was established in September 1993 to receive and investigate complaints that the Bank had not followed its own procedures concerning the design, appraisal, and/or implementation of Bank-supported projects.

Its members, comprising a full-time chairman and two part-time members, were appointed in April 1994. Panel members are proposed by the president of the Bank, and appointed by the executive directors, to whom the Panel reports. In August 1994 the Panel's operating procedures were adopted.

The first complaint, concerning the Arun III hydroelectric project in Nepal, was submitted in October 1994. It alleged that the Bank had not complied with its own operation policies and procedures with respect to the economic evaluation of investment operations, the disclosure of information, the environmental assessment, involuntary resettlement, and indigenous peoples. In November 1994 Bank management responded that it had complied with all requirements. The Panel then proceeded to investigate the complaint, and recommended a full investigation of possible violations of the Bank's policies with regard to environmental assessment, involuntary resettlement, and indigenous peoples. The Bank authorized this investigation, and the results will be presented to the Panel in due course.

World Bank Research Observer. First issued in 1986, this publication, which appears in January and July, includes articles on important issues in development economics, surveys of the literature, and reports on current Bank research.

World Development Report. This series of annual reports, first published in 1978, is intended to provide comprehensive assessments of current global development issues. In 1990, the *World Development Report* focused on poverty, and subsequent issues have dealt with such issues as health, infrastructure for development, and workers in an integrating world. The *Report* includes the *World Development Indicators* (also issued separately), which currently provide economic and natural resource indicators for 209 economies.

World Health Organization (WHO). Established in 1948, WHO is the central agency for directing international health activities. WHO's Special Programme for Research and Training in Human Reproduction was established in 1972, and since 1988 the World Bank has been one of its cosponsors. Since 1974 the Bank has been involved with WHO, the Food and Agriculture Organization, and the United Nations Development Programme in the Onchocerciasis Control Programme (q.v.) in West Africa, in which WHO is the executing agency. The Bank is responsible for raising funds and for coordinating donors. It also administers a fund supported by a number of donor nations and institutions. In 1975 WHO's Special Programme for Research and Training in Tropical Diseases was established, also sponsored by the Bank and the United Nations Development Programme (q.v.). A recent example of cooperation between the Bank and WHO occurred in September 1991, when the Children's Vaccine Initiative was launched. The initiative was sponsored by WHO, the United Nations Children's Fund, the United Nations Development Programme (qq.v.), the Rockefeller Foundation, and the World Bank.

World Tables. This annual publication, first issued in 1971, contains up-to-date economic, demographic, and social data for 178 countries and territories. It includes time series based on the Bank's collection of statistics concerning member countries, with emphasis on national accounts, international transactions, and other development indicators.

Statistical Appendix

TABLE 1. Subscriptions to IBRD Capital Stock and Voting Power
as of June 30, 1995
(expressed in millions of U.S. dollars)

Member	Shares	Votes
United States	255,590	255,840
Japan	93,770	94,020
Germany	72,399	72,649
France	69,397	69,647
United Kingdom	69,397	69,647
China	44,799	45,049
Canada	44,795	45,045
India	44,795	45,045
Italy	44,795	45,045
Russia	44,795	45,045
Saudi Arabia	44,795	45,045
Netherlands	35,503	35,753
Belgium	28,983	29,233
Switzerland	26,606	26,856
Brazil	24,946	25,196
Iran, Islamic Republic of	23,686	23,936
Spain	23,686	23,936
Australia	21,610	21,660
Mexico	18,804	19,054
Argentina	17,911	18,161
Indonesia	14,981	15,231
Sweden	14,974	15,224
South Africa	13,462	13,712
Kuwait	13,280	13,530
Nigeria	12,655	12,905
Venezuela	11,427	11,677
Austria	11,063	11,313

TABLE 1. Subscriptions to IBRD Capital Stock and Voting Power
as of June 30, 1995 (continued)
(expressed in millions of U.S. dollars)

Member	Shares	Votes
Poland	10,908	11,158
Ukraine	10,908	11,158
Denmark	10,251	10,501
Norway	9,982	10,232
Korea, Republic of	9,372	9,622
Pakistan	9,339	9,589
Finland	8,560	
Malaysia	8,244	8,494
Hungary	8,050	8,300
Libya	7,840	8,090
Turkey	7,379	7,629
New Zealand	7,236	7,486
Egypt	7,108	7,358
Chile	6,931	7,181
Philippines	6,844	7,094
Colombia	6,352	6,602
Thailand	6,349	6,599
Czech Republic	6,308	6,558
Portugal	5,460	5,710
Peru	5,331	5,581
Ireland	5,271	5,521
Bulgaria	5,215	5,465
Morocco	4,973	5,223
Bangladesh	4,854	5,104
Israel	4,750	5,000
Romania	4,011	4,261
Sri Lanka	3,817	4,067
Zimbabwe	3,325	3,575
Belarus	3,323	3,573
Slovak Republic	3,216	3,466
Iraq	2,808	3,058
Ecuador	2,771	3,021
Angola	2,676	2,926
Zaïre	2,643	2,893
Jamaica	2,578	2,828
Côte d'Ivoire	2,516	2,766
Uzbekistan	2,493	2,743
Myanmar	2,484	2,734
Kenya	2,461	2,711

TABLE 1. Subscriptions to IBRD Capital Stock and Voting Power
as of June 30, 1995 (continued)
(expressed in millions of U.S. dollars)

Member	Shares	Votes
United Arab Emirates	2,385	2,635
Croatia	2,293	2,543
Bolivia	1,785	2,035
Kazakhstan	1,675	1,925
Luxembourg	1,652	1,902
Azerbaijan	1,646	1,896
Georgia	1,584	1,834
Uruguay	1,578	1,828
Zambia	1,577	1,827
Oman	1,561	1,811
Trinidad and Tobago	1,495	1,745
Cyprus	1,461	1,711
Madagascar	1,422	1,672
Jordan	1,388	1,638
Moldova	1,368	1,616
Slovenia	1,261	1,511
Iceland	1,258	1,508
Mauritius	1,242	1,492
Syrian Arab Republic	1,236	1,486
Paraguay	1,229	1,479
Dominican Republic	1,174	1,424
Senegal	1,163	1,413
Armenia	1,139	1,389
Guatemala	1,123	1,373
Bahrain	1,103	1,353
Qatar	1,096	1,346
Malawi	1,094	1,344
Malta	1,074	1,324
Bahamas	1,071	1,321
Tajikistan	1,060	1,310
Guyana	1,058	1,308
Fiji	987	1,237
Ethiopia	978	1,228
Nepal	968	1,218
Barbados	948	1,198
Greece	945	1,195
Mozambique	930	1,180
Cameroon	857	1,107
Ghana	856	1,106

TABLE 1. Subscriptions to IBRD Capital Stock and Voting Power
as of June 30, 1995 (continued)

(expressed in millions of U.S. dollars)

Member	Shares	Votes
Namibia	855	1,105
Sudan	850	1,100
Lithuania	846	1,096
Albania	830	1,080
Latvia	777	1,027
Tanzania	727	977
Papua New Guinea	726	976
Guinea	725	975
Tunisia	719	969
Mali	652	902
Kyrgyz Republic	621	871
Togo	620	870
Uganda	617	867
Botswana	615	865
Nicaragua	608	858
Haiti	599	849
Rwanda	587	837
Belize	586	836
Vanuatu	586	836
Gabon	554	804
St. Lucia	552	802
Somalia	552	802
Vietnam	543	793
Grenada	531	781
Turkmenistan	526	776
Congo	520	770
Estonia	518	768
Solomon Islands	513	763
Cape Verde	508	758
Mauritania	505	755
Dominica	504	754
Benin	487	737
Burkina Faso	487	737
Central African Republic	484	734
Chad	484	734
Bhutan	479	729
Micronesia, Federated States of	479	729
Niger	478	728
Maldives	469	719
Mongolia	466	716
Liberia	463	713

TABLE 1.   Subscriptions to IBRD Capital Stock and Voting Power
as of June 30, 1995 (continued)

(expressed in millions of U.S. dollars)

Member	Shares	Votes
Swaziland	440	690
Macedonia, former Yugoslav Republic of	427	677
Suriname	412	662
Sierra Leone	403	653
Burundi	402	652
Equatorial Guinea	401	651
Panama	385	635
Lesotho	372	622
Honduras	360	610
Lebanon	340	590
Eritrea	333	583
Singapore	320	570
Djibouti	314	564
Gambia, The	305	555
Guinea-Bissau	303	553
Afghanistan	300	550
Western Samoa	298	548
Antigua and Barbuda	292	542
Comoros	282	532
St. Vincent and the Grenadines	278	528
São Tomé and Principe	278	528
Tonga	277	527
St. Kitts and Nevis	275	525
Marshall Islands	263	513
Seychelles	263	513
Kiribati	261	511
Costa Rica	233	483
Cambodia	214	464
El Salvador	141	391
Lao People's Democratic Republic	100	350
Totals, June 30, 1995*	1,462,574	1,507,074

*May differ from the sum of individual figures due to rounding.

Source: World Bank Annual Report 1995.

TABLE 2. Country Eligibility for Borrowing from the World Bank as of June 30, 1995

Countries Eligible for IBRD Funds Only

Income Category and Country	1994 GNP per capita (US$)
Per capita income over $5,055	
Argentina	8,060
Slovenia	7,140
Seychelles	6,210
Antigua and Barbuda	n.a.
Per capita income $2,896–$5,5055	
Uruguay	4,650
Mexico	4,010
Hungary	3,840
Trinidad and Tobago	3,740
Chile	3,560
Gabon	3,550
Malaysia	3,520
Brazil	3,370
Czech Republic	3,210
Mauritius	3,180
South Africa	3,010
St. Kitts and Nevis	n.a.
Per capita income $1,396–$2,895	
Estonia	2,820
Botswana	2,800
Venezuela	2,760
Panama	2,670
Belize	2,550
Croatia	2,530
Poland	2,470
Turkey	2,450
Costa Rica	2,380
Fiji	2,320
Latvia	2,290
Slovak Republic	2,230
Thailand	2,210
Belarus	2,160
Namibia	2,030
Russian Federation	1,910
Peru	1,890
Tunisia	1,800
Algeria	1,690
Colombia	1,620
Paraguay	1,570

TABLE 2. Country Eligibility for Borrowing from the World Bank
as of June 30, 1995 (continued)

Countries Eligible for IBRD Funds Only (continued)

Income Category and Country	1994 GNP per capita (US$)
Per capita income $1,396–$2,895 (continued)	
Ukraine	1,570
El Salvador	1,480
Jamaica	1,420
Iran, Islamic Republic of	n.a.
Lebanon	n.a.
Marshall Islands	n.a.
Micronesia	n.a.
Per capita income $726–$1,395	
Jordan	1,390
Lithuania	1,350
Dominican Republic	1,320
Ecuador	1,310
Romania	1,230
Guatemala	1,190
Bulgaria	1,160
Papua New Guinea	1,160
Morocco	1,150
Kazakhstan	1,110
Philippines	960
Uzbekistan	950
Moldova	870
Suriname	870
Indonesia	790
Swaziland	n.a.
Syrian Arab Republic	n.a.
Turkmenistan	n.a.

Countries Eligible for a Blend of IBRD and IDA Funds

Per capita income $2,896–$5,055	
St. Lucia	n.a.
Per capita income $1,396–$2,895	
Dominica	n.a.
Grenada	n.a.
St Vincent and the Grenadines	n.a.
Dominica	n.a.
Grenada	n.a.
Per capita income $726–$1,395	
Macedonia, FYR of	790

TABLE 2.   Country Eligibility for Borrowing from the World Bank
as of June 30, 1995 (continued)

Countries Eligible for a Blend of IBRD and IDA Funds (continued)

Income Category and Country	1994 GNP per capita (US$)
Per capita income $725 or less	
Egypt	710
Armenia	670
Kyrgyz Republic	610
China	530
Azerbaijan	500
Zimbabwe	490
Pakistan	440
India	310
Nigeria	280
Georgia	n.a.

Countries Eligible for IDA Funds Only

Per capita income $1,396–$2,895	
Tonga	n.a.
Per capita income $726–$1,395	
Vanuatu	1,150
Western Samoa	970
Cape Verde	910
Maldives	900
Bolivia	770
Angola	n.a.
Djibouti	n.a.
Kiribati	n.a.
Solomon Islands	n.a.
Per capita income $725 or less	
Cameroon	680
Congo	640
Sri Lanka	640
Senegal	610
Honduras	580
Guyana	530
Comoros	510
Côte d'Ivoire	510
Guinea	510
Mauritania	480
Equatorial Guinea	430
Ghana	430
Benin	370

TABLE 2. Country Eligibility for Borrowing from the World Bank
as of June 30, 1995 (continued)

Countries Eligible for IDA Funds Only (continued)

Income Category and Country	1994 GNP per capita (US$)
Per capita income $725 or less (continued)	
Central African Republic	370
Albania	360
Gambia, The	360
Tajikistan	350
Zambia	350
Mongolia	340
Nicaragua	330
Lao People's Democratic Republic	320
Togo	320
Burkina Faso	300
Yemen, Republic of	280
Mali	250
São Tomé and Principe	250
Guinea-Bissau	240
Bangladesh	230
Madagascar	230
Niger	230
Haiti	220
Nepal	200
Uganda	200
Chad	190
Vietnam	190
Burundi	150
Sierra Leone	150
Malawi	140
Ethiopia	130
Mozambique	80
Afghanistan	n.a.
Bhutan	n.a.
Cambodia	n.a.
Eritrea	n.a.
Kenya	n.a.
Lesotho	n.a.
Liberia	n.a
Myanmar	n.a.
Rwanda	n.a.
Somalia	n.a.
Sudan	n.a.

TABLE 2.   Country Eligibility for Borrowing from the World Bank
as of June 30, 1995 (continued)

Countries Eligible for IDA Funds Only (continued)

Income Category and Country	1994 GNP per capita (US$)
Per capita income $725 or less (continued)	
Tanzania	n.a.
Zaïre	n.a.

Source: World Bank Annual Report 1995.

n.a. Not available.

Per capita GNP figures are in 1994 U.S. dollars.

The estimate for Tajikistan is preliminary.

Countries are eligible for IDA assistance on the basis of (a) relative poverty and (b) lack of creditworthiness. To receive IDA resources, countries also meet tests of performance. In exceptional circumstances, IDA eligibility is extended on a temporary basis to countries undertaking major adjustment efforts that are not considered creditworthy for IBRD lending. Exceptions have also been made in the case of small island economies.

TABLE 3.   IBRD and IDA Lending, Fiscal Years 1994–95
(amounts in millions of dollars)

Sector	1994			1995		
	IBRD	IDA	Total	IBRD	IDA	Total
Agriculture	2,233.3	1,674.0	3,907.3	1,153.9	1,495.4	2,649.3
Education	1,499.9	658.1	2,158.0	1,280.6	816.2	2,096.8
Energy						
Oil, gas, coal	1,202.1	186.2	1,388.3	520.5	141.6	662.1
Power	1,368.5	—	1,368.5	1,743.5	439.0	2,182.5
Environment	640.5	17.3	657.8	444.1	40.5	484.6
Financial sector	1,093.5	411.1	1,504.6	2,435.4	129.3	2,564.7
Industry	422.7	272.2	694.9	175.0	56.2	231.2
Mining, other extractive	14.0		14.0		24.8	24.8
Multisector	606.3	815.9	1,422.2	2,295.0	870.5	3,165.5
Population, health, nutrition	366.0	519.7	885.7	451.3	711.0	1,162.3
Public sector management	370.6	322.6	693.2	1,411.2	294.4	1,705.6
Social sector	130.0	20.6	150.6	596.5	51.0	647.5
Telecommunications	405.0	18.0	423.0	325.0		325.0

TABLE 3. IBRD and IDA Lending, Fiscal Years 1994–95 (continued)
(amounts in millions of dollars)

Sector	1994			1995		
	IBRD	IDA	Total	IBRD	IDA	Total
Tourism	20.0		20.0			
Transportation	2,162.5	1,130.8	3,293.3	2,026.8	104.1	2,130.9
Urban development	837.0	442.4	1,279.4	1,263.5	186.0	1,449.5
Water supply and sewerage	872.0	103.2	975.2	730.3	309.2	1,039.5
Total	14,243.9	6,592.1	20,836.0	16,852.6	5,669.2	22,521.8

Source: World Bank Annual Report 1995.

Publications Issued by the World Bank

World Bank publications are listed in the bibliographic data file of the National Technical Information Service (NTIS). They are also available on CD-ROM through DIALOG, OCLC, and SilverPlatter. The Bank's *Index of Publications and Guide to Information Products and Services,* issued annually in printed form and on diskette, is also accessible through the Internet. Full information about ordering Bank publications is given in the *Index,* which lists all titles in print as of January 1 each year. Out-of-print titles, in microfiche or paper form, can be obtained from the National Technical Information Service, 5285 Port Royal Road, Springfield, Va 22161. The Bank also issues annually a catalog of its educational/classroom materials, and a guidebook to its most recent economic and social data collections. Videocassettes dealing with the Bank's activities or particular aspects of development are also available.

In 1993, the Bank's Executive Board approved a new information policy that makes certain operational documents, previously restricted to official users, available to the public. Although such documents are not listed in the Bank's *Index of Publications,* a catalog of them is available through the Internet. For more information, apply to the Bank's Public Information Center in Washington, D.C., or to the Bank's offices in London, Paris, and Tokyo.

Reports and Documents

Agreement between the United Nations and the World Bank, 1947.

Articles of Agreement, International Bank for Reconstruction and Development, 1993. Drawn up July 1944; entered into force December 27, 1945, after signature by twenty-nine member governments; amended December 17, 1965, and February 16, 1989. Also in French and Spanish.

By-Laws, as Amended through September 26, 1980, International Bank for Reconstruction and Development, 1991. Also in French and Spanish.

Decisions of the Executive Directors under Article IX of the Articles of Agreement on Questions of Interpretation of the Articles of Agreement, International Bank for Reconstruction and Development, 1991. Also in French and Spanish.

General Conditions Applicable to Loan and Guarantee Agreements dated January 1, 1985, International Bank for Reconstruction and Development, 1992. Also in French and Spanish.

Summary Proceedings of the . . . Annual Meetings of the Board of Governors, 1946 to date. Also in French and Spanish.

World Bank Annual Report, 1974 to date. Continues *Annual Report*/International Bank for Reconstruction and Development, 1945/46–1962/63; *Annual Report*/International Development Association, 1960/61–1962/63; and *World Bank and IDA Annual Report*/World Bank, International Development Association, 1963/64–1973. Also in Arabic, Chinese, French, German, Japanese, Russian, and Spanish.

Books

In some cases, the Oxford University Press, the Johns Hopkins University Press, or other presses or publishers are copublishers of World Bank publications.

Accelerated Development in Sub-Saharan Africa: An Agenda for Action, Elliot Berg, coordinator, 1981.

Adjustment in Africa: Reforms, Results, and the Road Ahead, Oxford University Press, 1994.

Adjustment Lending: An Evaluation of Ten Years of Experience, by World Bank, Country Economics Department, 1988.

Adjustment Lending and Mobilization of Private and Public Resources for Growth, by World Bank, Country Economics Department, 1992.

Adjustment Lending: How It Has Worked, How It Can Be Improved, edited by Vinod Thomas and Ajay Chhibber, 1989.

Adjustment Lending Policies for Sustainable Growth, by World Bank, Country Economics Department, 1990.

Advancing Gender Equality: From Concept to Action, by Anjana Bhushan, 1995.

Agricultural Extension: The Training and Visit System, by Daniel Benor, James Q. Harrison, and Michael Baxter, 1984.

An Agricultural Strategy for Albania: A Report Prepared by a Joint Team from the World Bank and the European Community, 1992.

Agricultural Trade Liberalization: Implications for Developing Countries, edited by Ian Goldin and Odin Knudsen, copublished by the World Bank and the Organisation for Economic Co-operation and Development, 1990.

Agroindustrial Project Analysis: Critical Design Factors, by James E. Austin, Johns Hopkins University Press, 1992. 2d ed.

Aid to African Agriculture: Lessons from Two Decades of Donors' Experience, edited by Uma Lele, Johns Hopkins University Press, 1992.

Albania and the World Bank: Building the Future, 1994.

Alleviation of Poverty under Structural Adjustment, by Lionel Demery and Tony Addison, 1987.

Annotated Glossary of Terms Used in the Economic Analysis of Agricultural Projects, 1994.

The Assault on World Poverty: Problems of Rural Development, Education, and Health, Johns Hopkins University Press, 1975.

Assessing Development Effectiveness: Evaluation in the World Bank and the International Finance Corporation, 1994.

Best Practices in Trade Policy Reform, by Vinod Thomas, John Nash, and associates, Oxford University Press, 1991.

Boom, Crisis, and Adjustment: The Macroeconomic Experience of Developing Countries, by Ian M. D. Little et al., Oxford University Press, 1994.

Brazil and the World Bank: Into the Fifth Decade, 1990.

Case Studies of Project Sustainability: Implications for Policy and Operations from Asian Experience, by Michael Bamberger and Shabbir Cheema, 1990.

Case Studies on Women's Employment and Pay in Latin America, edited by George Psacharopoulos and P. Zafiris Tzannatos, 1992.

China's Industrial Reform, edited by Gene Tidrick and Chen Jiyuan, Oxford University Press, 1987.

China's Rural Industry: Structure, Development, and Reform, edited by William A. Byrd and Lin Qingsong, Oxford University Press, 1990.

Chinese Industrial Firms under Reform, edited by William A. Byrd, Oxford University Press, 1992.

The Conable Years at the World Bank: Major Policy Addresses of Barber B. Conable, 1986–91, by Barber B. Conable, 1991.

Cost-Benefit Analysis: Issues and Methodologies, by Anandarup Ray, Johns Hopkins University Press, 1984.

The Design of Rural Development: Lessons from Africa, by Uma J. Lele, Johns Hopkins University Press, 1979. 3d printing.

Developing Electric Power: Thirty Years of World Bank Experience, by Hugh Collier, Johns Hopkins University Press, 1984.

Developing the Occupied Territories: An Investment in Peace, 1993. 6 vols.

Developing the Private Sector: The World Bank's Experience and Approach, by Enrique Rueda-Sabater and Brian Levy, 1991.

The Development Challenge of the Eighties: A. W. Clausen at the World Bank; Major Policy Addresses, 1981–1986, by A. W. Clausen, 1986.

Development Planning: Lessons of Experience, by Albert Waterston, assisted by C. J. Martin, August T. Schumacher, and Fritz A. Steuber, Johns Hopkins Press, 1969.

Disbursement Handbook, 1993.

Disease and Mortality in Sub-Saharan Africa, edited by Richard J. Feachem and Dean T. Jamison, Oxford University Press, 1991.

Disease Control Priorities in Developing Countries, edited by Dean T. Jamison et al., Oxford University Press, 1993.

Duckweed Aquaculture: A New Aquatic Farming System for Developing Countries, by Paul Skillicorn, William Spira, and William Journey, 1993.

Economic Analysis of Agricultural Projects, by James Price Gittinger, Johns Hopkins University Press, 1982. 2d ed.

Economic Analysis of Projects, by Lyn Squire and Herman G. van der Tak, Johns Hopkins University Press, 1975.

Economic Appraisal of Transport Projects: A Manual with Case Studies, by Hans A. Adler, Johns Hopkins University Press, 1987. Rev. ed.

Economic Development Projects and Their Appraisal: Cases and Principles from the Experience of the World Bank, by John Andrews King, Johns Hopkins Press, 1967.

The Economics of Rural Organization: Theory, Practice, and Policy, edited by Karla Hoff, Avishay Braverman, and Joseph E. Stiglitz, Oxford University Press, 1993.

Education for Development: An Analysis of Investment Choices, by George Psacharopoulos and Maureen Woodhall, Oxford University Press, 1985.

Education in Sub-Saharan Africa: Policies for Adjustment, Revitalization, and Expansion, by Peter R. Moock and Ralph Harbison, A World Bank Policy Study, 1988.

Educational Performance of the Poor: Lessons from Rural Northeast Brazil, by Ralph W. Harbison and Eric A. Hanushek, Oxford University Press, 1992.

Effective Family Planning Programs, 1993.

Energy Efficiency and Conservation in the Developing World: The World Bank's Role, 1993.

Enhancing Women's Participation in Economic Development, A World Bank Policy Paper, 1994.

Environment, Public Health, and Human Ecology: Considerations for Economic Development, by James A. Lee, Johns Hopkins University Press, 1985.

Environmental Economics and Natural Resource Management in Developing Countries, edited by Mohan Munasinghe, 1993.

Environmental, Health, and Human Ecologic Considerations in Economic Development Projects, 1974.

Environmental Management and Economic Development, edited by Gunter Schramm and Jeremy J. Warford, Johns Hopkins University Press, 1989.

Estimating Woody Biomass in Sub-Saharan Africa, edited by Andrew C. Millington et al., 1994.

The Evolving Role of the World Bank: Helping Meet the Challenge of Development, edited by K. Sarwar Lateef, 1995.

Financing Adjustment with Growth in Sub-Saharan Africa, 1986–90, 1986.

First Things First: Meeting Basic Needs in the Developing Countries, by Paul Streeten, Mahbub ul Haq, Norman Hicks, and Frances Stewart, Oxford University Press, 1981.

Forest Economics and Policy Analysis, by William F. Hyde and David H. Newman, 1991.

From the World Bank Journals: Selected Readings, by Douglas F. Barnes et al., 1995.

The Great Ascent: The Rural Poor in South Asia, by Inderjit Singh, Johns Hopkins University Press, 1990.

Health Care in Asia: A Comparative Study of Cost and Financing, by Charles C. Griffin, 1992.

Health of Adults in the Developing World, edited by Richard G. A. Feachem et al., Oxford University Press, 1992.

Implementing the World Bank's Strategy to Reduce Poverty: Progress and Challenges, 1993.

Improving Primary Education in Developing Countries, by Marlaine E. Lockheed, Adriaan M. Verspoor, and associates, Oxford University Press, 1991.

Industrial Adjustment in Sub-Saharan Africa, edited by Gerald M. Meier and William F. Steel with the assistance of Richard J. Carroll, Oxford University Press, 1989.

Institutional Development: Incentives to Performance, by Arturo Israel, Oxford University Press, 1987.

The International Bank for Reconstruction and Development, 1946–1953, Johns Hopkins Press, 1954.

Investing in Development: Lessons of World Bank Experience, by Warren C. Baum and Stokes M. Tolbert, Oxford University Press, 1985.

Labor-Based Construction Programs: A Practical Guide for Planning and Management, by Basil Coukis, Oxford University Press, 1983.

Labor Markets and Social Policy in Central and Eastern Europe: The Transition and Beyond, edited by Nicholas Barr, Oxford University Press, 1994.

Lessons of Tax Reform, 1991.

Listen to the People: Participant-Observer Evaluation of Development Projects, by Lawrence F. Salmen, Oxford University Press, 1987.

The Long-Term Perspective Study of Sub-Saharan Africa: Background Papers, 1990. 4 vols.

Mainstreaming the Environment: The World Bank Group and the Environment Since the Rio Earth Summit. 1995.

Making Adjustment Work for the Poor: A Framework for Policy Reform in Africa, by Tony Addison et al., 1990.

Making Development Sustainable: The World Bank Group and the Environment, Fiscal 1994, 1994.

Malnutrition: What Can Be Done? Lessons from World Bank Experience, by Alan Berg, Johns Hopkins University Press, 1987.

Managing Commodity Price Risk in Developing Countries, edited by Stijn Claessens and Ronald C. Duncan, Johns Hopkins University Press, 1994.

The McNamara Years at the World Bank: Major Policy Addresses of Robert S. McNamara, 1968–81, by Robert S. McNamara, Johns Hopkins University Press, 1981.

New Directions and New Partnerships, by James D. Wolfensohn, 1995.

The Open Economy: Tools for Policymakers in Developing Countries, edited by Rudiger Dornbusch and F. Leslie C. H. Helmers, 1988.

Pioneers in Development, edited by Gerald M. Meier and Dudley Seers, Oxford University Press, 1984.

Population Growth and Policies in Sub-Saharan Africa, 1986.

Poverty, Adjustment, and Growth in Africa, by Ismail Serageldin, 1989.

Poverty Reduction Handbook, 1993.

Private Provision of Public Services in Developing Countries, by Gabriel Roth, Oxford University Press, 1987.

Privatization: Principles and Practice, by David J. Donaldson and Dileep M. Wagle.* 1995.

The Project Cycle, by Warren C. Baum, 1982. Rev. ed.

Public Sector Deficits and Macroeconomic Performance, by William Easterly, Carlos A. Rodriguez, and Klaus Schmidt-Hebbel, Oxford University Press, 1994.

Putting People First: Sociological Variables in Rural Development, edited by Michael M. Cernea, Oxford University Press, 1991. 2d ed.

The Reform of State-Owned Enterprises: Lessons from World Bank Lending, by Mary M. Shirley, 1989.

Resettlement and Development: The Bankwide Review of Projects Involving Involuntary Resettlement, 1986–1993, by World Bank, Environment Department, 1994.

Restructuring Economies in Distress: Policy Reform and the World Bank, edited by Vinod Thomas, Ajay Chhibber, Mansoor Dailami, and Jaime de Melo, Oxford University Press, 1992.

Risk Analysis in Project Appraisal, by Louis Y. Pouliquen, Johns Hopkins Press, 1970.

Sociology, Anthropology, and Development: An Annotated Bibliography of World Bank Publications, 1975–1993, by Michael M. Cernea with the assistance of April Adams, 1994.

Striking a Balance: The Environmental Challenge of Development, 1989.

Sub-Saharan Africa: A Progress Report, 1983.

Sub-Saharan Africa: From Crisis to Sustainable Growth; a Long-Term Perspective Study, 1989.

Telecommunications and Economic Development, by Robert J. Saunders, Jeremy J. Warford, and Bjorn Wellenius, Johns Hopkins University Press, 1994. 2d ed.

Toward Sustained Development in Sub-Saharan Africa: A Joint Program of Action, 1984.

Tribal Peoples and Economic Development: Human Ecologic Considerations, by Robert J. A. Goodland, 1982.

Understanding the Developing Metropolis, by Rakesh Mohan, Oxford University Press, 1994.

Understanding the Social Effects of Policy Reform, edited by Lionel Demery et al., 1993.

Urban Policy and Economic Development: An Agenda for the 1990s, 1991.

Urban Public Finance in Developing Countries, by Roy W. Bahl and Johannes F. Linn, Oxford University Press, 1992.

Venezuela and the World Bank: Preparing for the Future, 1992.

Voting for Reform: Democracy, Political Liberalization, and Economic Adjustment, edited by Stephan Haggard and Steven B. Webb, 1994.

Welfare Consequences of Selling Public Enterprises: An Empirical Analysis, by Ahmed Galal et al., Oxford University Press, 1994.

Wildlands: Their Protection and Management in Economic Development, by George Ledec and Robert Goodland, 1988.

Women in Development: A Progress Report on the World Bank Initiative, 1990.

Women's Education in Developing Countries: Barriers, Benefits, and Policies, edited by Elizabeth M. King and Ann M. Hill, 1993.

The World Bank: A Financial Appraisal, by Eugene H. Rotberg, 1981.

The World Bank: A Global Partnership for Development, 1994. (8 pts. in folder)

The World Bank and Participation, by World Bank Operations Policy Department, 1994.

World Bank Glossary, 1993. Rev. and exp.

World Bank Group Organizational Directory, Apr. 1993.

The World Bank Inspection Panel, by Ibrahim F. I. Shihata, Oxford University Press, 1994.

World Bank Operations: Sectoral Programs and Policies, Johns Hopkins University Press, 1972.

World Bank Participation Sourcebook, 1996.

World Without End: Economics, Environment, and Sustainable Development, by David W. Pearce and Jeremy J. Warford, Oxford University Press, 1993.

Periodicals

The Bank's World, 1981 to date.

Commodity Markets and the Developing Countries: A World Bank Quarterly, 1993 to date.

Evaluation Results, by World Bank, Operations Evaluation Department, annual, 1975 to date. Title varies: *Annual Review of Project Performance Audit Results,* 1978–82; *Annual Review of Project Performance,* 1985; *Project Performance Results,* 1986–87. Also in French.

Finance and Development, quarterly, 1964 to date. Published jointly by the International Monetary Fund and the World Bank. Also in Arabic, Chinese, French, German, Portuguese, and Spanish. Selected articles are listed below:

   "The Allocation of Aid by the World Bank Group," by Andrew M. Kamarck, Vol. 9, No. 3 (Sept. 1972), pp. 22–29.

   "The Bank and Rural Poverty," by Leif E. Christoffersen, Vol. 15, No. 4 (Dec. 1978), pp. 18–22.

   "The Bank and the Development of Small Enterprises," by David L. Gordon, Vol. 16, No. 1 (March 1979), pp. 19–22.

   "The Bank and Urban Poverty," by Edward Jaycox, Vol. 15, No. 3 (Sept. 1978), pp. 10–13.

   "The Bank's Role in Resolving the Debt Crisis," by David R. Bock, Vol. 25, No. 2 (June 1988), pp. 6–8.

   "The Challenge of Development Today," by Ernest Stern, Vol. 20, No. 3 (Sept. 1983), pp. 2–5.

   "The Challenge of Economic Reforms in Eastern Europe," by Willi Wapenhans, Vol. 27, No. 4 (Dec. 1990), pp. 2–5.

"Changing Emphasis of the Bank's Lending Policies," by Mahbub ul Haq, Vol. 15, No. 2 (June 1978), pp. 12–14.

"Cofinancing of Bank and IDA Projects," by E. A. Hornstein, Vol. 14, No. 1 (June 1977), pp. 40–43.

"Community Participation in World Bank Projects," by Samuel Paul, Vol. 24, No. 4 (Dec. 1987), pp. 20–23.

"Development Theory and the Bank's Development Strategy: A Review," by John H. Adler, Vol. 14, No. 4 (Dec. 1977), pp. 31–34.

"Disbursing World Bank Loans," by Norman G. Jones, Vol. 4, No. 1 (March 1967), pp. 51–55.

"The Emerging Role of the Bank in Heavily Indebted Countries," by David R. Bock and Constantine Michalopoulos, Vol. 23, No. 3 (Sept. 1986), pp. 22–25.

"Evaluating the Bank's Development Projects," by Mervyn L. Weiner, Vol. 18, No. 1 (March 1981), pp. 38–40.

"Evolution of the World Bank's Environmental Policy," by Jeremy Warford and Zeinab Parton, Vol. 26, No. 4 (Dec. 1989), pp. 5–8.

"Financial Structure of the World Bank," by Robert W. Cavanaugh, Vol. 2, No. 4 (Dec. 1965), pp. 217–22.

"Financing the Mining Sector: The Bank's Role," by David M. Sassoon, Vol. 12, No. 3 (Sept. 1975), pp. 21–23, 41.

"Health and Development: The Bank's Experience," by Anthony R. Measham, Vol. 23, No. 4 (Dec. 1986), pp. 26–29.

"How the Bank Finances Its Operations," by Hakan Lonaeus, Vol. 25, no. 3 (Sept. 1988), pp. 40–42.

"IMF-World Bank Collaboration," by Hiroyuki Hino, Vol. 23, No. 3 (Sept. 1986), pp. 10–14.

"Impact of the Bank's Rural Development Lending," by Montague Yudelman, Vol. 16, No. 3 (Sept. 1979), pp. 24–28.

"Improving Nutrition: The Bank's Experience," by Alan Berg, Vol. 22, No. 2 (June 1985), pp. 32–35.

"Improving the Bank's Loan Currency Pool," by Barbara Opper, Vol. 26, No. 2 (June 1989), pp. 24–25.

"Improving the Quality of Education in Developing Countries," by Stephen P. Heyneman, Vol.20, No.1 (March 1983), pp. 18–21.

"Integrated Rural Development Projects: The Bank's Experience," by Montague Yudelman, Vol. 14, No. 1 (March 1977), pp. 15–18.

"Investing in Development: Lessons of World Bank Experience," by Warren C. Baum and Stokes M. Talbot, Vol. 22, No. 4 (Dec. 1985), pp. 26–37.

"Involuntary Resettlement and Development," by Michael M. Cernea, Vol. 25, No. 3 (Sept. 1988), pp. 44–46.

"Monitoring the Procurement Process," by David M. Sassoon, Vol. 12, No. 3 (June 1975), pp. 11–13.

"Nongovernmental Organizations and Development," by Vittorio Masoni, Vol. 22, No. 3 (Sept. 1985), pp. 38–41.

"Population and the World Bank," by Sundaram Sankaran, Vol. 10, No. 4 (Dec. 1973), pp. 18–21, 41.

"Procurement Under World Bank Projects," by John A. King, Vol. 12, No. 2 (June 1975), pp. 6–11, 31.

"Programming in the World Bank Group," by John H. Adler, Vol. 8, No. 2 (June 1971), pp. 10–15.

"Project Appraisal," by Hugh B. Ripman, Vol. 1, No. 3 (Dec. 1964), pp. 178–83.

"Project Supervision," by Hugh B. Ripman, Vol. 10, No. 2 (June 1973), pp. 14–18, 34.

"Promoting Agricultural Development," by Dinesh Bahl, Vol. 7, No. 2 (June 1970), pp. 38–43.

"Promoting the Private Sector," by Mary Shirley, Vol. 25, No. 1 (March 1988), pp. 40–43.

"Reorganizing the World Bank," by John A. King, Vol. 11, No. 1 (March 1974), pp. 5–8.

"Structural Adjustment Lending: Early Experience," by Pierre M. Landell-Mills, Vol. 18, No. 4 (Dec. 1981), pp. 17–21.

"The Technical Assistance amd Preinvestment Activities of the World Bank," by Norbert Koenig, Vol. 4, No. 2 (June 1967), pp. 132–42.

"Toward Better Project Implementation," by Arturo Israel, Vol. 15, No. 1 (March 1978), pp. 27–30.

"Training as an Element in Bank Group Projects," by Richard W. Van Wagenen, Vol. 9, No. 3 (Sept. 1972), pp. 34–39.

"What Is a 'World Bank Project?' " by Bernard Chadenet and John A. King, Jr., Vol. 9, No. 3 (Sept. 1972), pp. 2–12.

"The World Bank and Poverty in the 1980s," by David Beckmann, Vol. 23, No. 3 (Sept. 1986), pp. 26–29.

"The World Bank and the United Nations," by Lewis Perinban, Vol. 3, No. 4 (Dec. 1966), pp. 290–96.

"World Bank Bonds in the World's Capital Markets," by Raymond E. Deely, Vol. 3, No. 3 (Sept. 1966), pp. 179–85.

"World Bank Experience with Rural Development," by Julian Blackwood, Vol. 25, No. 4 (Dec. 1988), pp. 12–15.

"World Bank General Capital Increase," by Ernest Stern, Vol.25, No. 2 (June 1988), pp. 20–23.

"World Bank Goals in Project Lending," by Gerald M. Alter, Vol. 15, No. 2 (June 1978), pp. 23–25.

"The World Bank in a Changing Financial Environment," by Thomas Hoopengardner and Ines Garcia-Thoumi, Vol. 21, No. 2 (June 1984), pp. 12–15.

"World Bank Lending for Structural Adjustment," by Constantine Michalopoulos, Vol. 24, No. 2 (June 1987), pp. 7–10.

"World Bank Operations," by Geoffrey M. Wilson, Vol. 1, No. 1 (June 1964), pp. 15–25.

"The World Bank, Project Lending, and Cooperatives," by John A. King, Vol. 9, No. 1 (March 1972), pp. 30–35.

"The World Bank's Currency Swaps," by Christine I. Wallich, Vol. 21, No. 2 (June 1984), pp. 15–19.

"The World Bank's Mission in Eastern Africa," by David Gordon, Vol. 5, No. 1 (March 1968), pp. 37–41.

"The World Bank's Proposals for Supplementary Finance Measures," by Irving S. Friedman, Vol. 5, No. 2 (June 1968), pp. 13–16.

"The World Bank's Technical Assistance," by Francis Lethem and Vincent Riley, Vol. 19, No. 4 (Dec. 1982), pp. 16–21.

Financial Flows and the Developing Countries: A World Bank Quarterly, 1993 to date. Continues *Financial Flows to the Developing Countries,* September 1988–July 1993.

Global Economic Prospects and the Developing Countries, annual, 1991 to date.

Proceedings of the World Bank Annual Conference on Development Economics, 1989 to date. The *Proceedings* are issued as supplements to the *World Bank Economic Review* and the *World Bank Research Observer.* Listed below are the main themes of each conference:

1989: Development policy research; recent developments in the Uruguay Round of Trade Negotiations; saving in developing countries; role of institutions in development; noncompetitive theory of international trade and trade policy; policy response of agriculture.

1990: The transition from adjustment to sustainable growth; development and the environment; population change and economic development; public project appraisal.

1991: Transition in socialist economies; military expenditures and development; urbanization; role of governance in development.

1992: Growth and development theories; labor markets and development; technology; international capital flows.

1993: Financial policy revisited; regulation, including principles, capacity, and constraints; economics of regress; energy sector and the environment.

Transition: The Newsletter about Reforming Economies, monthly July/August combined issue), November 1990 to date. Continues *Socialist Economies in Transition,* April–October 1990.

World Bank and the Environment, annual, 1990 to date. Also in French and Spanish.

World Bank Economic Review, published three times a year (January, May, September), 1986 to date. Following are selected articles:

"Agricultural Incentives in Developing Countries: Measuring the Effect of Sectoral and Economywide Policies," by Anne O. Krueger, Maurice Schiff, and Alberto Valdes, Vol. 2, No. 3 (Sept. 1988), pp. 255–71.

"External Debt, Inflation, and the Public Sector: Toward Fiscal Policy for Sustainable Growth, by Sweder van Wijnbergen, Vol. 3, No. 3 (Sept. 1989), pp. 297–320.

"External Shocks and the Demand for Adjustment Finance," by Ricardo Martin and Marcelo Selowsky, Vol. 2, No. 1 (Jan. 1988), pp. 77–103.

"Food Aid: A Cause of Development Failure or an Instrument for Success?' by T. N. Srinivasan, Vol. 3, no. 1 (Jan. 1989), pp. 39–65.

"How Small Enterprises in Ghana Have Responded to Adjustment," by William F. Steel and Leila M. Webster, Vol. 6, No. 3 (Sept. 1992), pp. 423–38.

"Investment Incentives: New Money, Debt Relief, and the Critical Role of Conditionality in the Debt Crisis," by Stijn Claessens and Ishac Diwan, Vol. 4, No. 1 (Jan. 1990), pp. 21–41.

"Labor Markets and Adjustment in Open Asian Economies: The Republic of Korea and Malaysia," by Dipak Mazumdar, Vol. 7, No. 3 (Sept. 1993), pp. 349–80.

"The Management of the Developing Countries' Debt: Guidelines and Applications to Brazil," by Daniel Cohen, Vol. 2, No. 1 (Jan. 1988), pp. 105–21.

"Measuring Changes in Poverty: A Methodological Case Study of Indonesia During an Adjustment Period," by Martin Ravallion and Monika Huppi, Vol. 5, No. 1 (Jan. 1991), pp. 57–82.

"Measuring the Restrictiveness of Trade Policy," by James E. Anderson and Peter Neary, Vol. 8, No. 2 (May 1994), pp. 151–69.

"Modeling the Macroeconomic Effects of AIDS, with an Application to Tanzania," by John T. Cuddington, Vol. 7, No. 2 (May 1993), pp. 173–89.

"The Political Economy of Economic Liberalization," by Deepak Lal, Vol. 1, No. 2 (Jan. 1987), pp. 273–99.

"Project Evaluation and Uncertainty in Practice: A Statistical Analysis of Rate-of-Return Divergencies of 1,015 World Bank Projects," by Gerhard Pohl and Dubravko Mihaljek, Vol. 6, No. 2 (May 1992), pp. 255–77.

"The Short- and Long-Run Effects of Fiscal Policy," by Edward F. Buffie, Vol. 6, No. 2 (May 1992), pp. 331–51.

"Symposium on Inflation in Socialist Economies in Transition," by Simon Commander, Rudiger Dornbusch et al., Vol. 6, No. 1 (Jan. 1992), pp. 3–90.

"A Symposium Issue on the Analysis of Poverty and Adjustment," by Lyn Squire et al., Vol. 5, No. 2 (May 1991), pp. 177–393.

"A Symposium on Tax Policy in Developing Countries," by Javad Khalil-zadeh-Shirazi, Anwar Shah et al., Vol. 5, No. 3 (Sept. 1991), pp. 459–572.

"Trade Policies and the Highly Indebted Countries," by Sam Laird and Julio Nogues, Vol. 3, No. 2 (May 1989), pp. 241–61.

"A Valuation Model for Developing Country Debt with Endogenous Rescheduling," by Gerard Genotte, Homi J. Karas, and Sayeed Sadeq, Vol. 1, No. 2 (Jan. 1987), pp. 237–71.

World Bank Research Observer, published twice a year (January and July), 1986 to date. Selected articles follow:

"Agricultural Mechanization: A Comparative Historical Perspective," by Hans Binswanger, Vol. 1, No. 1 (Jan. 1986), pp. 27–56.

"AIDS and African Development," by Martha Ainsworth and Mead Over, Vol. 9, No. 2 (July 1994), pp. 203–40.

"A Benefit-Cost Analysis of Nutritional Programs for Anemia Reduction," by Stijn Claessens, Vol. 1, No. 2 (July 1986), pp. 219–45.

"Changes in Poverty and Inequality in Developing Countries," by Gary S. Fields, Vol. 4, No. 2 (July 1989), pp. 167–85.

"Charging for Roads," by David M. Newbery, Vol. 3, No. 2 (July 1988), pp. 119–38.

"The Coordinated Reform of Tariffs and Indirect Taxes," by Pradeep Mitra, Vol. 7, No. 2 (July 1992), pp. 195–218.

"The Debt Crisis: Where Do We Stand After Seven Years?" by Jeffrey Carmichael, Vol. 4, No. 2 (July 1989), pp. 121–42.

"The Earmarking of Government Revenue: A Review of Some World Bank Experience," by William McCleary, Vol. 6, No. 1 (Jan. 1991), pp. 81–104.

"The Economics of Malaria Control," by Jeffrey S. Hammer, Vol. 8, No. 1 (Jan. 1993), pp. 1–22.

"Export-Promoting Trade Strategy: Issues and Evidence," by Jagdish N. Bhagwati, Vol. 3, No. 1 (Jan. 1988), pp. 27–57.

"Issues in Medium-Term Macroeconomic Adjustment," by Stanley Fischer, Vol. 1, No. 2 (July 1986), pp. 157–69.

"Macroeconomic Adjustment in Developing Countries," by W. Max Corden, Vol. 4, No. 1 (Jan. 1989), pp. 51–64.

"Management of Public Industrial Enterprises,' by Mahmood A. Ayub and Sven O. Hegstad, Vol. 2, No. 1 (Jan. 1987), pp. 79–101.

"Options for Dismantling Trade Restrictions in Developing Countries," by Wendy E. Takacs, Vol. 5, No. 1 (Jan. 1990), pp. 25–46.

"Policy Instruments for Pollution Control in Developing Countries," by Gunnar S. Eskeland and Emmanuel Jimenez, Vol. 7, No. 2 (July 1992), pp. 145–69.

"Reform of Trade Policy: Recent Evidence from Theory and Practice," by Vinod Thomas and John Nash, Vol. 6, No. 2 (July 1991), pp. 219–40.

"Shelter Strategies for the Urban Poor in Developing Countries," by Stephen K. Mayo, Stephen Malpezzi, and David J. Cross, Vol. 1, No. 2 (July 1986), pp. 183–203.

"Stabilization Policies in Developing Countries," by Liaquat Ahamed, Vol. 1, No. 1 (Jan. 1986), pp. 79–110.

"The Value-Added Tax and Developing Countries," by Carl Shoup, Vol. 3, No. 2 (July 1988), pp. 139–56.

"What Do We Know about the Political Economy of Economic Policy Reform?" by Stephan Haggard and Steven B. Webb, Vol. 8, No. 2 (July 1993), pp. 143–68.

World Bank Research Program: Abstracts of Current Studies, annual, 1972 to date. Title varies; some years issued as: *Abstracts of Current Studies: The World Bank Research Program.*

World Development Report, 1978 to date. Each issue includes a statistical annex, *World Development Indicators* (q.v.), and deals with particular aspects of development. Currently also issued in Arabic, Chinese, French, German, Japanese, Portuguese, Russian, and Spanish. Listed below are the main themes of each report:

1978: Problems confronting the developing countries, and their relationship to trends in the international economy.

1979: Employment, industrialization, and urbanization in the developing countries.

1980: Adjustment and growth in the 1980s; poverty and human development.

1981: International context of development; country experiences in managing development.

1982: International development trends; agriculture and economic development.

1983: World economic recession and prospects for recovery; management in development.

1984: Recovery or relapse in the world economy; population and development.

1985: Contribution of international capital to development.

1986: Trends in the world economy and prospects for sustained growth; trade and pricing policies in world agriculture.

1987: Barriers to adjustment and growth in the world economy; industrialization and trade.

1988: Opportunities and risks in managing the world economy; public finance in development.

1989: Financial systems and development.

1990: Poverty and ways of relieving it.

1991: Challenge of development, and the lessons of more than forty years of development experience.

1992: Link between development and the environment.

1993: Investing in health.

1994: Infrastructure and development.

1995: Workers in an integrating world.

1996: Transition economies.

Conferences, Seminars and Symposia: Papers and Proceedings

Adjustment Lending Revisited: Policies to Restore Growth, 1992, edited by Vittorio Corbo, Stanley Fischer, and Steven B. Webb.

African External Finance in the 1990s, 1991, edited by Ishrat Husain and John Underwood.

Agricultural Extension by Training and Visit: The Asian Experience, 1983, papers presented at the Asian Regional Workshop on the T & V System of Extension sponsored by the World Bank and the United Nations Development Programme, held at Chiang Mai, Thailand, edited by Michael M. Cernea, John K. Coulter, and John F. A. Russell.

Agricultural Extension in Africa, 1989, edited by Nigel Roberts.

Agricultural Issues in the 1990s, 1991, proceedings of the Bank's eleventh Agriculture Sector Symposium, edited by Lisa Garbus, Anthony J. Pritchard, and Odin Knudsen.

Agricultural Marketing Strategy and Pricing Policy, 1987, edited by Dieter Elz.

The Agricultural Transition in Central and Eastern Europe and the Former U.S.S.R., 1993, edited by Avishay Braverman, Karen M. Brooks, and Csaba Csaki.

Agriculture and Environmental Challenges, 1993, papers presented at the Bank's Thirteenth Agricultural Sector Symposium, edited by Jitendra P. Srivastava and Harold Alderman.

Cities in Conflict: Studies in the Planning and Management of Asian Cities, 1985, edited by John P. Lea and John M. Courtney.

Civil Service Reform in Latin America and the Caribbean: Proceedings of a Conference, 1994, edited by Shahid A. Chaudhry, Gary J. Reid, and Walid H. Malik.

Culture and Development in Africa: Proceedings of an International Conference, 1994, edited by Ismael Serageldin and June Taboroff.

Dealing with the Debt Crisis, 1989, edited by Ishrat Husain and Ishac Diwan.

Developing and Improving Irrigation and Drainage Systems: Selected Papers from World Bank Seminars, 1992, edited by Guy Le Moigne, Shawki Barghouti, and Lisa Garbus.

Developing the Electronics Industry, 1993, edited by Bjorn Wellenius, Arnold Miller, and Carl J. Dahlman.

Development of Rainfed Agriculture under Arid and Semiarid Conditions, 1986, proceedings of the Bank's sixth Agriculture Sector Symposium, edited by Ted J. Davis.

Eastern Europe in Transition: From Recession to Growth? 1993, proceedings of a conference on the macroeconomic aspects of adjustment cosponsored by the International Monetary Fund and the World Bank, edited by Mario I. Blejer et al.

Economic Liberation and Stabilization Policies in Argentina, Chile, and Uruguay: Applications of the Monetary Approach to the Balance of Payments, 1984, edited by Nicolas Ardito Barletta, Mario I. Blejer, and Luis Landau.

Economic Reform in Sub-Saharan Africa, 1992, edited by Ajay Chhibber and Stanley Fischer.

The Economics of Urbanization and Urban Policies in Developing Countries, 1987, edited by George S. Tolley and Vinod Thomas.

Efficiency in Irrigation: The Conjunctive Use of Surface and Groundwater Resources, 1988, edited by Gerald T. O'Mara.

Environmental Accounting for Sustainable Development, 1989, edited by Yusuf J. Ahmad, Salah El Serafy, and Ernst Lutz, a UNEP-World Bank Symposium.

Environmental Assessment and Development, 1994, selected papers from the International Conference on Environmental Assessment, 1992, edited by Robert Goodland and Valerie Edmundson.

Exports of Developing Countries: How Direction Affects Performance, 1987, edited by Oli Havrylyshyn.

Groundwater Irrigation and the Rural Poor: Options for Development in the Gangetic Basin, 1993, edited by Friedrich Kahnert and Gilbert Levine.

Growth-Oriented Adjustment Programs, 1987, papers presented at a symposium held in Washington, D.C., organized jointly by the International Monetary Fund and the World Bank, edited by Vittorio Corbo, Morris Goldstein, and Mohsin Khan.

Horticultural Trade of the Expanded European Community: Implications for Mediterranean Countries, 1986, papers based on symposia held at the World Bank in Washington, D.C., and at the Food and Agriculture Organization in Rome, edited by Malcolm D. Bale.

Increasing Agricultural Productivity, 1982, proceedings of the Bank's third annual Agricultural Sector Symposium, edited by Ted J. Davis.

Innovation in Resource Management, 1989, proceedings of the Bank's ninth Agriculture Sector Symposium, edited by L. Richard Meyers.

International Debt and the Developing Countries, 1985, edited by Gordon Whitford Smith and John T. Cuddington.

Involuntary Resettlement in Africa: Selected Papers from a Conference on Environment and Resettlement Issues in Africa, 1994, edited by Cynthia C. Cook.

Macroeconomic Management in China: Proceedings of a Conference in Dalian, June 1993, 1994, edited by Peter Harrold, E. C. Hwa, and Lou Jiwei.

Managing External Debt in Developing Countries: Proceedings of a Joint Seminar, Jeddah, May 1990, 1992, edited by Thomas Klein.

Managing Fishery Resources: Proceedings of a Symposium Co-Sponsored by the World Bank and Peruvian Ministry of Fisheries Held in Lima, Peru, June 1992, 1994, edited by Eduardo A. Loayza.

Military Expenditure and Economic Development: A Symposium on Research Issues, 1992, edited by Geoffrey Lamb with Valeriana Kallab.

Monetary Policy Instruments for Developing Countries, papers presented at a conference sponsored by the Bank's Country Economics Department, 1991, edited by Gerard Caprio, Jr. and Patrick Honohan.

Multilateral Trade Negotiations and Developing-Country Interests, 1987, papers presented at a conference held in Bangkok, Thailand, under the auspices of the Thailand Development Research Institute and the World Bank, edited by Jagdish N. Bhagwati.

Overcoming Global Hunger: Proceedings of a Conference to Reduce Hunger World-wide, 1994, edited by Ismail Serageldin and Pierre Landell-Mills.

The Planning and Management of Agricultural Research, 1984, papers presented at a seminar sponsored by the Bank's Economic Development Institute and the International Service for National Agricultural Research (ISNAR), edited by Dieter Elz.

Population and Food, 1985, proceedings of the Bank's fifth Agriculture Sector Symposium, edited by Ted J. Davis.

Population Growth and Reproduction in sub-Saharan Africa, 1990, edited by George T. F. Acsadi, Gwendolyn Johnson-Acsadi, and Rodolfo A. Bulatao.

Proceedings of a Conference on Currency Substitution and Currency Boards, 1993, edited by Nissan Liviatan.

Proceedings of the {Bank's} Fourth Agriculture Sector Symposium, 1984, edited by Ted J. Davis.

Promoting Increased Food Production in the 1980s, 1981, proceedings of the Bank's second annual Agricultural Sector Symposium.

Public and Private Roles in Agricultural Development, 1992, proceedings of the Bank's twelfth Agriculture Sector Symposium, edited by Jock R. Anderson and Cornelis de Haan.

Reforming Central and Eastern European Economies: Initial Results and Challenges, 1991, papers presented at a conference held in Pultusk, Poland, organized by the Bank's Macroeconomic Adjustment and Growth Division, edited by Vittorio Corbo, Fabrizio Coricelli, and Jan Bossak.

Regulatory Reform in Transport: Some Recent Experiences, 1993, edited by Jose Carbajo.

Research-Extension-Farmer: A Two-Way Continuum for Agricultural Development, 1985, papers from an international workshop convened by the World Bank and the United Nations Development Programme held in Denpasar, Indonesia, edited by Michael M. Cernea, John K. Coulter, and John F. A. Russell.

Restructuring and Managing the Telecommunications Sector, 1989, papers presented at a seminar held in Kuala Lumpur, Malaysia, edited by Bjorn Wellenius et al.

Risk in Agriculture, 1990, proceedings of the tenth Agriculture Sector Symposium, edited by Dennis Holden, Peter Hazell, and Anthony J. Pritchard.

Social Accounting Matrices: A Basis for Planning, 1985, edited by Graham Pyatt and Jeffrey I. Round.

Tax Policy in Developing Countries, 1991, edited by Javad Khalilzadeh-Shirazi and Anwar Shah.

Toward Improved Accounting for the Environment, 1993, an UNSTAT-World Bank Symposium, edited by Ernst Lutz.

Trade, Aid, and Policy Reform, 1988, proceedings of the Bank's eighth Agriculture Sector Symposium, edited by Colleen Roberts.

Value Added Taxation in Developing Countries, 1990, edited by Malcolm Gillis, Carl S. Shoup, and Gerardo Sicat.

Valuing the Environment: Proceedings of the First Annual International Conference on Environmentally Sustainable Development, 1994, edited by Ismail Serageldin and Andrew Steer.

Water Policy and Water Markets: Selected Papers and Proceedings from the World Bank's Ninth Annual Irrigation and Drainage Seminar, Annapolis, Maryland, December 8–10, 1992, 1994, edited by Guy Le Moigne et al.

World Bank Infrastructure Symposium, 1993, papers presented at a symposium jointly sponsored by the Bank's Transportation, Water, & Urban Development Department, and by the Infrastructure Department of the International Finance Corporation.

Statistical Publications

Commodity Trade and Price Trends, annual, 1966 to date.

Price Prospects for Major Primary Commodities, biennial, 1989 to date.

Quarterly Review of Commodity Prices, 1966 to date.

Social Indicators of Development, annual, 1986 to date.

Trends in Developing Economies, annual, 1989 to date.

World Bank Atlas, annual, 1969 to date.

World Debt Tables: External Finance for Developing Countries, annual, 1973 to date.

World Development Indicators, annual, 1978 to date.

World Population Projections: Estimates and Projections with Related Demographic Statistics, biennial, 1984 to date.

Series

The following section contains a number of series published by the World Bank. In certain cases, where the subjects of individual papers are of particular interest, these papers and their authors are also listed under the series.

Some of the series listed below may include papers issued by individual Bank departments for distribution on a limited basis. For information about the availability of such papers, which are not included in the Bank's *Index of Publications,* application should be made to the originating department in the Bank.

AGREP Division Working Papers

Rural Projects through Urban Eyes: An Interpretation of the World Bank's New-Style Rural Development Projects, by Judith Tendler, 1982. No. 23.

Commodity Working Papers

Comparative Macroeconomic Studies

Macroeconomic Policies, Crises, and Growth in Sri Lanka, 1969–90, by Premachandra Athukorala and Sisira Jayusiya, 1994.
Macroeconomic Policies, Crises, and Long-Term Growth in Indonesia, 1965–90, by Wing Thye Woo, Bruce Glassburner, and Anwar Nasution, 1994.

Country Studies

Angola: An Introductory Economic Review, 1991.
Antigua and Barbuda: Economic Report, 1985.
Argentina: Economic Recovery and Growth, 1988.
Argentina: From Insolvency to Growth, 1993.
Argentina: Provincial Government Finances, 1990.
Argentina: Reallocating Resources for the Improvement of Education, by Bernardo Kugler with Robert W. McMeekin, 1991.
Argentina: Reforms for Price Stability and Growth, 1990.
Argentina: Social Sectors in Crisis, 1988.
Argentina: Tax Policy for Stabilization and Economic Recovery, 1990.
Armenia: The Challenge of Reform in the Agricultural Sector, 1995.
Azerbaijan: From Crisis to Economic Growth, 1993.
The Bahamas: Economic Report, 1986.
Bangladesh: Current Trends and Development Issues, 1979.
Bangladesh: From Stabilization to Growth, 1995.
Bangladesh: Promoting Higher Growth and Human Development, 1987.
Bangladesh: Strategies for Enhancing the Role of Women in Economic Development, 1990.
Bangladesh: Vocational and Technical Education Review, 1990.
Belize: Economic Report, 1984.
Bhutan: Development in a Himalayan Kingdom, 1984.
Bhutan: Development Planning in a Unique Environment, 1989.
Bosnia and Herzegovina: Toward Economic Recovery, 1996.

Brazil: Review of Agricultural Policies, 1982.

Brazil: An Interim Assessment of Rural Development Programs for the Northeast, 1983.

Brazil: Economic Memorandum, 1984.

Brazil: Finance of Primary Education, 1986.

Brazil: Financial Systems Review, 1984.

Brazil: Human Resources Special Report, 1979.

Brazil: Industrial Policies and Manufactured Exports, 1983.

Brazil: Integrated Development of the Northwest Frontier, 1981.

Brazil: The New Challenge of Adult Health, 1990.

Bulgaria: Crisis and Transition to a Market Economy, 1991. 2 vols.

The Caribbean: Export Preferences and Performance, 1988.

Caribbean Countries: Economic Situation, Regional Issues, and Capital Flows, 1988.

Caribbean Region: Access, Quality, and Efficiency in Education, 1993.

Caribbean Region: Current Economic Situation, Regional Issues, and Capital Flows, 1992, 1993.

Chad: Development Potential and Constraints, 1974.

Chile: Subnational Government Finance, 1993.

Chile: The Adult Health Policy Challenge, 1995.

China: Between Plan and Market, 1990.

China: Finance and Investment, 1988.

China: Financial Sector Policies and Institutional Development, 1990.

China: Foreign Trade Reform, 1994.

China: Growth and Development in Gansu Province, 1988.

China: Implementation Options for Urban Housing Reform, 1992.

China: Internal Market Development and Regulation, 1994.

China: Long-term Issues and Options in the Health Transition, 1992.

China: Macroeconomic Stability and Industrial Growth Under Decentralized Socialism, 1990.

China: Macroeconomic Stability in a Decentralized Economy, 1995.

China: Management and Finance of Higher Education, 1986.

China: Options for Reform in the Grain Sector, 1991.

China: Reform and the Role of the Plan in the 1990s, 1992.

China: Revenue Mobilization and Tax Policy, 1990.

China: Strategies for Reducing Poverty in the 1990s, 1992.

China: The Achievement and Challenge of Price Reform, 1993.

China: The Livestock Sector, 1987.

China: Urban Land Management in an Emerging Market, 1993.

The Chinese Economy: Fighting Inflation, Deepening Reforms, 1996.

Colombia: Economic Development and Policy under Changing Conditions, 1984.

Colombia: Industrial Competition and Performance, 1991.

Local Government Capacity in Colombia: Beyond Technical Assistance, 1995.

Poverty in Colombia, 1994.

Review of Colombia's Agriculture and Rural Development Strategy, 1996.

Colombia: Social Programs for the Alleviation of Poverty, 1990.

Colombia: The Investment Banking System and Related Issues in the Financial Sector, by World Bank, Latin America and the Caribbean Regional Office, 1985.

The Comoros: Current Economic Position and Prospects, by World Bank, Eastern Africa Regional Office, 1983.

The Comoros: Problems and Prospects of a Small Island Economy, by World Bank, Eastern Africa Regional Office, 1979.

Cyprus: A Long-Term Development Perspective, 1987.

Czechoslovakia: Transition to a Market Economy, 1991.

Dominica: Priorities and Prospects for Development, 1985.

Dominican Republic: Economic Prospects and Policies to Renew Growth, 1985.

Current Economic Position and Prospects of Ecuador, 1973.

Ecuador: An Agenda for Recovery and Sustained Growth, 1984.

Ecuador: Public Sector Reforms for Growth in the Era of Declining Oil Output, 1991.

Arab Republic of Egypt: An Agricultural Strategy for the 1990s, 1993.

Egypt: Alleviating Poverty during Structural Adjustment, 1990.

Egypt: Economic Management in a Period of Transition, 1980.

Estonia: The Transition to a Market Economy, 1993.

Fiji: A Transition to Manufacturing, 1987.

Gambia: Basic Needs in The Gambia, 1981.

Georgia: A Blueprint for Reforms, 1993.

Ghana: Policies and Program for Adjustment, 1984.

Guatemala: Economic and Social Position and Prospects, 1978.

Guyana: From Economic Recovery to Sustained Growth, 1993.

Guyana: Private Sector Development, 1993.

Guyana: Public Sector Review, 1993.

Haiti: Public Expenditure Review, 1987.

Hungary: Economic Developments and Reforms, 1984.

Hungary: Poverty and Social transfers, 1996.

Hungary: Reform of Social Policy and Expenditures, 1992.

Hungary: Structural Reforms for Sustainable Growth, 1995.

Gender and Poverty in India, 1991.

India: An Industrializing Economy in Transition, 1990.

Economic Development in India: Achievements and Challenges, 1995.

India: Poverty, Employment, and Social Services, 1989.

India: Recent Developments and Medium-Term Issues, 1989.

India: Recent Economic Developments and Prospects, 1995.

Indonesia: Employment and Income Distribution in Indonesia, 1980.

Indonesia: Environment and Development, 1994.

Indonesia: Family Planning Perspectives in the 1990s, 1990.

Indonesia: Health Planning and Budgeting, 1991.

Indonesia: A Strategy for a Sustained Reduction in Poverty, 1990.

Indonesia: Sustainable Development of Forests, Land, and Water, 1990.

Indonesia: Sustaining Development, 1994.

Indonesia: The Transmigration Program in Perspective, 1988.

Indonesia: Wages and Employment, 1985.

Jamaica: Economic Issues for Environmental Management, 1993.

Kazakhstan: The Transition to a Market Economy, 1993.

Kenya: Growth and Structural Change, by World Bank, Eastern Africa Regional Office, 1983.

Kenya: Population and Development, 1980.

Kenya: Re-Investing in Stabilization and Growth through Public Sector Adjustment, 1992.

Kenya: The Role of Women in Economic Development, 1989.

Korea: Development in a Global Context, 1984.

Korea: Managing the Industrial Transition, 1993. 2 vols.

Korea: The Management of External Liabilities, 1988.

Kyrgyzstan: Social Protection in a Reforming Economy, 1993.

Kyrgyzstan: The Transition to a Market Economy, 1993.

Latvia: The Transition to a Market Economy, 1993.

Lesotho: A Development Challenge, 1975.

Lithuania: The Transition to a Market Economy, 1993.

Madagascar: Financial Policies for Diversified Growth, 1993.

Madagascar: Recent Economic Developments and Future Prospects, by World Bank, Eastern Africa Regional Office, 1980.

Malaysia: Matching Risks and Rewards in a Mixed Economy Program, 1989.

The Maldives: An Introductory Economic Report, by World Bank, South Asia Regional Office, 1980.

Mauritius: Expanding Horizons, 1992.

Mauritius: Managing Success, 1989.

Mexico: Manufacturing Sector, by World Bank, Latin America and the Caribbean Regional Office, 1979.

Moldova: Moving to a Market Economy, 1994.

Mongolia: Toward a Market Economy, 1992.

Morocco: Industrial Incentives and Export Promotion, 1984.

Namibia: Poverty Alleviation with Sustainable Growth, 1992.

Nepal: Development Performance and Prospects, by World Bank, South Asia Regional Office, 1979.

Nepal: Policies for Improving Growth and Alleviating Poverty, 1989.

Nepal: Poverty and Incomes; A Joint Study, by World Bank, and United Nations Development Programme, 1991.

Pacific Island Economies: Building a Resilient Economic Base for the Twenty-First Century, 1996.

Pacific Island Economies: Towards Higher Growth in the 1990s, 1991.

Pakistan: Review of the Sixth Five-Year Plan, 1984.

Women in Pakistan: An Economic and Social Strategy, 1989.

Panama: Structural Change and Growth Prospects, 1985.

Papua New Guinea: Policies and Prospects for Sustained and Broad-Based Growth, 1988.

Paraguay: Country Economic Memorandum, 1992.

Peru: Policies to Stop Hyperinflation and Initiate Economic Recovery, 1989.

Philippines: Environment and Natural Resource Management Study, 1989.

Philippines: Framework for Economic Recovery, 1987.

Poland: Decentralization and Reform of the State, 1992.

Poland: Economic Management for a New Era, 1990.

Poland: Health System Reform, 1992.

Poland: Income Support and the Social Safety Net during the Transition, 1993.

Poland: Policies for Growth with Equity, 1994.

Poland: Reform, Adjustment, and Growth, 1987.

Understanding Poverty in Poland, 1995.

Portugal: Agricultural Sector Survey, by World Bank, Europe, Middle East and North Africa Regional Office, 1978.

Romania: Human Resources and the Transition to a Market Economy, 1992.

Romania: The Industrialization of an Agrarian Economy under Socialist Planning, 1979.

Fiscal Management in Russia, 1996.

Russia: The Banking System during Transition, 1993.

Russian Economic Reform: Crossing the Threshold of Structural Change, 1992.

Russian Federation: Toward Medium-Term Viability, 1996.

St. Lucia: Economic Performance and Prospects, 1985.

St. Vincent and the Grenadines: Economic Situation and Selected Development Issues, 1985.

Seychelles: Economic Memorandum, by World Bank, Eastern Africa Regional Office, 1980.

Slovakia: Restructuring for Recovery, 1994.

Sudan: Pricing Policies and Structural Balances, 1985.

Tajikistan, 1994.

Tajikistan: The Transition to a Market Economy, 1994.

Tanzania: Agriculture, 1994.

Tanzania: AIDS Assessment and Planning Study, 1992.

Thailand: Industrial Development Strategy in Thailand, by World Bank, East Asia and Pacific Regional Office, 1980.

Thailand: Managing Public Resources for Structural Adjustment, 1984.

Thailand: Pricing and Marketing Policy for Intensification of Rice Agriculture, 1985.

Thailand: Rural Growth and Employment, 1983.

Thailand: Toward a Development Strategy of Full Participation, 1980.

Trinidad and Tobago: A Program for Policy Reform and Renewed Growth, 1988.

Turkey: A Strategy for Managing Debt, Borrowings, and Transfers under Macroeconomic Adjustment, 1990.

Turkey: Industrialization and Trade Strategy, by World Bank, Europe, Middle East, and North Africa Regional Office, 1982.

Turkey: Informatics and Economic Modernization, 1993.

Turkey: Women in Development, 1993.

Turkmenistan, 1994.

Uganda: Agriculture, 1993.

Uganda: Growing out of Poverty, 1993.

Uganda: Social Sectors, 1993.

Uganda: The Challenge of Growth and Poverty Reduction, 1996.

Ukraine: The Agriculture Sector in Transition, 1994.

Ukraine: The Social Sectors During Transition, 1993.

Uruguay: The Private Sector, 1994.

Uzbekistan: An Agenda for Economic Reform, 1993.

Republic of Yemen: Health Sector Review, 1994.

Yugoslavia: Adjustment Policies and Development Perspectives, 1983.

Yugoslavia: Constraints and Prospects for Restructuring the Energy Sector, 1985.

Zaire: Current Economic Situation and Constraints, by World Bank, Eastern Africa Regional Office, 1980.

Zimbabwe: Financing Health Services, 1992.

Development Essays

Development in Practice Series

Better Health in Africa: Experience and Lessons Learned, 1994.

Enriching Lives: Overcoming Vitamin and Mineral Malnutrition in Developing Countries, 1994.

Governance: The World Bank's Experience, 1994.
Higher Education: The Lessons of Experience, 1994.
A New Agenda for Women's Health and Nutrition, 1994.
Population and Development: Implications for the World Bank, 1994.
Priorities and Strategies for Education: A World Bank Review, 1995.
Private Sector Development in Low-Income Countries, 1995.
Sustaining Rapid Development in East Asia and the Pacific, 1993.

Directions in Development

Investing in Development: The World Bank in Action, 1995.
Private and Public Initiatives: Working Together for Health and Education, by Jacques Van der Gaag, 1995.

Discussion Papers

Country Commitment to Development Projects, by Richard Heaver and Arturo Israel, 1986. No. 4.
Community Participation in Development Projects: The World Bank Experience, by Samuel Paul, 1987. No. 6.
The World Bank's Lending for Adjustment: An Interim Report, by Peter Nicholas, 1988. No. 34.
International Macroeconomic Adjustment, 1987–92: A World Model Approach, by Robert E. King and Helena Tang, 1989. No. 47.
Vocational Education and Training: A Review of World Bank Investment, by John Middleton and Terry Demsky, 1989. No. 51.
Pathways to Change: Improving the Quality of Education in Developing Countries, by Adriaan Verspoor, 1989. No. 53.
Managing Public Expenditure: An Evolving World Bank Perspective, by Robert M. Lacey, 1989. No. 56.
Improving Family Planning, Health, and Nutrition Outreach in India: Experience from Some World Bank-Assisted Programmes, by Richard Heaver, 1989. No. 59.
Public Sector Pay and Employment Reform: A Review of World Bank Experience, by Barbara Nunberg, 1989. No. 68.
How Adjustment Programs Can Help the Poor: The World Bank's Experience, by Helen Ribe et al., 1990. No. 71.
Ecuador's Amazon Region: Development Issues and Options, by Shelton H. Davis et al., 1990. No. 75.
The Greenhouse Effect: Implications for Economic Development, by Erik Arrhenius and Thomas W. Waltz, 1990. No. 78.

Why Educational Policies Can Fail: An Overview of Selected African Experiences, by George Psacharopoulos, 1990. No. 82.

Institutional Reforms in Sector Adjustment Operations: The World Bank's Experience, 1990. No. 92.

Assessment of the Private Sector: A Case Study and its Methodological Implications, by Samuel Paul, 1990. No. 93.

Public Sector Management Issues in Structural Adjustment Lending, by Barbara Nunberg, 1990. No. 99.

Social Security in Latin America: Issues and Options for the World Bank, by William Paul McGreevey, 1990. No. 110.

World Bank Lending for Small and Medium Enterprises: Fifteen Years of Experience, by Leila Webster, 1991. No. 113.

Designing Major Policy Reform: Lessons from the Transport Sector, by Ian Graeme Heggie, 1991. No. 115.

Public Enterprise Reform: Lessons from the Past and Issues for the Future, 1991. No. 119.

Research on Irrigation and Drainage Technologies: Fifteen Years of World Bank Experience, by Raed Safadi and Herve L. Plusquellec, 1991. No. 128.

Letting Girls Learn: Promising Approaches in Primary and Secondary Education, by Barbara Herz et al., 1991. No. 133.

A Strategy for Fisheries Development, by Eduardo Loayza in collaboration with Lucian M. Sprague, 1991. No. 135.

Developing Mongolia, by Shahid Yusuf and Shahid Javed Burki, 1991. No. 145.

The Urban Environment and Population Relocation, by Michael M. Cernea, 1991. No. 152.

Developing Agricultural Extension for Women Farmers, by Katrine A. Saito and Daphne Spurling, 1991. No. 156.

Civil Service Reform and the World Bank, by Barbara Nunberg and John Nellis, 1991. No. 161.

The Building Blocks of Participation: Testing Bottom-up Planning, by Michael M. Cernea, 1991. No. 166.

Common Property Resources: A Missing Dimension of Development Strategies, by N. S. Jodha, 1992. No. 169.

Combatting AIDS and Other Sexually Transmitted Diseases in Africa: A Review of the World Bank's Agenda for Action, by Jean-Louis Lamboray and A. Edward Elmendorf, 1992. No. 181.

Participatory Development and the World Bank: Potential Directions for Change, edited by Bhuvan Bhatnagar and Aubrey C. Williamson, 1992. No. 183.

Telecommunications: World Bank Experience and Strategy, Bjorn Wellenius et al., 1993. No. 192.

Borrower Ownership of Adjustment Programs and the Political Economy of Reform, by John H. Johnson and Sulaiman S. Wasty, 1993. No. 199.

The Contributions of Infrastructure to Economic Development: A Review of Experience and Policy Implications, by Christine Kessides, 1993. No. 213.

Maritime Transport Crisis, by Hans J. Peters, 1993. No. 220.

Toward an Environmental Strategy for Asia, by Carter Brandon and Ramesh Ramankutty, 1993. No. 224.

Agricultural Extension in Africa, by Aruna Bagchee, 1994. No. 231.

Pesticide Policies in Developing Countries: Do They Encourage Excessive Use? by Jumanah Farah, 1994. No. 238.

International Inland Waters: Concepts for a More Active World Bank Role, by Syed Kirmani and Robert Rangeley, 1994. No. 239.

Women in Higher Education: Progress, Constraints, and Promising Initiatives, by K. Subbarao, 1994. No. 244.

Projectizing the Governance Approach to Civil Service Reform: An Institutional Environment Assessment for Preparing a Sectoral Adjustment Loan in The Gambia, by Rogerio F. Pinto with assistance from Angelous J. Mrope, 1994. No. 252.

Violence against Women: The Hidden Health Burden, by Lori Heise, Jacqueline Pitanguy, and Adrienne Germain, 1994. No. 255.

World Bank-Financed Projects with Community Participation: Procurement and Disbursement Issues, by Gita Gopal and Alexandre Marc, 1994. No. 265.

The Evolution of the World Bank's Railway Lending, by Alice Galenson and Lewis S. Thompson, 1994. No. 269.

Small Enterprises Adjusting to Liberalization in Five African Countries, by Ronald L. Parker, Randall Riopelle, and William F. Steel, 1995. No. 271.

Social Action Programs and Social Funds: A Review of Design and Implementation in Sub-Saharan Africa, by Marc Alexandre et al., 1995. No. 274.

Investing in Young Children, by Mary E. Young, 1995. No. 275.

Managing Primary Health Care: Implications of the Health Transition, by Richard Heaver, 1995. No. 276.

Restructuring Banks and Enterprises: Recent Lessons from Transition Countries, by Michael S. Borish, Michel Noel, and Millard Long, 1995. No. 279.

Agriculture, Poverty, and Policy Reform in Sub-Saharan Africa, by Kevin M. Cleaver and W. Graeme Donovan, 1995. No. 280.

The Diffusion of Information Technology: Experience of Industrial Countries and Lessons for Developing Countries, by Nagy Hanna, Ken Guy, and Erik Arnold, 1995. No. 281.

Meeting the Challenge of Chinese Enterprise Reform, by Harry G. Broadman, 1995. No. 283.

Desert Locust Management: A Time for Change, by Steen Joffe, 1995. No. 284.

East Asia's Environment: Principles and Priorities for Action, by Jeffrey S. Hammer and Sudhir Shetty, 1995. No. 287.

Africa's Experience with Structural Adjustment: Proceedings of the Harare Seminar, May 23–24, 1994, edited by Kapil Kapoor, 1995. No. 288.

Rethinking Research on Land Degradation in Developing Countries, by Yvan Biot et al., 1995. No. 289.

Decentralizing Infrastructure: Advantages and Limitations, edited by Antonio Estache, 1995. No. 290.

Regulated Deregulation of the Financial System in Korea, by Ismail Dalla and Deena Khatkhate, 1995. No. 292.

Design Issues in Rural Finance, by Orlando J. Sacay and Bikki K. Randhawa, 1995. No. 293.

Financing Health Services through User Fees and Insurance: Case Studies from Sub-Saharan Africa, edited by R. Paul Shaw and Martha Ainsworth, 1995. No. 294.

Reforming the Energy Sector in Transition Economies: Selected Experience and Lessons, by Dale Grey, 1995. No. 296.

Assessing Sector Institutions: Lessons of Experience from Zambia's Education Sector, by Rogerio F. Pinto and Angelous J. Mrope, 1995. No. 297.

Uganda's AIDS Crisis: Its Implications for Development, by Jill Armstrong, 1995. No. 298.

Review and Outlook for the World Oil Market, by Shane S. Streifel, 1995. No. 301.

Institutional Adjustment and Adjusting to Institutions, by Robert E. Klitgaard, 1995. No. 303.

Putting Institutional Economics to Work: From Participation to Governance, by Robert Picciotto, 1995. No. 304.

Pakistan's Public Agricultural Enterprises: Inefficiencies, Market Distortions, and Proposals for Reform, by Rashid Faruqee, Ridwan Ali, and Yusuf Choudhry, 1995. No. 305.

Grameen Bank: Performance and Sustainability, by Shahidur R. Khandker, Baqui Khalily, and Zahed Khan, 1995. No. 306.

The Uruguay Round and the Developing Economies, edited by Will Martin and L. Alan Winters, 1995. No. 307.

Bank Governance Contracts: Establishing Goals and Accountability in Bank Restructuring, by Richard P. Roulier, 1995. No. 308.

Practical Lessons for Africa from East Asia in Industrial and Trade Policies, by Peter Harrold, Malathi Jayawickrama, and Deepak Bhattasali, 1996. No. 310.

The Impact of the Uruguay Round on Africa, by Peter Harrold, 1995. No. 311.

Harnessing Information for Development: A Proposal for a World Bank Group Strategy, by Eduardo Talero and Philip Gaudette, 1996. No. 313.

Colombia's Pension Reform: Fiscal and Macroeconomic Effects, by Klaus Schmidt-Hebbel, 1995. No. 314.

Sustainability of a Government Targeted Credit Program: Evidence from Bangladesh, by Shahidur R. Khandker, Zahed Khan, and Baqui Khalily, 1995. No. 316.

Selected Social Safety Net Programs in the Philippines: Targeting, Cost-Effectiveness, and Options for Reform, by Khalanidhi Subbarao, Akhter U. Ahmed, and Tesfaye Teklu, 1996. No. 317.

Education Achievements and School Efficiency in Rural Bangladesh, by Shahidur R. Khandker, 1996. No. 319.

Evaluating Public Spending: A Framework for Public Expenditure Reviews, by Sanjay Pradhan, 1996. No. 323.

Discussion Papers. Africa Technical Department Series

Environment Papers

Conservation of West and Central African Rainforests: Selected Papers, edited by Kevin M. Cleaver et al., 1992. No. 1. In English and French.

Sustainable Development Concepts: An Economic Analysis, by John Pezzey, 1992. No. 2.

Environmental Economics and Sustainable Development, by Mohan Munasinghe, 1993. No. 3.

Trees, Land, and Labor, by Peter A. Dewees, 1993. No. 4.

Land Resource Management in Machakos District, Kenya, 1930–1990, by John English, Mary Tiffen, and Michael Mortimore, 1994. No. 5.

Incorporating Environmental Concerns into Power Sector Decision making: A Case Study of Sri Lanka, by Peter Meier and Mohan Munasinghe, 1993. No. 6.

Alternative Policies for the Control of Air Pollution in Poland, by Robin Bates, Janusz Cofala, and Michael Toman, 1994. No. 7.

Economic and Institutional Analyses of Soil Conservation Projects in Central America and the Caribbean, by Ernst Lutz, Stefano Pagiola, and Carlos Reiche, 1993. No. 8.

Poverty, Institutions, and the Environmental-Resource Base, by Partha Dasgupta and Karl-Goran Maler, 1994. No. 9.

Economywide Policies and the Environment: Lessons from Experience, by Mohan Munasinghe and Wilfrido Cruz, 1995. No. 10.

Environmentally Sustainable Development Series:
Occasional Papers
Proceedings
Studies and Monographs

The World Bank's Strategy for Reducing Poverty and Hunger: A Report to the Development Community, by Hans P. Binswanger and Pierre Landell-Mills, 1995. No. 4.

The Evolving Role of the World Bank

The Challenge of Africa, by Ishrat Husain. 1994.

The East Asian Economic Miracle, by Vinod Thomas and Peter Stephens, 1994.

The First Half Century: An Overview, by K. Sarwar Lateef, 1994.

From Reconstruction to Development in Europe and Japan, by Caroline Doggart, 1994.

The Latin American Debt Crisis, by Sebastian Edwards. 1994.

Mobilizing Private Savings for Development: IBRD and the Capital Markets, by Kenneth G. Lay, 1994.

South Asia's Food Crisis: The Case of India, by Uma J. Lele and Balu Bumb, 1994.

The Transition in Central and Eastern Europe and the Former Soviet Union, by Kemal Dervis, Marcelo Selowsky, and Christine Wallich, 1994.

Lessons of East Asia Series
LSMS [Living Standards Measurement Study] Working Papers
MADIA [Managing Agricultural Development in Africa]
Discussion Papers
Operations Evaluation Studies

The Aga Khan Rural Support Program in Pakistan: Second Interim Evaluation, 1990.

Agricultural Marketing: The World Bank's Experience, 1974–85, 1990.

Cotton Development Programs in Burkina Faso, Cote d'Ivoire, and Togo, 1988.

Educational Development in Thailand: The Role of World Bank Lending, 1989.

Forestry: The World Bank's Experience, 1991.

Ghana Country Assistance Review: A Study in Development Effectiveness, by Robert P. Armstrong, 1995.

The Jengka Triangle Projects in Malaysia: Impact Evaluation Report, 1987.
New Lessons from Old Projects: The Workings of Rural Development in Northeast Brazil, 1993.
Population and the World Bank: Implications from Eight Case Studies, 1992.
Renewable Resource Management in Agriculture, 1989.
Rural Development: World Bank Experience, 1965–1986, 1988.
Sri Lanka and the World Bank: A Review of a Relationship, 1987.
Trade Policy Reforms under Adjustment Programs, 1992.
The World Bank and Irrigation, by William I. Jones, 1995.
World Bank Approaches to the Environment in Brazil: A Review of Selected Projects, 1993.
World Bank Support for Industrialization in Korea, India, and Indonesia, 1992.
The World Bank's Role in Human Resource Development in Sub-Saharan Africa: Education, Training, and Technical Assistance, 1994.

Policy Papers

Assistance Strategies to Reduce Poverty, 1991.
Energy Efficiency and Conservation in the Developing World: The World Bank's Role, 1993.
Enhancing Women's Participation in Economic Development, 1994.
The Forest Sector, 1991.
Housing: Enabling Markets to Work, 1993.
Primary Education, by Marlaine E. Lockheed and Deborah Bloch, 1990.
Urban Policy and Economic Development: An Agenda for the 1990s, 1991.
Vocational and Technical Education and Training, 1991.
Water Resources Management, 1994. 2d printing.
The World Bank's Role in the Electric Power Sector: Policies for Effective Institutional, Regulatory, and Financial Reform, 1993.

Policy, Research, and External Affairs Working Papers

Institutional Development Work in the Bank: A Review of 84 Bank Projects, by Cheryl Williamson Gray, Lynn S. Khadiagala, and Richard J. Moore, 1990. No. 437.
World Bank Treatment of the Social Impact of Adjustment Programs, by Helena Ribe and Soniya Carvalho, 1990. No. 521.
The Bretton Woods Agencies and Sub-Saharan Africa in the 1990s: Facing the Tough Questions, by Richard E. Feinberg, 1991. No. 661.

African Financing Needs in the 1990s, by Jorge Culagovski et al., 1991. No. 764.

Policy Research Reports

Policy Research Working Papers

Sources of World Bank Estimates of Current Mortality Rates, by Eduard Bos, My T. Vu, and Patience W. Stephens, 1992. No. 851.

World Bank Adjustment Lending and Economic Performance in Sub-Saharan Africa in the 1980s: A Comparison with Other Low-Income Countries, by Ibrahim Elbadawi, Ghura Dhaneshwar, and Gilbert Uwujaren, 1992. No. 1000.

World Bank Project-Financed Research on Population, Health, and Nutrition, by J. Price Gittinger and Carol Bradford, 1992. No. 1046.

Structural Adjustment, Economic Performance, and Aid Dependency in Tanzania, by Nisha Agrawal et al., 1993. No. 1204.

Kenya: Structural Adjustment in the 1980s, by Gurushri Swami, 1994. No. 1238.

Macroeconomic Reform and Growth in Africa: Adjustment in Africa Revisited, by Lawrence Bouton, Christine Jones, and Miguel Kiguel, 1994. No. 1394.

Restructuring Uganda's Debt: The Commercial Debt Buy-Back Operation, by Kapil Kapoor, 1995. No. 1409.

The World Bank and Legal Technical Assistance: Initial Lessons, by World Bank, Legal Department, 1995. No. 1414.

Policy Studies

Agricultural Mechanization: Issues and Options, by Hans P. Binswanger et al., 1987.

Education in Sub-Saharan Africa: Policies for Adjustment, Revitalization, and Expansion, by Peter R. Moock et al., 1988.

Financing Health Services in Developing Countries: An Agenda for Reform, by John Akin, Nancy Birdsall, and David De Ferranti, 1987.

Population Growth and Policies in Sub-Saharan Africa, 1986.

Poverty and Hunger: Issues and Options for Food Security in Developing Countries, by Shlomo Reutlinger and Jack van Holst Pellekaan, 1986.

Road Deterioration in Developing Countries: Causes and Remedies, by Clell G. Harral et al., 1988.

Urban Transport, 1986.

Poverty and Social Policy Series

Intended to encourage governments in sub-Saharan Africa to include social considerations in plans for structural adjustment, this series includes *Surveys and Statistics, Policy Analysis,* and *Program Design and Implementation.* It replaces a former series, *Social Dimensions of Adjustment in Sub-Saharan Africa Working Papers.*

Regional and Sectoral Studies

Adjustment in Africa: Lessons from Country Case Studies, edited by Ishrat Husain and Rashid Faruqee, 1994.

Administering Targeted Social Programs in Latin America: From Platitudes to Practice, by Margaret E. Grosh, 1994.

Commodity Price Stabilization and Policy Reform: An Approach to the Evaluation of the Brazilian Price Band Proposals, by Avishay Braverman et al., 1992.

Crop-Livestock Interaction in Sub-Saharan Africa, by John McIntire, Daniel Bourzat, and Prabhu Pingali, 1992.

The Determinants of Reproductive Change in Bangladesh: Success in a Challenging Environment, by John Cleland et al., 1994.

Education in Asia: A Comparative Study of Cost and Financing, by Jee-Peng Tan and Alain Mingat, 1992.

The Effects of Protectionism on a Small Country: The Case of Uruguay, edited by Michael Conolly and Jaime de Melo, 1994.

Implementing Reforms in the Telecommunications Sector: Lessons of Experience, by Bjorn Wellenius and Peter A. Stern, 1994.

Including the Poor, by Michael Lipton and Jacques van der Gaag, 1993.

Indigenous People and Poverty in Latin America: An Empirical Analysis, edited by George Psacharopoulos and Harry Anthony Patrinos, 1994.

Rapid Appraisal Methods, by Krishna Kumar, 1993.

Rehabilitating Government: Pay and Employment Reform in Africa, by David L. Lindauer and Barbara Nunberg, 1994.

Russia and the Challenge of Fiscal Federalism, edited by Christine I. Wallich, 1994.

Transition from Socialism in Eastern Europe: Domestic Restructuring and Foreign Trade, edited by Arye L. Hillman and Branko Milanovic, 1992.

Unfair Advantage: Labor Market Discrimination in Developing Countries, edited by Nancy Birdsall and Richard Sabot, 1991.

Women's Employment and Pay in Latin America: Overview and Methodology, edited by Georgem Psacharopoulos and P. Zafiris Tzannatos, 1992.

Staff Working Papers

Social and Cultural Dimensions of Tourism, by Raymond Noronha, 1979. No. 326.

Evaluation of Shelter Programs for the Urban Poor: Principal Findings, by Douglas H. Keare and Scott Parris, 1982. No. 547.

Using Communication Support in Projects: The World Bank's Experience, by Heli E. Perrett, 1982. No. 551.

Adjustment Policies in Developing Countries, 1979–83: An Update, by Bela A. Balassa and F. Desmond McCarthy, 1984. No. 675.

How Should Developing Countries Adjust to External Shocks in the 1980s? An Examination of Some World Bank Macroeconomic Models, by Warren C. Sanderson and Jeffrey G. Williamson, 1985. No. 708.

Structural Adjustment Lending: An Evaluation of Program Design, by Fahrettin Yagci, Steven Kamin, and Vicki Rosenbaum, 1985. No. 735.

Institutional Considerations in Rural Roads Projects, by Cynthia C. Cook et al., 1985. No. 748.

Studies of Economies in Transformation

Food and Agricultural Policy Reforms in the Former USSR: An Agenda for the Transition, by World Bank, Europe and Central Asia Region, Country Department III, 1992. No. 1.

Trade and Payments Arrangements for States of the Former USSR, by Constantine Michalopoulos and David Tarr, 1992. No. 2.

Statistical Handbook: States of the Former USSR, by World Bank, Europe and Central Asia Region, Country Department III, 1992. No. 3.

Income Transfers and the Social Safety Net, by Nicholas Barr, 1992. No. 4.

Foreign Direct Investment in the States of the Former USSR, prepared under the supervision of Keith Crane, 1992. No. 5.

Fiscal Decentralization: Intergovernmental Relations in Russia, by Christine Wallich, 1992. No. 6.

Trade Issues in the New Independent States, by Constantine Michalopoulos, 1993. No. 7.

Statistical Handbook: States of the Former USSR, by World Bank, Europe and Central Asia Region, Country Department III, 1994. No. 8.

Transport Strategies for the Russian Federation, by Jane Holt, 1993. No. 9.

The Role of Women in Rebuilding the Russian Economy, by Monica S. Fong, 1993. No. 10.

Private Service Firms in a Transitional Economy: Findings of a Survey in St. Petersburg, by Martha De Melo and Gur Ofer, 1994. No. 11.

Macroeconomic Consequences of Energy Supply Shocks in Ukraine, by H. Quan Chu and Wafik Grais, 1994. No. 12.

Trade in the New Independent States, by Constantine Michalopoulos and David Tarr, 1994. No. 13.

Russia: Creating Private Enterprises and Efficient Markets, edited by Ira W. Lieberman and John R. Nellis, 1994. No. 15.

Mass Privatization in Central and Eastern Europe and the Former Soviet Union, by Ira W. Lieberman et al., 1995. No. 16.

Investment Policy in Russia, by Philippe H. Le Houerou, 1995. No. 17.

Foreign Trade Statistics in the USSR and Successor States, edited by Misha V. Belkindas and Olga V. Ivanova, 1995. No. 18.

Foreign Trade in the Transition: The International Environment and Domestic Policy, by Barlomiej Kaminski, Zhen Kun Wang, and L. Alan Winters, 1996. No. 20.

Symposium Series

Technical Papers

The African Trypanosomiases: Methods and Concepts of Control and Eradication, edited by C. W. Lee and J. M. Maurice, 1983. No. 2.

Meeting the Needs of the Poor for Water Supply and Waste Disposal, by Frederick L. Golladay, 1983. No. 9.

Managing Elephant Depredation in Agricultural and Forestry Projects, by John Seidensticker, 1984. No. 16.

Industrialization in Sub-Saharan Africa: Strategies and Performance, by William F. Steel and Jonathan W. Evans, 1984. No. 25.

Small Enterprise Development: Economic Issues from African Experience, by John M. Page and William F. Steel, 1984. No. 26.

Recycling from Municipal Refuse: A State-of-the-Art Review, by Sandra Johnson Cointreau et al., 1984. No. 30.

The Management of Cultural Property in World Bank-Assisted Projects: Archaeological, Historical, Religious, and Natural Unique Sites, by Robert Goodland and Maryla Webb, 1987. No. 62.

Desertification Control and Renewable Resource Management in the Sahelian and Sudanian Zones of West Africa, edited by Francois Falloux and Aleki Mukendi, 1987. No. 70.

Water Pollution Control: Guidelines for Project Planning and Financing, by Ralph C. Palange and Alfonso Zavala, 1987. No. 73.

Involuntary Resettlement in Development Projects: Policy Guidelines in World Bank-Financed Projects, by Michael M. Cernea, 1988. No. 80.

Techniques of Privatization of State Enterprises, by Charles Vuylsteke et al., 1988. Nos. 88–90. 3 vols.

Safe Disposal of Hazardous Wastes: The Special Needs and Problems of Developing Countries, edited by Roger Batstone, James E. Smith, and David Wilson, 1989. No. 93. 3 vols.

Improving the Supply of Fertilizers to Developing Countries: A Survey of the World Bank's Experiences, by World Bank, Asia Technical Department, 1989. No. 97.

World Software Industry and Software Engineering: Opportunities and Constraints for Newly Industrialized Economies, by Robert Schware, 1989. No. 104.

Dams and the Environment: Considerations in World Bank Projects, by John A. Dixon, Lee M. Talbot, and Guy Le Moigne, 1989. No. 110.

Helping Women Improve Nutrition in the Developing World: The Zero Sum Game, by Judith S. McGuire and Barry M. Popkin, 1990. No. 114.

Dryland Management: The "Desertification" Problem, by Ridley Nelson, 1990. No. 116.

Lending by the World Bank for Agricultural Research: A Review of the Years 1981 through 1987, by Anthony J. Pritchard, 1990. No. 118.

Flood Control in Bangladesh: A Plan for Action, by World Bank, Asia Energy Technical Department, 1990. No. 119.

Coconut Production: Present Status and Priorities for Research, edited by Alan H. Green, 1991. No. 136.

Environmental Assessment Sourcebook, vols. 1–3, 1991. No. 140.

Rural Roads in Sub-Saharan Africa: Lessons from World Bank Experience, by John D. N. Riverson, Juan Gaviria, and Sydney Ihriscutt, 1991. No. 141.

Fisheries and Aquaculture Research Capabilities in Asia: Studies of India, Thailand, Malaysia, Indonesia, the Philippines, and the ASEAN Region, 1991. No. 147.

Fisheries and Aquaculture Research Capabilities and Needs in Africa: Studies of Kenya, Malawi, Mozambique, Zimbabwe, Mauritania, and Senegal, 1991. No. 149.

Successful Small-Scale Irrigation in the Sahel, by Ellen P. Brown and Robert Nooter, 1992. No. 171.

Water Users' Associations in World Bank-Assisted Irrigation Projects in Pakistan, by Kerry J. Byrnes, 1993. No. 173.

The World Bank's Treatment of Employment and Labor Market Issues, by Arvil A. Adams et al., 1992. No. 177.

Developing and Improving Irrigation and Drainage Systems: Selected Papers from World Bank Seminars, edited by Guy Le Moigne, Shawki Barghouti, and Lisa Garbus, 1992. No. 178.

Balancing Water Demands with Supplies: The Role of Management in a World of Increasing Scarcity, by Kenneth D. Frederick, 1993. No. 189.

Settlement and Development in the River Blindness Control Zone, by Della E. McMillan, Thomas Painter, and Thayer Scudder, 1993. No. 192.

Conserving Biological Diversity: A Strategy for Protected Areas in the Asia-Pacific Region, by Susan Braatz et al., 1992. No. 193.

The Development of Cooperatives and Other Rural Organizations: The Role of the World Bank, by Pekka Hussi et al., 1993. No. 199.

A Strategy to Develop Agriculture in Sub-Saharan Africa and a Focus for the World Bank, by Kevin M. Cleaver, 1993. No. 203.

Participatory Evaluation Tools for Managing Change in Water and Sanitation, by Deepa Narayan, 1993. No. 207.

Integrated Pest Management and Pesticide Regulation in Developing Asia, by Uwe-Carsten Wiebers, 1993. No. 211.

Improving Cash Crops in Africa: Factors Influencing the Productivity of Cotton, Coffee, and Tea Grown by Smallholders, by Stephen J. Carr, 1993. No. 216.

Bibliography of Publications: Technical Department, Africa Region, July 1987 to December 1992, edited by P. C. Mohan, 1993. No. 218.

Alcohol-Related Problems as an Obstacle to the Development of Human Capital: Issues and Policy Options, by James Anthony Cercone, 1993. No. 219.

Strategies for Family Planning Promotion, by Phyllis T. Piotrow et al., 1994. No. 223.

Involuntary Resettlement in Africa: Selected Papers . . . edited by Cynthia C. Cook, 1994. No. 227.

Providing Enterprise Development and Financial Services to Women: A Decade of Bank Experience in Asia, by Lynn Bennett and Mike Goldberg, 1993, No. 236.

International Inland Waters: Concepts for a More Active World Bank Role, by Syed S. Kirmani and Robert Rangeley, 1994. No. 239.

Newly Privatized Russian Enterprises, by Leila M. Webster, 1994. No. 241.

What Makes People Cook with Improved Biomass Stoves? A Comparative International Review of Stove Programs, by Douglas F. Barnes, 1994. No. 242.

External Debt Management: An Introduction, by Thomas M. Klein, 1994. No. 245.

Agricultural Extension: A Step beyond the Next Step, by Charles Ameur, 1994. No. 247.

A Strategy for the Forest Sector in Sub-Saharan Africa, by Narendra P. Sharma et al., 1994. No. 251.

Protected Agriculture: A Global Review, by Merle H. Jensen and Alan J. Malter, 1995. No. 253.

Governance Capacity and Economic Reform in Developing Countries, by Leila L. Frischtak, 1994. No. 254.

Design and Operation of Smallholder Irrigation in South Asia, by Donald Campbell, 1995. No. 256.

Managing the Quality of Health Care in Developing Countries, by Willy De Geyndt, 1995. No. 258.

Provision for Children with Special Educational Needs in the Asia Region, by James Lynch, 1994. No. 261.

Organic and Compost-Based Growing Media for Tree Seedling Nurseries, by Joan H. Miller and Norman Jones, 1994. No. 264.

Rehabilitation of Degraded Forests in Asia, by Ajit Kumar Banerjee, 1995. No. 270.

Health Expenditures in Latin America, by Ramesh Govindaraj, Christopher J. L. Murray, and Gnanaraj Chellaraj, 1995. No. 274.

Management and Financing of Roads: An Agenda for Reform, by Ian Graeme Heggie, 1995. No. 275.

Applying Environmental Economics in Africa, by Frank J. Convery, 1995. No. 277.

Air Quality Management: Considerations for Developing Countries, by Lakdasa Wijetilleke and Suhashini A. R. Karunaratne, 1995. No. 278.

The Case for Solar Energy Investments, by Dennis Anderson and Kulsum Ahmed, 1995. No. 279.

Judicial Reform in Latin America and the Caribbean, edited by Malcolm Rowat, Waleed Haider Malik, and Maria Dakolias, 1995. No. 280.

Cost-Benefit Analysis of the Onchocerciasis Program (OCP), by Aehyung Kim and Bruce Benton, 1995. No. 282.

Clean Coal Technologies for Developing Countries, by E. Stratos Tavoulareas and Jean-Pierre Charpentier, 1995. No. 286.

Cotton Production Prospects for the Next Decade, by Fred E. M. Gillham et al., 1995. No. 287.

Restoring and Protecting the World's Lakes and Reservoirs, by Ariel Dinar, 1995. No. 289.

Creating Capital Markets in Central and Eastern Europe, by Gerhard Pohl, Gregory T. Jedrzejczak, and Robert E. Anderson, 1995. No. 295.

Small-Scale Gasifiers for Heat and Power: A Global Review, by Hubert E. Stassen, 1995. No. 296.

Key Indicators for Family Planning Projects, by Rodolfo A. Bulatao, 1995. No. 297.

Girls and Schools in Sub-Saharan Africa: From Analysis to Action, by Adhiambo Odaga and Ward Heneveld, 1995. No. 298.

Technologies for Rainfed Agriculture in Mediterranean Climates: A Review of World Bank Experiences, by Peter A. Oram and Cornelis de Haan, 1995. No. 300.

Schools Count: World Bank Project Designs and the Quality of Primary Education in Sub-Saharan Africa, by Ward Heneveld and Helen Craig, 1996. No. 303.

Photovoltaic Applications in Rural Areas of the Developing World, by Gerald Foley, 1995. No. 304.

Improving State Enterprise Performance: The Role of Internal and External Incentives, by Russell Muir and Joseph P. Saba, 1995. No. 306.

Energy Use, Air Pollution, and Environmental Policy in Krakow: Can Economic Incentives Really Help? By Seabron Adamson et al., 1995. No. 308.

World Bank Lending for Small Enterprises, 1989–1993, by Leila M. Webster, Randall Riopelle, and Anne-Marie Chidzero, 1996. No. 311.

Project Finance at the World Bank: An Overview of Policies and Instruments, by Philippe Benoit, 1995. No. 312.

Airport Infrastructure: The Emerging Role of the Private Sector, by Anil Kapur, 1995. No. 313.

Urban Management Program Papers
World Bank Country Studies *See* **Country Studies.**
World Bank Development Essays
World Bank Discussion Papers *See* **Discussion Papers.**
World Bank Technical Papers *See* **Technical Papers.**

Pamphlets

Assessing Development Effectiveness: Evaluation in the World Bank and the International Finance Corporation, 1994.

Getting Results: The World Bank's Agenda for Improving Development Effectiveness, 1993.

Governance: The World Bank's Experience, 1994.

Guidelines: Procurement Under IBRD Loans and IDA Credits, 1995. 5th ed.

The World Bank and the Poorest Countries: Support for Development in the 1990s, 1994.

The World Bank Policy on Disclosure of Information, 1994. Also in French and Spanish.

General Bibliography

Acheson, A. L. K., J. F. Chant, and M. F. J. Prachowny, eds. *Bretton Woods Revisited: Evaluations of the International Monetary Fund and the International*

Bank for Reconstruction and Development, University of Toronto Press (Toronto, 1972).

Afshar, Haleh, and Carolyne Dennis, eds. *Women and Adjustment Policies in the Third World,* St. Martin's Press (New York, 1992).

Amerasinghe, C. F. *Principles of the Institutional Law of International Organizations,* Cambridge Studies in International and Comparative Law, Cambridge University Press (Cambridge, 1996).

Anderson, Robert S., and Walter Huber. *The Hour of the Fox: Tropical Forests, the World Bank, and Indigenous People in Central India,* University of Washington Press (Seattle, Washington, 1988).

Ascher, William. "The World Bank and U.S. Control," in *The United States and Multilateral Institutions: Patterns of Changing Instrumentality and Influence,* edited by Margaret P. Karns and Karen A. Mingst, Unwin Hyman (Boston, Massachusetts, 1990), pp. 115–39.

Assetto, Valerie J. *The Soviet Bloc in the IMF and the IBRD,* Westview Press (Boulder, Colorado, 1988).

Ayittey, George B.N. "Why Structural Adjustment Failed in Africa," *Trans-Africa Forum,* Vol. 8, No. 2 (Summer 1991), pp. 43–65.

Ayres, Robert L. *Banking on the Poor: The World Bank and World Poverty,* MIT Press (Cambridge, Massachusetts, 1983).

Babai, Don. "The World Bank and the IMF: Rolling Back the State or Backing its Role?" in *The Promise of Privatization: A Challenge for U.S. Policy,* edited by Raymond Vernon, Council on Foreign Relations (New York, 1988), pp. 254–85.

Bandow, Doug, and Ian Vasquez, eds. *Perpetuating Poverty: The World Bank, the IMF, and the Developing World,* Cato Institute (Washington, D.C., 1994).

Bello, Walden F., with Shea Cunningham, and Bill Rau. *Dark Victory: The United States, Structural Adjustment, and Global Poverty,* Pluto Press (London, 1994).

Bello, Walden F., David Kinley, and Elaine Elinson. *Development Debacle: The World Bank in the Philippines,* Institute for Food and Development Policy (San Francisco, California, 1982).

Bird, Graham. "Changing Partners: Perspectives and Policies of the Bretton Woods Institutions," *Third World Quarterly,* Vol. 15, No. 3 (Sept. 1994), p. 483–502.

———. "Sisters in Economic Development: The Bretton Woods Institutions and the Developing Countries," *Journal of International Development,* Vol. 5, No. 1 (Jan./Feb. 1993), pp. 1–25.

Black, Eugene R. "The World Bank at Work," *Foreign Affairs,* Vol. 30, No. 3 (April 1952), pp. 402–11.

Bleicher, Samuel A. "UN v. IBRD: A Dilemma of Functionalism," *International Organization,* Vol. 24, No. 1 (Winter 1970), pp. 31–47.

Boughton, James M., and K. Sarwar Lateef, eds. *Fifty Years After Bretton Woods: The Future of the IMF and the World Bank; Proceedings of a Conference Held in Madrid, Spain, September 29–30, 1994,* International Monetary Fund; World Bank Group (Washington, D.C., 1995).

Bretton Woods Commission. *Bretton Woods: Looking to the Future; Commission Report, Staff Review, Background Papers* (Washington, D.C., 1994).

Brietzke, Paul. "The World Bank's *Accelerated Development in Sub-Saharan Africa*: A Symposium," *African Studies Review,* Vol. 27, No. 4 (Dec. 1984), pp. 1–60.

Broad, Robin. *Unequal Alliance: The World Bank, the International Monetary Fund, and the Philippines,* University of California Press (Berkeley, California, 1988).

Broches, Aron. "International Legal Aspects of the Operations of the World Bank," *Recueil des Cours de l'Academie de Droit International, Collected Courses of the Hague Academy of International Law,* Vol. 98 (1959), pp. 297–408.

————. *Selected Essays: World Bank, ICSID, and Other Subjects of Public and Private International Law,* M. Nijhoff (Dordrecht; Boston, 1995).

Brown, Bartram Stewart. *The United States and the Politicization of the World Bank: Issues of International Law and Policy,* Publication of the Graduate Institute of International Studies, Geneva; Kegan Paul International (London; New York, 1992).

Brydon, Lynne, and Karen Legge. *Adjusting Society: The World Bank, the IMF, and Ghana,* International Library of African Studies, No.5, Tauris Academic Studies (London; New York, 1996).

Cairncross, Alexander. *The International Bank for Reconstruction and Development,* Essays in International Finance, No. 33, International Finance Section, Department of Economics, Princeton University (Princeton, New Jersey, 1959).

Campbell, Bonnie K., and John Loxley, eds. *Structural Adjustment in Africa,* International Political Economy Series, St. Martin's Press (New York, 1989).

Carreau, Dominique. "Why not Merge the International Monetary Fund with the International Bank for Reconstruction and Development?" *Fordham Law Review,* Vol. 62, No. 7 (May 1994), pp. 1989–2000.

Cavanaugh, John, Daphne Wysham, and Marcos Arruda, eds. *Beyond Bretton Woods: Alternatives to the Global Economic Order,* Pluto Press, with the

Institute for Policy Studies and Transnational Institute (Boulder, Colorado, 1994).

Christin, Ivan. *La Banque Mondiale,* Que sais-je? No. 2330, Presses universitaires de France (Paris, 1995).

Clark, William. "Robert McNamara at the World Bank," *Foreign Affairs,* Vol. 60, No. 1 (Fall 1981), pp. 167–84.

Clough, Paul, and Gavin Williams. "Decoding Berg: The World Bank in Rural Northern Nigeria," in *State, Oil, and Agriculture in Nigeria,* edited by Michael Watts, Institute of International Studies, University of California (Berkeley, California, 1987), pp. 168–201.

Commander, Simon, ed. *Structural Adjustment & Agriculture: Theory & Practice in Africa & Latin America,* Overseas Development Institute (London, 1989).

Commins, Stephen K. *Africa's Development Challenges and the World Bank: Hard Questions, Costly Choices,* L. Rienner (Boulder, Colorado, 1988).

Commission on International Development. *Partners in Development: Report,* Praeger (New York, 1969).

Cornia, Giovanni Andrea, and Gerald K. Helleiner, eds. *From Adjustment to Development in Africa: Conflict, Controversy, Convergence, Consensus?* St. Martin's Press (New York, 1994).

Cornia, Giovanni Andrea, Richard Jolly, and Frances Stewart, eds. *Adjustment with a Human Face,* Oxford University Press (Oxford, England, 1987). 2 vols.

Crane, Barbara B., and Jason L. Finkle. "Organizational Impediments to Development Assistance: The World Bank's Population Program," *World Politics,* Vol. 33, No. 4 (July 1981), pp. 516–53.

Danaher, Kevin, ed. *50 Years is Enough: The Case Against the World Bank and the International Monetary Fund,* South End Press (Boston, Massachusetts, 1994).

De Vries, Barend A. *Remaking the World Bank,* Seven Locks Press (Washington, D.C., 1987).

Dominguez, Kathryn M. "The Role of International Organizations in the Bretton Woods System," in *A Retrospective on the Bretton Woods System: Lessons for International Monetary Reform,* edited by Michael D. Bordo and Barry J. Eichengreen, A National Bureau of Economic Research Project Report, University of Chicago Press (Chicago, 1993), pp. 357–97.

Donaldson, Graham. "Government-Sponsored Rural Development: The Experience of the World Bank," in *Agriculture and the State: Growth, Employment, and Poverty in Developing Countries,* edited by C. Peter Timmer, Cornell University Press (Ithaca, New York, 1991), pp. 156–90.

Drischler, Alvin Paul, and Munir P. Benjenk, eds. *U.S. Policy toward the Bretton Woods Institutions,* Foreign Policy Institute, School of Advanced International Studies, Johns Hopkins University (Washington, D.C., 1988).

Duncan, Alex, and John Howell, eds. *Structural Adjustment and the African Farmer,* Overseas Development Institute, in association with J. Currey; Heinemann (London; Portsmouth, New Hampshire, 1992).

Fatouros, A. A. "The World Bank's Impact on International Law: A Case Study in the International Law of Cooperation," in *Jus et Societas: Essays in Tribute to Wolfgang Friedmann,* Gabriel M. Wilner, principal editor, Nijhoff (The Hague, 1979), pp. 62–95.

Feder, Ernst. "The World Bank and the Expansion of Industrial Monopoly Capital into Underdeveloped Agriculture," *Journal of Contemporary Asia,* Vol. 12, No. 1 (1982), pp. 34–60.

Feinberg, Richard E. "The Changing Relationship between the World Bank and the International Monetary Fund," *International Organization,* Vol. 42, No. 3 (Summer 1988), pp. 545–60.

Fischer, Stanley. "The IMF and the World Bank at Fifty," in *The International Monetary System: Its Institutions and its Future,* edited by Hans Genberg, Springer (Berlin, 1995), pp. 171–200.

Fried, Edward R., and Henry D. Owen, eds. *The Future Role of the World Bank: Addresses by Robert S. McNamara, George P. Shultz, Edward R. Fried, R.T. McNamar, David Rockefeller, Manfred Lahnstein, A.W. Clausen; Presented at a Conference at the Brookings Institution on January 7, 1982,* Brookings Institution (Washington, D.C., 1982).

Gardner, Richard N. *Sterling-Dollar Diplomacy: The Origins and Prospects of our International Economic Order,* Columbia University Press (New York, 1975). Rev. ed. (repr. 1980).

George, Susan. *A Fate Worse than Debt,* Penguin Books (London, 1988).

George, Susan, and Fabrizio Sabelli. *Faith and Credit: The World Bank's Secular Empire,* Westview Press (Boulder, Colorado, 1994).

Gibbon, Peter. "The World Bank and African Poverty, 1973–91," *Journal of Modern African Studies,* Vol. 30 (June 1992), pp. 193–220.

Gibbon, Peter, et al. *A Blighted Harvest: The World Bank and African Agriculture,* Africa World Press (Trenton, New Jersey, 1993).

Gold, Joseph. "The Relationship Between the International Monetary Fund and the World Bank," *Creighton Law Review,* Vol. 15, No. 2 (1980/81), pp. 499–521.

Gold, Sonia S. "Shifting Emphasis on Macro- and Micro-Levels in Development Planning: The IBRD Experience 1946–1973," *Journal of Developing Areas,* Vol. 11, No. 1 (Oct. 1976), pp. 13–38.

Group of Twenty-Four. *International Monetary and Financial Issues for the 1990s: Research Papers for the Group of Twenty-Four,* United Nations (New York, 1992–94). 4 vols.

Guessan, Tchetche. "The Socioeconomic Impact of the World Bank and the African Development Bank on African Countries: The Case of the Ivory Coast," in *Brazil and the Ivory Coast: The Impact of International Lending, Investment, and Aid,* edited by Werner Baer and John F. Due, JAI Press (Greenwich, Connecticut, 1987), pp. 57–89.

Gwin, Catherine. *U.S. Relations with the World Bank, 1945–1992,* Brookings Occasional Papers, Brookings Institution (Washington, D.C., 1994).

Haggard, Stephan, and Robert R. Kaufman, eds. *The Politics of Economic Adjustment: International Constraints, Distributive Conflicts, and the State,* Princeton University Press (Princeton, New Jersey, 1992).

Haq, Mahbub ul, Richard Jolly, and Khadija Haq, eds. *The UN and the Bretton Woods Institutions: New Challenges for the Twenty-First Century,* St. Martin's Press (New York, 1995).

Havnevik, Kjell J., ed. *The IMF and the World Bank in Africa: Conditionality, Impact, and Alternatives,* Scandinavian Institute of African Studies (Uppsala, Sweden, 1987).

Helleiner, Gerald K., ed. *The International Monetary and Financial System: Developing Country Perspectives,* St. Martin's Press (New York, 1996).

Hirschman, Albert O. *Development Projects Observed,* Brookings Institution (Washington, D.C., 1967).

Hürni, Bettina S. *The Lending Policy of the World Bank in the 1970s: Analysis and Evaluation,* Westview Press (Boulder, Colorado, 1980).

Humphreys, Norman K. *Historical Dictionary of the International Monetary Fund,* Scarecrow Press (Metuchen, N.J.; London, 1993).

Hutchful, Eboe. "Adjustment in Africa and Fifty Years of the Bretton Woods Institutions: Change or Consolidation?" *Canadian Journal of Development Studies,* Vol. 16, No. 3 (1995), pp. 391–417.

Independent Commission on International Development Issues. *The Brandt Commission Papers: Selected Background Papers,* Independent Bureau for International Development Issues (Geneva, 1981).

———. *Common Crisis North-South: Cooperation for World Recovery,* MIT Press (Cambridge, Massachusetts, 1983).

————. *North-South: A Programme for Survival,* MIT Press (Cambridge, Massachusetts, 1980).

Jacobson, Harold Karan, and Michel Oksenberg. *China's Participation in the IMF, the World Bank, and GATT: Toward a Global Economic Order,* University of Michigan Press (Ann Arbor, Michigan, 1991).

Jones, Philip W. *World Bank Financing of Education: Lending, Learning, and Development,* Routledge (London; New York, 1992).

Kardam, Nüket. *Bringing Women in: Women's Issues in International Development Programs,* L. Rienner (Boulder, Colorado, 1991).

————. "Development Approaches and the Role of Policy Advocacy: The Case of the World Bank," *World Development,* Vol. 21, No. 11 (Nov. 1993), pp. 1773–86.

Kenen, Peter B., ed. *Managing the World Economy: Fifty Years After Bretton Woods,* Institute for International Economics (Washington, D.C., 1994).

Keynes, John Maynard. *The Collected Writings of John Maynard Keynes,* Vols. 25–26, Macmillan, St. Martin's Press, for the Royal Economic Society (London; New York, 1977–79).

Kindleberger, Charles P. "Bretton Woods Reappraised," *International Organization,* Vol. 5, No. 1 (Feb. 1951), pp. 32–47.

Kirshner, Orin, ed. *The Bretton Woods-GATT System: Retrospect and Prospect After Fifty Years,* M.E. Sharpe (Armonk, New York, 1995).

Kremmydas, Nicholas. "The Cross-Conditionality Phenomenon: Some Legal Aspects," *International Lawyer,* Vol. 23, No. 3 (Fall 1989), pp. 651–75.

Lawrence, Peter R., ed. *World Recession and the Food Crisis in Africa,* J. Currey for the *Review of African Political Economy* (London, 1986).

Le Prestre, Philippe G. *The World Bank and the Environmental Challenge,* Susquehanna University Press (Selinsgrove, Pennsylvania, 1989).

Lewis, John P., and Ishan Kapur, eds. *The World Bank Group, Multilateral Aid, and the 1970s,* Lexington Books (Lexington, Massachusetts, 1973).

Lewis, John P., and Richard Webb with Devesh Kapur. *History of the World Bank as a Development-Promoting Institution,* Brookings Institution (Washington, D.C., Forthcoming). 2 vols.

Lipton, Michael, and John Toye. *Does Aid Work in India?* Routledge (New York, London, 1990).

Lipton, Michael, and Robert Paarlberg. *The Role of the World Bank in Agricultural Development in the 1990s,* International Food Policy Research Institute (Washington, D.C., 1990).

Loxley, John, ed. *Debt and Disorder: External Financing for Development,* Westview Press (Boulder, Colorado, 1986).

Martens, Todd K. "Ending Tropical Deforestation: What is the Proper Role for the World Bank?" *Harvard International Law Review,* Vol. 13, No. 2 (1991), pp. 485–515.

Mason, Edward Sagendorph, and Robert E. Ascher. *The World Bank Since Bretton Woods: The Origins, Policies, Operations, and Impact of the International Bank for Reconstruction and Development and the Other Members of the World Bank Group: The International Finance Corporation, the International Development Association, the International Centre for Settlement of Investment Disputes,* Brookings Institution (Washington, D.C., 1973).

McCloy, John J. "The Lesson of the World Bank," *Foreign Affairs,* Vol. 27, No. 4 (July 1949), pp. 551–60.

McNamara, Robert S. *One Hundred Countries, Two Billion People: The Dimensions of Development,* Praeger (New York, 1973).

Michalopoulos, Constantine. *Financing Needs of Developing Countries: Proposals for International Action,* Essays in International Finance, No. 110, International Finance Section, Department of Economics, Princeton University (Princeton, New Jersey, 1975).

Mikesell, Raymond F. *The Bretton Woods Debates: A Memoir,* Essays in International Finance, No. 192, International Finance Section, Department of Economics, Princeton University (Princeton, New Jersey, 1994).

Miller, Morris. *Coping Is Not Enough: The International Debt Crisis and the Roles of the World Bank and International Monetary Fund,* Dow-Jones Irwin (Homewood, Illinois, 1989).

Moore, Frederick T. "The World Bank and its Economic Missions," *Review of Economics and Statistics,* Vol. 42, No. 1 (Feb. 1960), pp. 81–93.

Morris, James. *The Road to Huddersfield: A Journey to Five Continents,* Pantheon Books (New York, 1963).

Morse, Bradford W., and Thomas Berger. *Sardar Sarovar: Report of the Independent Review,* Resource Futures International (Ottawa, 1992).

Morss, Elliott R., and David D. Gow. *Implementing Rural Development Projects: Lessons from AID and World Bank Experience,* Westview Press (Boulder, Colorado, 1985).

Mosley, Paul. *Conditionality as Bargaining Process: Structural-Adjustment Lending, 1980–86,* Essays in International Finance, No. 168, International Finance Section, Dept. of Economics, Princeton University (Princeton, New Jersey, 1986).

———. "Privatisation, Policy-Based Lending, and World Bank Behaviour," in *Privatisation in Less Developed Countries,* ed. by Paul Cook and Colin Kirkpatrick, Wheatsheaf Press (Brighton, England, 1988), pp. 125–40.

Mosley, Paul, Jane Harrigan, and John F.J.Toye. *Aid and Power: The World Bank and Policy-Based Lending,* Routledge (London, 1991). 2 vols. 2d ed. Routledge (New York, 1995–   ).

Mullen, Joseph, ed. *Rural Poverty Alleviation: International Development Perspectives,* Avebury (Aldershot, 1995).

Nafziger, E. Wayne. *The Debt Crisis in Africa,* Johns Hopkins University Press (Baltimore, Maryland, 1993).

Nelson, Paul J. *The World Bank and Non-Governmental Organizations: The Limits of Apolitical Development,* St. Martin's Press (New York, 1995).

Oliver, Robert Warner. *Early Plans for a World Bank,* Essays in International Finance, No. 29, International Finance Section, Department of Economics, Princeton University (Princeton, New Jersey, 1971).

———. *George Woods and the World Bank,* L. Rienner (Boulder, Colorado, 1995).

———. *International Economic Co-Operation and the World Bank,* Macmillan (London, 1975).

Onimode, Bade. *The IMF, the World Bank, and the African Debt,* Zed Books (London, 1989). 2 vols.

Paarlberg, Robert, and Michael Lipton. "Changing Missions at the World Bank," *World Policy Journal,* Vol. 8, No. 3 (Summer 1991), pp. 475–98.

Parfitt, Trevor W., and Stephen P. Riley. *The African Debt Crisis,* Routledge (London; New York, 1989).

Payer, Cheryl. *The World Bank: A Critical Analysis,* Monthly Review Press (New York, 1982).

———. "The World Bank and the Small Farmer," *Monthly Review,* Vol. 32, No. 6 (Nov. 1980), pp. 30–46.

Please, Stanley. *The Hobbled Giant: Essays on the World Bank,* Westview Press (Boulder, Colorado, 1984).

———. "The World Bank: Lending for Structural Adjustment," in *Adjustment Crisis in the Third World,* edited by Richard E. Feinberg and Valeriana Kallab, Transaction Books (New Brunswick, New Jersey, 1984), pp. 83–98.

Price, David. *Before the Bulldozer: The Nambiquara Indians and the World Bank,* Seven Locks Press (Cabin John, Maryland, 1989).

Ravenhill, John, ed. *Africa in Economic Crisis,* International Political Economy Series, Macmillan (Basingstoke, England, 1986).

Rees, David. *Harry Dexter White: A Study in Paradox,* Coward, McCann & Geoghegan (New York, 1973).

Rees, David, ed. *Structural Adjustment and the Environment,* Westview Press (Boulder, Colorado, 1992).

Reid, Escott. *Strengthening the World Bank,* Adlai Stevenson Institute (Chicago, Illinois, 1973).

Rich, Bruce. "The Emperor's New Clothes: The World Bank and Environmental Reform," *World Policy Journal,* Vol. 7, No. 1 (Spring 1990), pp. 305–29.

———. *Mortgaging the Earth: The World Bank, Environmental Impoverishment, and the Crisis of Development,* Beacon Press (Boston, Massachusetts, 1990).

Richardson, Richard W., and Jonas H. Haralz. *Moving to the Market: The World Bank in Transition,* Policy Essay, No. 17, Overseas Development Council (Washington, D.C., 1995).

Rodriguez, Ennio, and Stephany Griffith-Jones, eds. *Cross-Conditionality, Banking Regulation and Third World Debt,* Macmillan (Basingstoke, England, 1992).

Rotberg, Eugene H. "The Financial Operations of the World Bank," in *Bretton Woods: Looking to the Future,* Bretton Woods Commission (Washington, D.C, 1984), pp. C.185–214.

Sachs, Jeffrey D. "Conditionality, Debt Relief, and the Developing Country Debt Crisis," in *Developing Country Debt and Economic Performance, Vol. 1: The International Financial System,* edited by Jeffrey D. Sachs, University of Chicago Press (Chicago, Illinois, 1989), pp. 255–95.

Salda, Anne C.M. *World Bank,* International Organizations Series, vol. 4, Clio Press (Oxford, England, 1994).

Shapley, Deborah. *Promise and Power: The Life and Times of Robert McNamara,* Little, Brown (Boston, Massachusetts, 1993).

Shihata, Ibrahim F.I. *Legal Treatment of Foreign Investment: "The World Bank Guidelines,"* M. Nijhoff (Dordrecht; Boston, 1993).

———. *The World Bank in a Changing World: Selected Essays,* ed. by Franziska Tschofen and Antonio R. Parra, M. Nijhoff (Dordrecht; Boston, 1991–95). 2 vols.

Stein, Howard. "Deindustrialization, Adjustment, the World Bank and the IMF in Africa," *World Development,* Vol. 20, No. 1 (Jan. 1992), pp. 83–95.

Stern, Ernest. "World Bank Financing of Structural Adjustment," in *IMF Conditionality,* edited by John Williamson, Institute for International Economics (Washington, D.C., 1983), pp. 87–107.

Stewart, Frances, ed. *Adjustment and Poverty: Options and Choices,* Routledge (London, New York, 1995).

Ugalde, Antonio, and Jeffrey T. Jackson. "The World Bank and International Health Policy: A Critical Review," *Journal of International Development,* Vol. 7, No.3 (May/June 1995), pp. 525–41.

United Nations Monetary and Financial Conference, Bretton Woods, New Hampshire, 1944. *Proceedings and Documents,* International Organization and Conference Series; Department of State Publication, 2866 (Washington, D.C., 1944).

U.S. Congress. House. Committee on Banking and Currency. *Bretton Woods Agreements Act: Hearings . . . March 7–May 11, 1945,* Government Printing Office (Washington, D.C., 1945). 2 vols.

————. *International Bank for Reconstruction and Development: Hearing . . . May 23, 1949,* Government Printing Office (Washington, D.C., 1949).

U.S. Congress. House. Committee on Banking and Financial Services. Subcommittee on Domestic and International Monetary Policy. *The World Bank: Hearing . . . March 27, 1995,* Government Printing Office (Washington, D.C., 1995).

U.S. Congress. House. Committee on Banking, Finance, and Urban Affairs. *General Capital Increase for the World Bank: Hearing . . . June 15, 1988,* Government Printing Office (Washington, D.C., 1988).

U.S. Congress. House. Committee on Banking, Finance, and Urban Affairs. Subcommittee on International Institutions and Finance. *Increasing IMF-World Bank Cooperation: Joint Hearing before the Subcommittee on International Development Institutions and Finance and the Subcommittee on International Finance, Trade, and Monetary Policy . . . July 25, 1985,* Government Printing Office (Washington, D.C., 1985).

————. *A Mandate for Development: The Future of the World Bank; Hearing . . . September 5, 1985,* Government Printing Office (Washington, D.C., 1985).

————. *The Proposed General Capital Increase for the World Bank: Hearing . . . May 4, 11, 18, and 24, 1988,* Government Printing Office (Washington, D.C.).

U.S. Congress. House. Committee on Banking, Finance, and Urban Affairs. Subcommittee on International Development, Finance, Trade, and Monetary Policy. *World Bank Lending to the People's Republic of China: Hearing . . . May 8, 1990,* Government Printing Office (Washington, D.C., 1990).

U.S. Congress. House. Committee on Science, Space, and Technology. *Sardar Sarovar Dam Project: Hearing before the Subcommittee on Natural Resources, Agriculture Research, and Environment . . . October 24, 1989,* Government Printing Office (Washington, D.C., 1990).

U.S. Congress. Senate. Committee on Banking and Currency. *Bretton Woods Agreements Act: Hearings . . . June 12–28, 1945,* Government Printing Office (Washington, D.C., 1945).

U.S. Congress. Senate. Committee on Banking, Housing, and Urban Affairs. *Impact of IMF/World Bank Policies Toward Russia and the Russian Economy: Hearing . . . February 8, 1994*, Government Printing Office (Washington, D.C., 1994).

Van de Laar, Aart J.M. "The World Bank and the World's Poor," *World Development*, Vol. 4, Nos. 10/11 (Oct./Nov. 1976), pp. 837–51.

Wallich, Christine I. "What's Right and Wrong with World Bank Involvement in Eastern Europe," *Journal of Comparative Economics*, Vol. 20, No. 1 (Feb. 1995), pp. 57–94.

Walrafen, Thierry, ed. *Bretton Woods: Mélange pour un Cinquantenaire*, Association d'Economie financière (Paris, 1994).

Walters, Alan Arthur. *Do we Need the IMF and the World Bank?* Institute of Economic Affairs (London, 1994).

Weiss, Charles, and Nicolas Jequier, eds. *Technology, Finance, and Development: An Analysis of the World Bank as a Technological Institution*, Lexington Books (Lexington, Massachusetts, 1984).

Wilson, Carol R. *The World Bank Group: A Guide to Information Services*, Garland (New York, 1991).

"The World According to Wolfensohn," *Euromoney*, No. 317 (Sept. 1995), pp. 45–59.

World Bank Affiliates (World Bank Group) and Associated Institutions
Consultative Group on International Agricultural Research (CGIAR)

CGIAR Priorities and Future Strategies, by Consultative Group on International Agricultural Research, Technical Advisory Committee, Food and Agriculture Organization of the United Nations (Rome, 1987).

International Agricultural Research Gears Up for the 21st Century: The CGIAR Enters its Third Decade, by Donald L. Plucknett, 1993.

Partners Against Hunger: The Consultative Group on International Agricultural Research, by Warren C. Baum, with Michael L. LeJeune, 1986.

Science and Food: The CGIAR and its Partners, by Jock R. Anderson, Robert W. Herdt, and Grant McDonald Scobie, 1988.

CGIAR Annual Report, 1984 to date.

CGIAR Study Papers

The International Agricultural Research Centers: Their Impact on Spending for National Agricultural Research and Extension, by Robert E. Evenson, 1987. No. 22.

Governance and Management of the CGIAR Centers, by Selcuk Ozgediz, 1991. No. 27.

"The CGIAR: Investing in Agricultural Research [Special Section]" *Finance and Development,* Vol.29, No.1 (March 1992), pp. 25–37.

Development Committee

(Joint Ministerial Committee of the Boards of Governors of the World Bank and the International Monetary Fund on the Transfer of Real Resources to Developing Countries)

Development Committee Series

The Development Committee: Its First Ten Years, 1974–1984, 1984. No. 1.

Current Development Issues: Reports by the President of the World Bank to the Development Committee . . . , 1984. No. 2.

Linkages Between Trade and the Promotion of Development, 1985. No. 3.

Resources for Development, 1985. No. 4.

Developing Countries: Medium-Term Prospects, 1985. No. 5.

Trade and Development, 1985. No. 6.

Report of the Task Force on Concessional Flows, 1985. No. 7.

Aid for Development: The Key Issues . . . , 1986. No. 8.

Status Report on Concessional Flows, 1986. No. 9.

A Strategy for Restoration of Growth in Middle-Income Countries that Face Debt-Servicing Difficulties, 1986. No. 10.

Opening Statements to the Meetings of the Development Committee by Ghulam Ishaq Khan, Chairman . . . , 1987. No. 11.

Annual Report of the Development Committee, July 1985-June 1986, 1987. No. 12.

Protecting the Poor During Periods of Adjustment, 1987. No. 13.

Environment, Growth, and Development, 1987. No. 14.

Market Prospects of Raw Materials, 1987. No. 15.

Proposals for Enhancing Assistance to Low-Income Countries that Face Exceptional Difficulties, 1988. No. 16.

Environment and Development: Implementing the World Bank's New Policies, 1988. No. 17.

The Adequacy of Resource Flows to Developing Countries, 1988. No. 18.

Strengthening Efforts to Reduce Poverty, 1989. No. 19.

The Impact of the Industrial Policy of Developed Countries on Developing Countries, 1989. No. 20.

Progress of Initiatives to Benefit Sub-Saharan Africa, 1990. No. 21.
World Bank Support for the Environment: A Progress Report, 1990. No. 22.
Problems and Issues in Structural Adjustment, 1990. No. 23.
Development Issues: Presentations to the Meeting{s} of the Development Committee, semiannual (April and October). Nos. 24, 26-, 1990 to date.
The Development Committee: Its Origins and Achievements, 1974–1990, 1990. No. 25.

Economic Development Institute (EDI)

Agricultural Project Analysis: Case Studies and Exercises, 1979. 3 vols.
Economic Development Institute: General Information, 1985.
Economic Development Projects and Their Appraisal: Cases and Principles from the Experience of the World Bank, by John A. King, 1967.
EDI/20: Memoir of a Fellowship, by Michael Lindsay Hoffman, 1976.
Municipal Water Supply Project Analysis: Case Studies, edited by Frank H. Lamson-Scribner and John W. Huang, 1977.
National Economic Policy-Making: The Key Elements, edited by Yin-Kann Wen and Elie Canetti, 1987.

EDI Development Policy Case Studies: Analytical Case Studies
EDI Development Policy Case Studies: Teaching Cases
EDI Development Studies
EDI Policy Seminar Reports
EDI Seminar Papers
EDI Seminar Series

Financial Sector Reforms, Economic Growth, and Stability: Experiences in Selected Asian and Latin American Countries, edited by Ravi Gulhati, 1994.
Financial Systems and Development in Africa: Collected Papers from an EDI Policy Seminar Held in Nairobi, Kenya, from January 29 to February 1, 1990, edited by Philippe Callier, 1991.
Increasing the International Competitiveness of Exports from Caribbean Countries: Collected Papers from an EDI Policy Seminar held in Bridgetown, Barbados, May 22–24, 1989, edited by Yin-Kann Wen and Jayshree Sengupta, 1991.
The Making of Economic Policy in Africa, edited by Ravi Gulhati, 1990.
Managing Policy Reform in the Real World: Asian Experiences, edited by Geoffrey Lamb and Rachel Weaving, 1992.
Monitoring and Evaluating Development Projects: The South Asian Experience, edited by Viqar Ahmed and Michael Bamberger, 1989.

Textbooks in the Developing World: Economic and Educational Choices, edited by Joseph P. Farrell and Stephen P. Heyneman, 1989.

EDI Series in Economic Development

Agroindustrial Project Analysis: Critical Design Factors, by James E. Austin, 1992. 2d ed.

Aspects of Development Bank Management, edited by William Diamond and V. S. Raghavan, 1982.

Compounding and Discounting Tables for Project Analysis with a Guide to their Applications, by J. Price Gittinger, 1984. 2d ed.

Economic Analysis of Agricultural Projects, by J. Price Gittinger, 1982. Rev. ed.

Economic Appraisal of Transport Projects: A Manual with Case Studies, by Hans A. Adler, 1987. Rev. ed.

Food Policy: Integrating Supply, Distribution, and Consumption, edited by J. Price Gittinger, Joanne Leslie, and Caroline Hoisington, 1987.

Metropolitan Management: The Asian Experience, by K. C. Sivaramakrishnan and Leslie Green, 1986.

The Open Economy: Tools for Policymakers in Developing Countries, edited by Rudiger Dornbusch and F. L. C. H. Hazlewood, 1986.

Pricing Policy for Development Management, edited by Gerald M. Meier, 1983.

The Private Provision of Public Services in Developing Countries, by Gabriel Roth, 1987.

EDI Training Materials
EDI Working Papers

De Lusignan, Guy. "The Bank's Economic Development Institute," *Finance and Development,* Vol. 23, No. 2 (June 1986), pp. 28–31.

Global Environment Facility (GEF)

Global Environment Facility: The Pilot Phase and Beyond, 1992.

Instrument for the Establishment of the Restructured Global Environment Facility, 1994.

Quarterly Operational Report, 1994 to date.

Project Documents
Reports by the Chairman
Working Papers

Implementing the Framework Convention on Climate Change: Incremental Costs and the Role of the GEF, by Irving M. Mintzer, 1993. No. 4.

The Cost-Effectiveness of GEF Projects, by Dennis Anderson and Robert H. Williams, 1993. No. 6.
From Idea to Reality: The Creation of the Global Environment Facility, by Helen Sjoberg, 1994. No. 10.

United Nations Development Programme, United Nations Environment Programme, and World Bank. *Global Environment Facility: Independent Evaluation of the Pilot Phase,* World Bank (Washington, D.C., 1994).
U.S. Congress. House. Committee on Banking, Finance, and Urban Affairs. Subcommittee on International Development, Finance, Trade, and Monetary Policy. *Authorizing Contributions to IDA, GEF, and ADF: Hearing . . . May 5, 1993.* Government Printing Office (Washington, D.C., 1994).

International Centre for Settlement of Investment Disputes (ICSID)

Convention on the Settlement of Investment Disputes Between States and Nationals of Other States: Documents Concerning the Origin and Formulation of the Convention, 1968–70. 4 vols. in 5.
ICSID Basic Documents, 1985.
ICSID Bibliography, 1994.
ICSID Cases, 1994.
ICSID Regulations and Rules for Arbitration Proceedings, 1983.

Annual Report, 1967 to date. Also in French and Spanish.
ICSID Review, Foreign Investment Law Journal, semiannual, 1984 to date.
News from ICSID, semiannual, 1984 to date.

Bondzi-Simpson, P. Ebow. *Legal Relationships between Transnational Corporations and Host States,* Quorum Books (New York, 1990).
Broches, Aron. "The Convention on the Settlement of Investment Disputes between States and Nationals of Other States," *Recueil des Cours de l'Académie de Droit International, Collected Courses of the Hague Academy of International Law,* Vol. 136 (1972), pp. 330–410.
Cherian, Joy. *Investment Contracts and Arbitration: The World Bank Convention on the Settlement of Investment Disputes,* A. W. Sijthoff (Leiden, 1975).
Hirsch, Moshe. *The Arbitration Mechanism of the International Centre for the Settlement of Investment Disputes,* International Arbitration Law Library, M. Nijhoff (Dordrecht, 1993).
Rowat, Malcolm D. "Multilateral Approaches to Improving the Investment Climate of Developing Countries: The Cases of ICSID and MIGA,"

Harvard International Law Journal, Vol. 33, No. 1 (Winter 1992), pp. 103–44.

Schmidt, John T. "Arbitration under the Auspices of the International Centre for Settlement of Investment Disputes (ICSID): Implications of the Decision on Jurisdiction in Alcoa Minerals of Jamaica, Inc. v. Government of Jamaica," *Harvard International Law Journal,* Vol. 17, No. 1 (Winter 1976), pp. 90–109.

Shihata, Ibrahim F. I. *Towards a Greater Depoliticization of Investment Disputes: The Roles of ICSID and MIGA,* 1992.

Soley, David A. "ICSID Implementation: An Effective Alternative to International Conflict," *International Lawyer,* Vol. 19, No. 2 (Spring 1985), pp. 521–44.

"25th Anniversary of ICSID," *ICSID Review, Foreign Investment Law Journal,* Vol. 6, No. 2 (Fall 1991), pp.321–616.

International Development Association (IDA)

Articles of Agreement, Effective September 24, 1960; and, Report of the Executive Directors of the International Bank for Reconstruction and Development on the Articles of Agreement. 2d printing. [1993].

By-Laws, as Amended through March 2, 1981, 1991.

Decision of the Executive Directors under Article X of the Articles of Agreement on Questions of Interpretation of the Articles of Agreement, 1991.

IDA in Retrospect: The First Two Decades of the International Development Association, Oxford University Press for the World Bank (New York, 1982).

Baldwin, David A. "International Development Association: Theory and Practice," *Economic Development and Cultural Change,* Vol. 10 (Oct. 1961), pp. 86–96.

Bretton Woods Committee. *IDA and the U.S. Interest: A Report on the World Bank's International Development Association* (Washington, D.C., 1987).

Burki, Shahid Javed, and Norman Hicks. "International Development Association in Retrospect," *Finance and Development,* Vol. 19, No. 4 (Dec. 1982), pp. 22–25.

Fleming, Alexander, and Mary Oakes Smith. "Raising Resources for IDA: The Eighth Replenishment," *Finance and Development,* Vol. 24, No. 3 (Sept. 1987), pp. 23–26.

Katz, Jeffrey. "The Evolving Role of IDA," *Finance and Development,* Vol. 26, No. 2 (June 1989), pp. 16–19.

Stern, Ernest. "Mobilizing Resources for IDA: The Ninth Replenishment," *Finance and Development,* Vol. 27, No. 2 (June 1990), pp. 20–23.

U.S. Congress. House. Committee on Banking and Currency. Subcommittee on International Finance. *Providing for Additional U.S. Contributions to the Asian Development Bank and the International Development Association: Hearings . . . November 14; December 3 and 6, 1973,* Government Printing Office (Washington, D.C., 1973).

U.S. Congress. House. Committee on Banking, Finance, and Urban Affairs. Subcommittee on International Development, Finance, Trade, and Monetary Policy. *Authorizing Contributions to IDA, GEF, and ADF: Hearing . . . May 5, 1993,* Government Printing Office (Washington, D.C., 1994).

———. *The Ninth Replenishment of the International Development Association: Hearing . . . March 28, 1990,* Government Printing Office (Washington, D.C., 1990).

U.S. Congress. House. Committee on Banking, Finance, and Urban Affairs. Subcommittee on International Development Institutions and Finance. *U.S. Participation in the International Development Association Seventh Replenishment: Hearings . . . February 29 and March 1, 1984,* Government Printing Office (Washington, D.C., 1984).

U.S. Congress. Senate. Committee on Foreign Relations. *International Development Association: Hearings . . . to Provide for the Participation of the United States in the International Development Association, March 18 and 21, 1960,* Government Printing Office (Washington, D.C., 1960).

Weaver, James H. *The International Development Association: A New Approach to Foreign Aid,* Praeger (New York, 1965).

International Finance Corporation (IFC)

Articles of Agreement, as Amended through April 28, 1993, 1994. Original Articles in 1956, subsequently amended September 21, 1961, and September 1, 1965.

By-Laws, as Amended through February 18, 1980, 1991.

International Finance Corporation: Policy on Disclosure of Information, 1994.

Private Sector Development: The IFC Perspective, by Jannik Lindbaek, 1994.

Small-Scale Privatization in Russia: The Nizhny-Novgorod Model, 1992. 3 vols.

Annual Report, 1956 to date.

IFC and the Environment: Annual Review, 1992 to date.

FIAS {Foreign Investment Advisory Service} Occasional Papers
IFC Discussion Papers

Private Business in Developing Countries: Improved Prospects, by Guy P. Pfefferman, 1986. No. 1.

Debt-Equity Swaps and Foreign Direct Investment in Latin America, by Joel Bergsman and Wayne Edisis, 1987. No. 2.

Prospects for the Business Sector in Developing Countries, by Economics Department, IFC, 1988. No. 3.

Strengthening Health Services in Developing Countries Through the Private Sector, by Charles C. Griffin, 1989. No. 4.

The Development Contribution of IFC Operations, by Economics Department, IFC, 1990. No. 5.

Trends in Private Investment in Thirty Developing Countries, by Guy P. Pfefferman and Andrea Madarassy, 1990. No. 6.

Automotive Industry Trends and Prospects for Investment in Developing Countries, by Yannis Karmokolias, 1990. No. 7.

Exporting to Industrial Countries: Prospects for Businesses in Developing Countries, by Economics Department, IFC, 1990. No. 8.

African Entrepreneurs—Pioneers of Development, by Keith Marsden, 1991. No. 9.

Privatizing Telecommunications Systems: Business Opportunities in Developing Countries, by William W. Ambrose, Paul R. Hennemeyer, and Jean-Paul Chapon, 1991. No. 10.

Trends in Private Investment in Developing Countries, 1990–91 Edition, by Guy P. Pfefferman and Andrea Madarassy, 1991. No. 11.

Financing Corporate Growth in the Developing World, by Economics Department, IFC, 1992. No. 12.

Venture Capital: Lessons from the Developed World for Developing Markets, by Silvia B. Sagari with Gabriella Guidotti, 1992. No. 13.

Trends in Private Investment in Developing Countries, 1992 Edition, by Guy P. Pfefferman and Andrea Madarassy, 1992. No. 14.

Private Sector Electricity in Developing Countries: Supply and Demand, by Jack D. Glen, 1993. No. 15.

Trends in Private Investment in Developing Countries 1993: Statistics for 1970–91, by Guy P. Pfefferman and Andrea Madarassy, 1993. No. 16.

How Firms in Developing Countries Manage Risk, by Jack D. Glen, 1994. No. 17.

Coping with Capitalism: The New Polish Entrepreneurs, by Bohdan Wyznikiewicz, Brian Pinto, and Maciej Grabowski, 1994. No. 18.

Intellectual Property Protection, Foreign Direct Investment, and Technology Transfer, by Edwin Mansfield, 1994. No. 19.

Trends in Private Investment in Developing Countries 1994: Statistics for 1970–92, by Robert R. Miller and Mariusz A. Sumlinski, 1994. No. 20.

IFC Technical Papers

Baker, James Calvin. *The International Finance Corporation: Origin, Operations, and Evaluation,* Praeger (New York, 1968).

Bell, Carl. "Promoting Private Investment: The Role of the International Finance Corporation," *Finance and Development,* Vol. 18, No. 3 (Sept. 1981), pp. 16–19.

"IFC: Promoting Private Sector Development [Special Section]" *Finance and Development,* Vol. 25, No. 4 (Dec. 1988), pp. 21–40.

Leeds, Roger S. "IFC's New Approach to Project Promotion," *Finance and Development,* Vol. 22, No. 1 (March 1985), pp. 5–7.

Lowe, John W. "IFC and the Agribusiness Sector," *Finance and Development,* Vol. 14, No. 1 (March 1977), pp. 25–28.

Matecki, B.E. *Establishment of the International Finance Corporation and United States Policy: A Case Study in International Organization,* Praeger (New York, 1957).

Peters, Hans Heinrich. *Internationale Entwicklungsfinanzierung: die Rolle der International Finance Corporation im Entwicklungsprozess* [International Financing of Development: The Role of the International Finance Corporation in the Development Process], H. Edmann (Tubingen, 1978).

U.S. Congress. House. Committee on Banking, Finance, and Urban Affairs. Subcommittee on International Development, Finance, Trade, and Monetary Policy. *International Finance Corporation: Hearing . . . May 24, 1990,* Government Printing Office (Washington, D.C., 1990).

U.S. Congress. Senate. Committee on Banking and Currency. *International Finance Corporation: Hearings Before a Subcommittee of the Committee on Banking and Currency . . . June 6 and 7, 1955,* Government Printing Office (Washington, D.C., 1955).

Multilateral Investment Guarantee Agency (MIGA)

By-Laws, Adopted June 8, 1988, 1991.

Convention Establishing the Multilateral Investment Guarantee Agency, and Commentary on the Convention, 1985.

General Conditions of Guarantee for Equity Investments, 1989.

Investment Guarantee Guide, 1991.

MIGA: The First Five Years and Future Challenges, 1994.

Requirements for Membership in the Multilateral Investment Guarantee Agency, 1990.

M.I.G.A. Annual Report, 1989 to date. Also in Arabic, French, and Spanish.

Chen, Zhongxun. "The Multilateral Investment Guarantee Agency and U.S. Investment in China," *Social Sciences in China,* Vol. 14, No. 4 (Winter 1993), pp. 84–98.

Ebenroth, Carsten Thomas, and Joachim Karl. *Die Multilaterale Investitions-Garantie-Agentur: Kommentar zum MIGA-Ubereinkommen* [The Multilateral Investment Guarantee Agency: Commentary on the MIGA Convention], Verlag Recht und Wirtschaft (Heidelberg, 1989).

Shihata, Ibrahim F.I. *MIGA and Foreign Investment: Origins, Operations, Policies, and Basic Documents of the Multilateral Investment Guarantee Agency,* M. Nijhoff (Dordrecht; Boston, 1988).

Sinn, Stefan. "Direct Investments: Second Thoughts on MIGA," *Intereconomics: Review of International Trade and Development,* Vol. 21, No. 6 (Nov./Dec. 1988), pp. 269–76.

Voss, Jurgen. "The Multilateral Investment Guarantee Agency: Status, Mandate, Concept, Features, Implications," *Journal of World Trade Law,* Vol. 21, No. 4 (Aug. 1987), pp. 5–23.

About the Author

Anne C. M. Salda was a staff member of the Joint Bank-Fund Library in Washington, D.C. from 1966 until her retirement in 1987. During the years 1974–84, she continued the bibliography, initiated by Martin L. Loftus, entitled "The IMF: A Selected Bibliography", which was published in the IMF's *Staff Papers*. As the Library's Bibliography Librarian, Mrs. Salda was responsible for its monthly list of periodical articles, and its collection of research papers. After her retirement, she prepared bibliographies on the International Monetary Fund and the World Bank, which were published by the Clio Press, Oxford. Mrs. Salda, a graduate of Oxford University, was born in Singapore but educated mainly in England. Before coming to the United States she was on the staff of the Victoria & Albert Museum Library in London.